INDIA AND THE INDIAN OCEAN

Shaping Pathways for Peace and Security

INDIA AND THE INDIAN OCEAN

Shaping Pathways for Peace and Security

Edited by

Anurag Bisen

Esha Banerji

Vivekananda International Foundation

PENTAGON PRESS LLP

First published in 2026 by
PENTAGON PRESS LLP
206, Peacock Lane, Shahpur Jat
New Delhi-110049, India
Contact: 011-26490600

Typeset in Times New Roman, 11 Point
Printed at Aegean Offset Printers, Greater Noida

ISBN 978-81-994764-8-6

www.pentagonpress.in

Contents

Foreword

For centuries, the Indian Ocean Region has stood at the helm of global interaction, and has served as both a bridge and a boundary across continents, cultures and spheres of power. Stretching between resource-rich Africa, the dynamic economies of South and Southeast Asia, and the strategic chokepoints connecting the region to the wider Indo-Pacific, it today shapes the trajectory of not only economic growth, but also technological evolution and geopolitical realignment. Yet, its centrality, which is anchored by maritime trade and energy flows, is increasingly tested by the co-existence of cooperation and competition, opportunity and challenge, continuity and transformation.

The region stands at a pivotal historical juncture. India's ascent as an Indo-Pacific power is inseparable from its maritime legacy and destiny. As economic interdependence intensifies and the seas become ever-more critical for the free movement of goods, energy and data, India finds itself called upon not only to champion its own security and prosperity but also to shoulder broader responsibilities. Nowhere is this more evident than in its leadership position within the Indian Ocean Rim Association (IORA), an organisation that echoes India's vision to nurture peace, security and shared growth for all regional stakeholders. Furthermore, these evolving dynamics are deeply rooted in India's civilisational heritage as well as the contemporary strategic imperatives.

Today, the Indian Ocean Region faces foundational questions: How can the interests and aspirations of coastal and island nations be harmonised amidst great power competition? In what ways can the region's unique diversity, be it ethnic, civilisational or political—be channelled into new forms of cooperative and inclusive regionalism? And how might India, through its vision, leadership and institution building, catalyse pathways toward maritime stability that uplift the region as a whole?

The Indian Ocean has shaped India's destiny for millennia. Indians have been engaged in maritime trade since the time of the Indus Valley Civilisation.

Historically, Lothal in the Indian state of Gujarat is considered to be the oldest port in the world. Indian Ocean Region now occupies an increasingly prominent place in India's policies. India seeks peace, stability, collaboration and cooperation, growth and prosperity in the Indian Ocean Region. The Indian Ocean should not become an arena of great power contestation.

Drawing upon the doctrines of Security and Growth for All in the Region (SAGAR) and the Mutual and Holistic Advancement for Security and Growth Across Regions (MAHASAGAR) Vision, India has demonstrated its determination to act as a provider of public goods in the maritime domain. These frameworks reimagine the Indian Ocean not merely as a strategic theatre but as a 'shared common', which encompasses responsibilities for humanitarian assistance and disaster relief, climate adaptation and the protection of undersea infrastructure that supports the region's digital and economic future. A whole-of-nation approach, rooted in pragmatism and partnership, remains essential to overcome the pressing threats posed by illegal, unregulated fishing, organized transnational crime, cyber vulnerabilities and climate crisis. India was historically a maritime nation. The neglect of maritime capabilities opened the way for colonial penetration with disastrous results for India. India is determined to set right the past neglect, build its maritime capabilities while promoting the doctrine of security and growth for all in the region.

India's distinctive strength lies in its focus on strengthening the region's institutional landscape. Mechanisms such as IORA, the Indian Ocean Naval Symposium (IONS), the Bay of Bengal Initiative for Multi-Sectoral Technical and Economic Cooperation (BIMSTEC) and the Djibouti Code of Conduct offer platforms for collaboration. However, operational fragmentation, limited information-sharing and underdeveloped protocols have hampered the emergence of a resilient regional order. Addressing these gaps through standardised operational procedures, improved incident response coordination and trust-building measures is crucial. Peace and stability rest not only on the hard architecture of security alliances but also on the softer links of shared information and norms and a common vision.

The growing significance of dialogue partners and extra-regional actors plays an equally important role. As emerging technologies reshape maritime operations and as the architecture of regional order changes, India's engagement with partner countries is crucial for fostering resilience, technological exchange and harmony across the vast Indian Ocean region. The increasing importance of domains such as autonomous maritime systems, subsea cables and digital infrastructure underscores India's forward-looking approach and the integrated nature of modern security.

In presenting this book to the reader, there is cause for both hope and resolve. Hope rests in the region's extraordinary capacity for renewal, its history of trade, mingling of civilisations and adaptability in the face of change. Resolve is found in India's readiness to match vision with action, and in the commitment of all those invested in peaceful and cooperative seas. This book, ***India and the Indian Ocean: Shaping Pathways for Peace and Security***, brings together these ideas with analytical depth and strategic foresight, inviting readers to engage with the evolving narrative of the Indian Ocean and India's enduring leadership within it. May it inspire thoughtful engagement, informed policy and a renewed sense of purpose as India and its partners navigate these consequential waters together.

13 Nov 2025

Dr Arvind Gupta
Director
Vivekananda International Foundation

Editor's Note

Anurag Bisen and Esha Banerji

For centuries, the Indian Ocean Region has stood at the crossroads of global interaction, at once a bridge connecting continents and cultures, and a threshold that has long defined the reach and limits of geopolitical power. Stretching from the resource-rich coastline of Africa to the vibrant economies of South and Southeast Asia, and encompassing the strategic chokepoints that link it with the wider Indo-Pacific, the region continues to define the trajectory of global economic growth, technological advancement, and strategic realignment. Its centrality, long anchored in maritime trade and energy flows, is today increasingly shaped by the interplay of cooperation and competition, opportunity and uncertainty, continuity and disruption.

It is against this backdrop that this edited volume is released, coinciding with the dialogue *"India and the Indian Ocean: Shaping Pathways for Peace and Security,"* co-organised by the **Vivekananda International Foundation (VIF)** and the **Centre for Humanitarian Dialogue (HD)** in New Delhi. Bringing together scholars, practitioners, and policy leaders, the book offers a nuanced examination of India's evolving maritime role, engaging the region's challenges and possibilities with analytical depth and clarity. It seeks not only to interpret the changing dynamics of the Indian Ocean but also to provide grounded perspectives on India's enduring stakes and emerging responsibilities.

In Chapter 1, **Rear Admiral K. Raja Menon (Retd)** examines India's maritime evolution from its early dominance in Indian Ocean trade to the contemporary strategic environment shaped by China's rise. It outlines how Beijing's long-term strategy, marked by global port acquisitions and maritime expansion, poses challenges to India's security and influence. Menon argues that India must respond through a comprehensive maritime grand strategy that strengthens naval capabilities and leverages initiatives such as SAGAR and MAHASAGAR. The chapter concludes that India's ability to manage asymmetry with China will depend on its strategic use of the Indian Ocean as a domain of influence and deterrence.

Saudiptendu Ray explores India's civilisational maritime legacy in Chapter 2. The chapter traces the evolution of India's seafaring traditions from the dockyards of the Indus Valley to the naval power of the Cholas, illustrating how the Indian Ocean served as a corridor of trade, culture, and faith rather than a frontier of conquest. It examines the integration of maritime activity with India's economic, religious, and philosophical life, highlighting the roles of ancient ports, merchant guilds, and Buddhist and Hindu exchanges across Asia. Concluding with a discussion on contemporary revival efforts—such as *Sagarmala*, *Project Mausam*, and the Lothal Maritime Heritage Complex—Ray underscores how India's historical maritime consciousness continues to shape its modern Indo-Pacific outlook.

In Chapter 3, **Raghvendra Singh** explores the outreach of India's maritime heritage, tracing how the Indian Ocean served as a conduit for trade, religion, and cultural exchange linking India with Africa, the Middle East, and Southeast Asia. He emphasises the need to recover and reinterpret these shared legacies through collaborative research, maritime museums, and UNESCO heritage frameworks. The chapter calls for an "*Indian Ocean Maritime Heritage Project*" to document and revitalise both tangible and intangible cultural linkages, ranging from shipbuilding and trade routes to literature and spiritual traditions. He concludes that reviving these networks can enhance India's cultural diplomacy and reaffirm its historic maritime centrality in the Indian Ocean world.

India's evolving approach to maritime governance is explored in Chapter 4 by **Commodore Abhay Kumar Singh (Retd)**. The chapter analyses India's transition from a defence-centric maritime strategy to a comprehensive governance model integrating security, economic growth, and environmental sustainability. It traces this evolution from the SAGAR to the MAHASAGAR initiative, marking India's shift from a "Net Security Provider" to a "Preferred Security Partner." Examining India's engagement through frameworks such as IORA, IONS, and the Colombo Security Conclave, the chapter highlights ongoing challenges of institutional fragmentation, capacity asymmetries, and strategic competition, concluding that effective leadership depends on coherent, inclusive, and sustainable maritime governance.

Rear Admiral Monty Khanna (Retd), in Chapter 5, examines how India can reframe its maritime vision by aligning the MAHASAGAR initiative with existing regional architectures in the Indian Ocean. The chapter argues for consolidating India's multiple maritime frameworks under a single, clearly articulated MAHASAGAR policy, supported by a dedicated institutional mechanism capable of coordinating development assistance, capacity building, and strategic engagement across the Global South. Rear Admiral Khanna proposes aligning MAHASAGAR's implementation with IORA's six priority areas to enhance coherence, visibility, and regional leadership, while retaining bilateral and sub-regional platforms—such as IONS, BIMSTEC, and the Colombo Security Conclave—for higher-end security cooperation. He concludes that India's ability to operationalise MAHASAGAR and strengthen its role as a preferred security partner will depend on building robust domestic capacities, particularly through the success of *Sagarmala* and related maritime sector reforms.

Chapter 6 by **Captain Anurag Bisen (Retd)** examines how India is translating its maritime vision into a unified national strategy. It traces the country's maritime heritage, its decline under colonial rule, and the present-day renewal shaped by initiatives such as *SAGAR*, *Sagarmala*, and *Maritime India Vision 2030*. The chapter reviews developments in port capacity, inland waterways, the blue economy, maritime legislation, renewable energy, and security coordination, while identifying persistent challenges in shipbuilding, fleet expansion, and institutional alignment. It concludes by proposing a six-pillar, PMO-led *MAHASAGAR* framework integrating diplomacy (*Sagar Sambandh*), defence (Sagar *Suraksha*), connectivity (*Sagarmala*), scientific research (*Sagar Shodh*), culture (*Sagar Sanskriti*), and resource management (*Sagar Sansadhan*) to guide India's re-emergence as a leading maritime nation.

Vice Admiral A.K. Chawla (Retd), in Chapter 7, analyses the maritime security interlinkages among IORA, IONS, BIMSTEC and the Indo-Pacific Oceans Initiative (IPOI), highlighting how these frameworks collectively shape a multilayered security architecture across the Indian Ocean and wider Indo-Pacific. He outlines the region's diverse traditional and non-traditional threats—ranging from piracy and trafficking to climate-induced disasters and emerging technological risks—and examines how each organisation addresses these challenges at different functional levels: IORA and BIMSTEC through diplomatic and policy-driven cooperation, IONS through operational coordination among navies, and IPOI through a broader strategic and developmental vision. The chapter emphasises growing complementarities, such as the IORA–BIMSTEC MoU and the integration of information-sharing mechanisms like IFC-IOR, while also noting persistent political, capacity, and resource constraints.

Commodore Anil Jai Singh, in Chapter 8, examines the role of extra-regional powers in shaping the emerging maritime security architecture of the Indian Ocean. He traces their long historical presence—first as colonisers, later as strategic actors, and now as partners driven by economic and security imperatives—and explains how the Indo-Pacific's geopolitical shift has deepened their engagement. Analysing the region's defining geographic features, strategic chokepoints, vulnerability to non-traditional threats, climate risks, and China's expanding maritime footprint, the chapter argues that no single littoral state can secure the region alone. Commodore Singh outlines the diverse multilateral mechanisms at play, from IORA and IONS to the DCOC, CMF, and EU initiatives, noting both complementarities and fragmentation.

In Chapter 9, **Captain Sarabjeet Singh Parmar (Retd)** analyses India's maritime security challenges and strategic choices in the increasingly complex IOR. He highlights how instability at key chokepoints, intensifying great-power competition, and the rise of non-traditional maritime threats have reshaped the region into a multi-actor security space central to India's economic and geopolitical interests. The chapter traces India's gradual shift from a primarily continental focus to a more outward-looking maritime posture, reflected in its roles as "Preferred Security Partner" and "First Responder." Assessing gaps in capability, coordination, and regional engagement, Captain Parmar argues that India's ability to shape the IOR will depend on strengthening maritime domain awareness, leveraging regional platforms like IORA, IONS, and BIMSTEC, and aligning national capacity with its broader ambition to act as a stabilising force in the region.

Prof. Sudhir Saxena, in Chapter 10, examines the need for a collaborative maritime Intelligence, Surveillance and Reconnaissance (ISR) framework for the IORA. The chapter outlines the region's dense concentration of global trade, critical chokepoints, subsea cable networks, and resource-rich waters, highlighting how these factors generate complex security challenges for member states. Prof. Saxena argues that existing IORA mechanisms remain limited and that an effective maritime security architecture depends on shared ISR capabilities, technology-driven monitoring, and inclusive information-sharing structures. He proposes a common ISR framework that accommodates capability asymmetries among member states, with India—given its geography and technological strengths—well positioned to anchor a dedicated regional information-sharing infrastructure, thereby strengthening collective maritime domain awareness and security.

Dr Neha Kumar, in Chapter 11, examines how disruptions to undersea communication cables can influence India's strategic and nuclear stability. She argues that the growing reliance on data-driven intelligence and real-time maritime awareness introduces new operational vulnerabilities for India. The chapter analyses China's expanding technological and maritime footprint, India's limited repair capacity, and the concentration of cable landing stations as key risks. It concludes by recommending indigenous repair capabilities, diversified landing sites, strengthened seabed surveillance, and the integration of undersea infrastructure protection into India's wider maritime and nuclear deterrence framework.

Dr. Richa Srimal and **Dr. Shishir Shrotriya**, in Chapter 12, analyse India's evolving maritime trade strategy within the complex geopolitical and economic dynamics of the Indian Ocean. The chapter outlines the region's significance as a global trade hub and identifies emerging challenges such as piracy, geopolitical tensions, supply chain disruptions, and China's expanding influence. It examines India's responses through frameworks like SAGAR, Maritime India Vision 2030, and MAHASAGAR, alongside legislative reforms, digitalisation, and strategic port investments. Concluding with a systems-based approach, the authors emphasise the need for regional cooperation, sustainable blue-economy practices, and resilient supply chains to strengthen India's role as a leading maritime and trade power in the Indian Ocean.

In Chapter 13, **Dr. Pooja Bhatt** examines international governance frameworks designed to combat illegal, unreported, and unregulated (IUU) fishing and assesses their relevance for the Indian Ocean context. The chapter analyses legal, institutional, and technological mechanisms—from the *Port State Measures Agreement* and Regional Fisheries Management Organisations to emerging AI-based monitoring systems—highlighting both their potential and implementation gaps. It argues that fragmented governance, limited enforcement, and geopolitical tensions undermine effective regulation in the region. Dr. Bhatt concludes by advocating a hybrid, multi-layered model integrating legal harmonisation, technology-driven surveillance, and regional cooperation through platforms like IORA, BIMSTEC, and IONS to strengthen sustainable fisheries management in the Indian Ocean.

Ruchita Beri, in Chapter 14, examines India's expanding humanitarian assistance and disaster relief (HADR) cooperation with African states in the IOR, highlighting how India has emerged as a reliable first responder to crises ranging from cyclones and floods to pandemics and environmental emergencies. She situates India's approach within long-standing cultural principles of *dāna* and *Vasudhaiva Kutumbakam*, as well as the broader frameworks of SAGAR and MAHASAGAR. The chapter details India's demand-driven, consent-based relief operations—led by the armed forces and coordinated by the MEA—across countries such as Mozambique, Madagascar, Mauritius, Comoros, Kenya, and Djibouti. Beri shows how India's rapid deployment capabilities, food and medical assistance, vaccine diplomacy, and naval outreach have strengthened its role as a key partner for African littorals.

Dr. Sanjeet Ruhal explores cyber-physical threats at sea in Chapter 15, analysing how the digitalisation of the maritime domain has exposed critical vulnerabilities within existing international legal frameworks. The chapter argues that the *United Nations Convention on the Law of the Sea (UNCLOS)*, conceived in a pre-digital era, is ill-equipped to address cyber incidents that can trigger physical and environmental harm at sea. Dr. Ruhal identifies three key governance gaps: inadequate enforcement of flag-state responsibilities for "cyber-worthiness," unresolved jurisdictional limits for coastal states, and the absence of accountability for technology manufacturers. He proposes interpretive and structural reforms to enhance legal clarity, establish technical cyber-resilience standards, and redistribute liability across the maritime ecosystem. The chapter concludes by suggesting that India's chairmanship of the IORA offers an opportunity to promote regional cooperation and legal innovation to strengthen maritime cybersecurity governance.

Dr. Rasik Ravindra looks at deep ocean exploration and science-based cooperation in Chapter 16. The chapter examines how the Indian Ocean's living and non-living resources, such as polymetallic nodules, cobalt crusts, gas hydrates, and fisheries, can be sustainably harnessed through research, technology, and regional collaboration. It discusses India's *Deep Ocean Mission* as a central initiative for advancing marine science, blue economy development, and disaster preparedness. Emphasising data sharing and cooperative frameworks among Indian Ocean Rim countries, Dr. Ravindra highlights the importance of science-led governance for equitable resource utilisation and environmental stewardship in the Indo-Pacific region.

Dr. K. Kathiresan and **Dr. J.R. Bhatt**, in Chapter 17, examine the environmental attributes of the Indian Ocean and the opportunities they create for strengthened regional cooperation. They outline the ocean's exceptional ecological richness—from mangroves and coral reefs to seagrasses, seaweeds, and diverse marine fauna—and highlight how these ecosystems underpin fisheries, coastal livelihoods, tourism, and climate regulation for nearly one-third of the world's population. The chapter also details the mounting pressures of overexploitation, pollution, habitat loss, and climate change, alongside the uneven distribution of vulnerability among IORA member states. Emphasising the need for coordinated conservation and sustainable resource management, the authors point to IORA, IOC, UNEP Regional Seas programmes, and global frameworks as critical platforms for collective action.

For policymakers, practitioners, strategic thinkers and academics, this volume serves as a touchstone for understanding a maritime world in motion and for contributing to the collective enterprise of shaping its future. May it inspire thoughtful engagement, informed policy, and a sustained sense of purpose as India and its partners navigate the shifting tides of the Indian Ocean together.

List of Contributors

Commodore Anil Jai Singh (Retd) is an Honorary Adjunct Fellow at the National Maritime Foundation and Senior Vice President of a leading European MNC in India. A former submariner with over three decades of service, he commanded four submarines and a Fleet ship. A specialist in Anti-Submarine Warfare, he has held key appointments in Naval Headquarters and also served as Defence and Naval Adviser in the UK. He is Vice President of the Indian Maritime Foundation and the Navy Foundation (Delhi Chapter).

Commodore Abhay Kumar Singh (Retd) is a Research Fellow at the Military Affairs Centre, IDSA, New Delhi. An Indian Navy veteran with 27 years of distinguished service, he has commanded multiple warships, and later served as Director (Military Affairs) at MEA. His research focuses on maritime geopolitics in the Indo-Pacific. He has authored a book on India-China relations and has co-edited a book on the Ukraine war.

Captain Anurag Bisen (Retd) is a veteran submariner who commanded a Sindhughosh-class submarine and later served eight years in the National Security Council Secretariat as Senior Defence Specialist shaping key maritime policy, including India's 2022 Arctic Policy. He is an Honorary Adjunct Fellow at the National Maritime Foundation, a Senior Fellow at Vivekananda International Foundation, New Delhi and is currently pursuing PhD in National Security Studies from Jawaharlal Nehru University.

Captain Sarabjeet Parmar (Retd), a Sea King pilot and NDA–DSSC alumnus, commanded two ships and a frontline ASW helicopter squadron, contributed to India's maritime strategy and doctrine development, worked at IDSA and NMF, and is currently a Distinguished Fellow at CSDR and USI, New Delhi, and AII and IPSC, Melbourne.

Dr. J.R. Bhatt is the Distinguished Fellow in an honorary capacity at Vivekananda International Foundation, Research and Information System for Developing Countries, New Delhi and National Institute of Advanced Studies, Bangalore; formerly Scientist at the Ministry of Environment, Forest and Climate Change, Government of India.

Dr. K. Kathiresan is an honorary Professor of Marine Biology in Annamalai University, Tamil Nadu, formerly the Dean and Director at Centre of Advanced Study in Marine Biology of Annamalai University. He has spent practically most of his research and teaching career on marine ecology particularly on mangroves.

Dr. Neha Kumar is Associate Professor and Head, Department of Liberal Arts and Humanities, Chandigarh University, Mohali, India. A former Visiting Fellow at the Institute for National Defense and Security Research (INDSR), Taiwan, she writes extensively on China, nuclear weapons, deterrence strategy, and nuclear security.

Associate Prof. (Dr) Pooja Bhatt is a maritime security scholar and author of *Nine-Dash Line*. She works extensively on Indo-Pacific and South China Sea issues, has published internationally, contributed to *A Decade of Transformation: The Indian Navy 2011–21*, previously served at MEA, and is Stimson Centre South Asia Visiting Fellow 2025.

Dr Rasik Ravindra, former Director of NCPOR, Goa is the current Chairman of its Research Advisory Committee. He also heads the INSA–SCAR National Committee. He has led scientific expeditions to the Arctic, Antarctica and Himalaya, including the South Pole and has made long-standing contributions to polar science and policy.

Dr. Richa Srimal is an award-winning case writer and academician. Her areas of specialization are International Business, International Shipping and Logistics. Her case studies are listed at The UK Case Centre and one of her cases has also won the prestigious John Molson International Case Writing Award-2025.

Ruchita Beri is a Senior Fellow at the Vivekananda International Foundation and a leading scholar and commentator on African studies with over three decades of research experience. Formerly Senior Research Associate and Centre Coordinator for Africa, LAC and UN at MP-IDSA, she serves on several national and international boards, publishes widely, and regularly lectures at premier Indian institutions.

Dr. Sanjeet Ruhal is an international maritime security law scholar, serving since 2018 as The Nippon Foundation Lecturer at the IMO-IMLI (UN), where he leads the M.Jur. and PhD research programmes. He is also Adjunct Professor of Law at Gujarat Maritime University and actively mentors the next generation of maritime legal specialists.

Dr. Shishir Shrotriya, is currently the Head Centre for Maritime Economy and Connectivity (CMEC) at RIS, is an IIT Delhi alumnus (MTech, PhD) specialising in maritime technology and strategy. His key previous assignments include, Head of Faculty (ECE) at the Indian Naval Academy, Counsellor (S&T) at the Embassy of India, Moscow. He has recently edited the 2024 Taylor & Francis volume on *Waste to Wealth.*

Prof. Sudhir Saxena is a Senior Fellow at the Vivekananda International Foundation and a Visiting Faculty at the Indian Institute of Technology Kanpur. He has served in National Security organizations, including the Institute for Defence Studies and Analysis, New Delhi. He specialises in Data/Signals Fusion and Analysis.

A former member of the Indian Administrative Service, **Raghvendra Singh** has headed The National Archives, The Nehru Memorial Museum and Library and the National Library. He was Secretary Culture and Textiles in the Government of India. He worked extensively in the sector of Museology. He has also authored a book called *India's Lost Frontiers: The Story of North-West Frontier Province of Pakistan*. He is currently working on two projects: *Gilgit* and *Syama Prasad Mukherjee.*

Gold medallist from NDA, **Rear Admiral K. Raja Menon (Retd)** is a former Indian Navy submarine specialist who commanded seven ships and retired as Assistant Chief of Naval Staff (Operations) in 1994. He later authored major works on maritime and nuclear strategy, served on key national defence committees, and is currently writer on Strategy affecting Geopolitical Scenarios.

Rear Admiral Monty Khanna, AVSM, NM (Retd), served in the Indian Navy from 1983 to 2019. A graduate of NDA, DSSC Wellington, and the U.S. Naval War College, he commanded INS Sindhuvijay, INS Krishna, and INS Gomati, and later served as Assistant Chief of Naval Staff (Foreign Cooperation &

Intelligence) and Commandant, Naval War College. He is currently a member of the National Security Advisory Board.

Saudiptendu Ray is a Research Associate at the Vivekananda International Foundation. He holds Master's degrees in Modern Indian History from the University of Delhi and in Museology from the National Museum Institute. With over seven years of experience in the museum sector, he has contributed to major national projects and documented more than a hundred Partition oral histories. His research focuses on Indian culture, civilisation, and heritage studies.

Vice Admiral A.K. Chawla (Retd) is a Navigation specialist who commanded major warships including INS Viraat, served as Defence Attaché (Jakarta), led key capability and policy reforms at Naval HQ, commanded the Western Fleet, later became DG Naval Operations, and FOC-in-C Southern Naval Command. He is a VSM, AVSM, PVSM awardee.

List of Abbreviations

ADB	Asian Development Bank
AI	Artificial Intelligence
AIKEYME	Africa–India Key Maritime Engagement
AIMS	Africa Integrated Maritime Strategy
AIS	Automatic Identification System
ASEAN	Association of Southeast Asian Nations
BBNJ	Biodiversity Beyond National Jurisdiction
BGP	Border Gateway Protocol
BIMSTEC	Bay of Bengal Initiative for Multi-Sectoral Technical and Economic Cooperation
BRI	Belt and Road Initiative
CAGR	Compound Annual Growth Rate
CISF	Central Industrial Security Force
CMF	Combined Maritime Forces
CMS	Convention on Migratory Species
COP	Conference of the Parties
COVAXIN	COVID-19 Vaccine (Bharat Biotech)
CRI	Climate Risk Index
CRIMARIO	Critical Maritime Routes Indian Ocean
CSS	Coastal Security Scheme
CTF	Combined Task Force
DCOC	Djibouti Code of Conduct
DGH	Directorate General of Hydrocarbons
DoT	Department of Telecommunications
EEZ	Exclusive Economic Zone
EODB	Ease of Doing Business

EU	European Union
EUNAVFOR	EU Naval Force
EXIM	Export-Import
FAO	Food and Agriculture Organization
G20	Group of Twenty
GCC	Gulf Cooperation Council
GCRMN	Global Coral Reef Monitoring Network
GDP	Gross Domestic Product
GHG	Greenhouse Gas/Greenhouse Gas Emissions
GPS	Global Positioning System
HADR	Humanitarian Assistance and Disaster Relief
HCQ	Hydroxychloroquine
IFC	Information Fusion Centre (Singapore)
IFC-IOR	Information Fusion Centre – Indian Ocean Region
IMAC	Information Management and Analysis Centre
IMEC	India–Middle East–Europe Corridor
IMO	International Maritime Organization
INR	Indian Rupee
INS	Indian Naval Ship
INSTC	International North–South Transport Corridor
IOC	Indian Ocean Commission
IOC–UNESCO	Intergovernmental Oceanographic Commission of UNESCO
IONS	Indian Ocean Naval Symposium
IOR	Indian Ocean Region
IORA	Indian Ocean Rim Association
IORIS	Indian Ocean Regional Information Sharing
IOTC	Indian Ocean Tuna Commission
IPCC	Intergovernmental Panel on Climate Change
IPOI	Indo-Pacific Oceans Initiative
ISL	International Shipping Lane
ISR	Intelligence, Surveillance and Reconnaissance
ITLOS	International Tribunal for the Law of the Sea
IUU	Illegal, Unreported and Unregulated

LNG	Liquefied Natural Gas
LPG	Liquefied Petroleum Gas
MAHASAGAR	Mutual and Holistic Advancement for Security and Growth Across Regions
MAITRI	Master Application for International Trade and Regulatory Interface
MDA	Maritime Domain Awareness
MEA	Ministry of External Affairs
MIV/MIV 2030	Maritime India Vision 2030
MoES	Ministry of Earth Sciences
MoU	Memorandum of Understanding
MPA/MPAs	Marine Protected Area(s)
MR	Maritime Reconnaissance
MSR	Maritime Silk Road
MSS	Ministry of State Security (China)
NAM	Non-Aligned Movement
NATO	North Atlantic Treaty Organization
NC3I	National Command, Control, Communications & Intelligence
NCPOR	National Centre for Polar and Ocean Research
NDCs	Nationally Determined Contributions
NDMA	National Disaster Management Authority (appears but *not* in list)
NGRI	National Geophysical Research Institute
NIO	National Institute of Oceanography
NIOT	National Institute of Ocean Technology
NMF	National Maritime Foundation
NMSC	National Maritime Security Coordinator
NOAA	National Oceanic and Atmospheric Administration
NOCs	Network Operation Centres
NSCS	National Security Council Secretariat
OECD	Organisation for Economic Cooperation and Development
OPEC	Organization of the Petroleum Exporting Countries
PCA	Permanent Court of Arbitration

PLA	People's Liberation Army
PMN	Polymetallic Nodules
PPE	Personal Protective Equipment
QUAD	Quadrilateral Security Dialogue
R2P	Responsibility to Protect
RCOC	Regional Centre for Operational Coordination
RMIDC	Regional Maritime Information and Data Centre
RMSA	Regional Maritime Security Architecture
ROV	Remotely Operated Vehicle
RRC	Rapid Response Cell
SAARC	South Asian Association for Regional Cooperation
SAGAR	Security and Growth for All in the Region
SAR	Search and Rescue
SDG	Sustainable Development Goal
SHADE	Shared Awareness and Deconfliction
SLOC	Sea Lines of Communication
SOP	Standard Operating Procedure
STEM	Science, Technology, Engineering, Mathematics
SWIOFC	South West Indian Ocean Fisheries Commission
UDA	Underwater Domain Awareness
UK	United Kingdom
UN	United Nations
UNCLOS	United Nations Convention on the Law of the Sea
UNCTAD	United Nations Conference on Trade and Development
UNEP	United Nations Environment Programme
UNESCO	United Nations Educational, Scientific and Cultural Organization
US	United States
USD	United States Dollar
UUV	Unmanned Underwater Vehicle
VTC	Virtual Trade Corridor
WGMSS	Working Group on Maritime Safety and Security

1

The Indian Ocean: Theatre of Destiny in the 21st Century

Rear Admiral K. Raja Menon (Retd)

There was a time when Peninsula India dominated the Indian Ocean, through trade, the movement of people and the transfer of cultural values. These movements go back in time to the pre-Christian era, as evidenced by the discovery of an ivory statuette, probably representing *Lakshmi* found in the archaeological dig at Pompei, destroyed by the eruption of volcanic Mount Vesuvius.[1] Equally well known is the complaint of Pliny, the Elder, a Roman senator, of the annual transfer of gold to India to pay for the huge amount of luxury Indian goods imported into Rome. Indian mariners on the West coast who had figured out the seasonal pattern of the monsoon winds, took their cargo up to Berenice in the Red Sea, for transfer to camel caravans that conveyed the goods to the 'Great' bend in the Nile, to Alexandria, Rome, and in the Middle Ages, to Venice. Similarly, Indian mariners on the East Coast took regular voyages to the Malay Peninsula, around Singapore (*Singha-pura*) to Thailand, Cambodia and even quite a way up the Viet Nam coast, as far as Da Nang. The Pallava dynasty in Kanchipuram, saw the transfer of a cultural Inspiration to enable the Khmer King Suryavarman to build Angkor Wat[2], the largest religious site in the world. Later on, of course under Raja Raja Chola and Rajendra Chola, Indian maritime empires were set up in Southeast Asia. The Indian maritime sailing tradition went into relative decline owing to a number of reasons of complex origin, but which resulted in their missing out on the five great inventions or discoveries of the marine compass, the computation of star tables, the building of the sextant, the development of the chromometer (for accurate time) and the development of Engineering Drawing, to construct large vessels. Even so, Indian merchants continued to finance the entire Indian Ocean trade, and their descendants are the *Kachchhis* of East Africa, Yemen and the Chettiars of the Tamil Nadu coast.[3] Eventually of course, the wealth of India attracted the Portuguese, the Dutch and the English, whose superior maritime skills replaced those of the Indian mariners. Even so, a nascent Indian modern shipbuilding effort by the Wadia family in Bombay so alarmed British strategic and commercial interests that Whitehall banned the East India company navy and transferred the maritime defence of India to the Royal Naval C-in-C Far East Fleet, based in Singapore.

In the post-Independence period, with the 1962 Chinese attack on an unprepared India, New Delhi's threat perceptions have shifted between Pakistan and China, as the countries that pose threats to our well-being and prosperity. However, one is never quite sure over which threat predominates at any time. Of course, we can't forget that in 1965 the Pakistani army actually had plans to conduct a blitzkrieg into Indian Punjab with the intention of detaching Kashmir territorially. Yet, two years later in 1967 it was China again in the news after the standoff at Nathu La. However, looking back 50 or 60 years, there is one act that stands out as the ultimate evil in anti-India projects. That was, the deliberate and cold-blooded transfer of nuclear weapon technology by China, to Pakistan, over nine long years in the 1980s that enabled Islamabad to have an air deliverable nuclear bomb in 1987, eleven years before Indian nuclear weapon test in Pokhran.[4] So, it is evident that China appears to have made up its mind about tying India down in South Asia as a long-term project, while India still had an open mind about such things. There is very little literature available about Beijing's strategic thinking of those days, perhaps, because during the cold war, the US had co-opted China as an ally against its primary enemy—the USSR. The defining of China as the long-term threat by the US was still three decades away. As discussed in *The Hundred-Year Marathon* by Michael Pillsbury (2015), this reassessment only emerged after what Pillsbury described as five major American misconceptions about China. The first was that engaging with China would bring about cooperation. The second was that China would eventually embrace Democracy. The third was that the Chinese communist government was fragile, and that, if pressed, it would collapse, leading to chaos. The fourth was that China eventually wanted to be the like the US and the fifth and final assumption was that the 'hawks' in China were in a minority.

International events changed dramatically in the 1990s, particularly for people in New Delhi. The Soviet Union collapsed, and this event is remembered by different people in different ways. For us, in India, and particularly for those serving in the Navy, the event was marked by the arrival of the US C-in-C Pacific Fleet to the Naval War Room in New Delhi, where, in a candid confession, he admitted that the US Pacific command had been misled for many years, by US intelligence that we in India had given our naval facilities in Visakhapatnam to the Soviet Navy, for their use[5]. This was followed by the series of Malabar naval exercises between the US and Indian Navies eventually leading to a growing maritime outlook in South Block. Of course, there were other earth-shaking events, mainly the Indian economic reforms of 1991 that set us on the path of economic growth and national resurgence.

In the meanwhile, transformative events were taking place in China which, under the reforms of Deng Xiaoping, led to the country growing at an average rate of over 9 percent per year for 18 consecutive years. The rise of China has permanently altered the landscape of international affairs in the 21st century. For strategic thinkers in India, this became evident when a group of us were invited to a conference in Istanbul by the legendary American strategist Andrew Marshall, to discuss if and when China might overtake the United States as the world's richest nation. This was in the year 2010[6].

Today, of course, this subject is at the center of discussions in all forums on international affairs. Everyone is familiar with the current numbers—which stand at $4.2 trillion for India, $19.6 trillion for China, and $29.4 trillion for the United States. More importantly, the question most frequently asked is: what will these numbers look like in 2050 or beyond? Since it is accepted that China, with a history of governance spanning over two millennia, thinks in terms of centuries, we too must adopt a similar long-term perspective in any competition with Beijing. India, however, has two significant advantages on its side—its relatively young population and its position as the world's fastest-growing major economy.

The Indian strategic environment, however, will be determined by the outcome of the Sino–US competition. This competition can broadly be divided into five factors: economic, technological, military, geopolitical, and social and cultural. The United States carries a huge debt burden, which China does not, but the supremacy of the dollar continues to protect the US, while Trump's efforts to reinvent global supply chains will shape the long-term outcomes.

The US is self-sufficient in energy, whereas China is heavily energy-deficient, with 80 percent of its energy imports transiting the Indian Ocean.

At one stage, the US was supreme in technology, particularly in semiconductors, but has been deficient in STEM education. China, meanwhile, is the manufacturer to the world and has recently overtaken the US in both research publications and patent filings. It also has more engineers and scientists, though the US remains the global leader in innovation.

Militarily, the US is a true world power, with a worldwide command infrastructure and global military reach. China, on the other hand, feels locally invulnerable and seeks to replicate its sea denial strategy in other regions. However, China is ahead of the US in its ability to sustain prolonged military conflict, owing to its strong engineering infrastructure.

In geopolitical terms, the Indian Ocean will be critical, and it represents India's best opportunity to emerge as a decisive factor. The US currently controls most of the world's sea lanes. Socially and culturally, the US continues to lead with its soft power, though President Trump's actions are eroding the country's cultural cohesion—an area where China presently enjoys relative stability. Of the two, the US is better equipped to absorb shocks, while China's one-party system may prove socially fragile.

While this paper was being written, a new and uncertain factor emerged: the extent to which the innovative genius of the American people might be constrained by President Trump's attacks on immigration and restrictions on American universities—particularly since many US Nobel laureates have been of immigrant origin.

With all this background in economic rejuvenation, in Asia and the world, how is India's old enemy Pakistan doing? Quite badly it would seem, as it is now dependent on the IMF to bail it out of repetitive crises. So much so, that many of us had given up looking at Pakistan as an existential threat until Pahalgam and Op *Sindoor* happened. This has rekindled all the old fears of Beijing's use of Pakistan as a proxy to tie India down in South Asia, a game which started in 1980, and was evident during Op *Sindoor* in 2025[7].

Politically, what has China done to approach victory in what is now openly perceived as the competition to become the world's hegemon? To answer that, we must look at the grand strategies currently in play. During the run-up to Xi Jinping's takeover of the Chinese Politburo in 2013, he articulated a vision for

China in a speech where he spokc of the "Chinese Dream." Subsequent white papers and official documents issued by Beijing clearly indicate the existence of a comprehensive Chinese Grand Strategy, with distinct silos for economic development, technological supremacy, living standards, social welfare, and military rejuvenation[8].

China unabashedly claims to challenge U.S. hegemony and to establish its own dominance over Asia. Given our experience of what China did in the 1980s, along with its clearly enunciated strategy of using Pakistan as a proxy, we should fully grasp what that implies. Therefore, this author does not subscribe to the prevailing belief in Delhi that China's threat to India is confined to the Himalayan border. The real threat, as he sees it, is to India's prosperous and democratic rise in Asia, which, in time, could challenge China's primacy in the region.

To understand that threat better, we must examine Beijing's military strategy, which is deeply interconnected with the rest of its grand strategy. The strongest component of its military grand strategy is its maritime dimension. In India, we often speak of China's entry into the Indian Ocean and its preparation to use four key ports—in Myanmar, Sri Lanka, Pakistan, and Djibouti. But these four are merely the tip of the iceberg. Beijing today controls 129 ports in 65 countries worldwide. In a sweeping westward arc, these ports span Eurasia, Africa, Western Europe, South America, and even across the Atlantic at the Panama Canal—Trump was correct on that one.

Figure 1: China's Westward Global Sweep taking control of 129 Ports in 65 countries

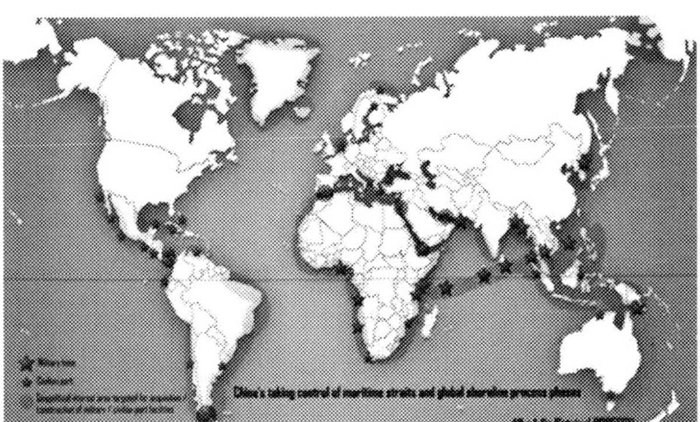

Source: Popescu, Alba Iulia Catrinel. "The 'China's Dream'—the Grand Strategy of Transforming China into a Global Maritime Power."[9]

The best estimates, including those generated by AI-based analyses, suggest that the PLA Navy accounts for nearly 70 percent of the capital budget of China's three armed services. Its commercial fleet now stands at 254 million gross tons—the largest merchant fleet in the world. Moreover, China is now the largest trading partner of 100 countries worldwide, including all of India's neighbours.

The purpose of taking over these ports is both commercial and military. The commercial objective is self-eminent. The military objective is to replicate worldwide, a continuous series of Sea denial areas based upon the littoral countries which have been brought under Chinese hegemony.

Figure 2: China's Global Port Investment

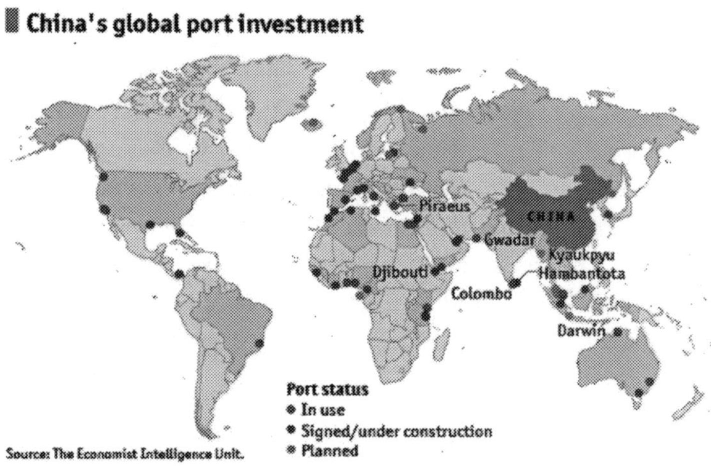

Source: IMR. "CHINA Strategic Ports Worldwide under Chinese Control."[10]

So, the question of whether China can make up the ten trillion dollars gap with the US, is now a moot question. The answer may lie in two new books that have been published. The first is by an Indian American, Rush Doshi, whose book *The Long Game: China's Grand Strategy to Displace American Order*, which states that China has long term plans to displace the US as the world's hegemon in an asymmetric way that will circumvent the current strength of the US. The second book is *Breakneck*[11] by a Chinese origin author Dan Wang, probably the most talked about book today, says that China is a country of Engineers, while the US is a country of lawyers. China will therefore out build American with brilliant metropolises that will create the innovators that will eventually overtake the US. What is our strategic response to all these inputs? Unfortunately, we have a poor Himalayan geography, being dominated by the Tibetan plateau. But on the contrary, China has a poor maritime geography with 60 percent of its overseas trade and 80 percent of its energy transiting the Malacca Straits – a feature which is in our power to control. Beijing is so obsessed with its Malacca dilemma that it continuously maintains a two billion barrels oil strategic reserve. We, on the other hand are blessed with a sublime maritime geography, virtually dominating the Indian ocean, and are best placed to threaten China's maritime strategy of the grand sweep westwards. But we are unlikely to achieve that with 14 percent of the defence budget being allocated to the Navy. True, things are changing. We have articulated *SAGAR* and *MAHASAGAR* vision of ports and their connectivity.[12]

India's approach to the changing dynamics of the Indian ocean follows two separate tracks. The first is a developmental and trade approach that includes humanitarian issues and being the first responder that sheds all transactional motives. This approach is brought out in *MAHASAGAR*, an acronym for *Mutual and Holistic Advancement for Security and Growth Across Regions*. Its inspiration comes from what the Indian ocean was in pre-colonial days and is a significant departure from China's attempts to gain littoral footholds in the Indian ocean region (IOR), which is purely extractive. This approach is inclusive of security considerations, where many African nations are keen to engage in maritime security exercises like AIKEYME[13] (Africa-India Key Maritime Engagement) which included harbour training as well as exercises in seagoing skills. *MAHASAGAR i*ncluded some transfer of hardware as well as the inauguration of the airstrip and jetty on Agaléga Island. It seeks to provide assistance to the littoral nations of the Indian ocean on India being a dependable partner in all circumstances. India's diplomatic initiative of the Indian Ocean Rim Initiative (IORA) supports Africa's littoral initiative of Africa Integrated Maritime Strategy (AIMS).

The second track would ideally be a grand maritime military strategy of our own that encompasses all the good points of *MAHASAGAR*. As stated earlier, there is an existing fifteen trillion dollars gap between the GDPs of India and China. Fortunately, the Indian GDP is growing faster, and India still has the democratic dividend. A comparative table of projected GDPs in 2050 is shown below as estimated by some agencies.

World GDPs in 2050 in $ Trillions

Agency	*China*	*US*	*India*
Price Waterhouse Cooper	49.85	34.10	28.02
Goldman Sachs	41.9	37.2	22.2

Source: Compiled by the Author

While the figures themselves may be open to question, the fact remains that the big take from this table is that we in India may have to live in asymmetry with China in the 21st century. What kind of a grand strategy can New Delhi craft that enables India to live in a just world, with:

- China likely to be the hegemon in both Asia and the World.
- China having given early indications ever since 1980 of what Beijing views India's place in the world.

This Paper is not about any conflict with China, but about how New Delhi can manage the long-term competition with a hegemonic China. As stated earlier, our poor Himalayan geography precludes our ability to create any anxieties in Beijing. Certainly, the Indian army can "defend" our northern border, but that is unlikely to worry Xi Jinping. On the other hand, a well-crafted military maritime Grand strategy in the Indian ocean, leveraging our favourable maritime geography and China's Malacca Dilemma, can act as the only card India has to play to keep Beijing quiescent. The military maritime quotient will have to be raised dramatically in which Naval Headquarters can use the modern war gaming facilities in Goa to arrive at an optimum force mix. *Prima facie*, we cannot escape the need to dominate the battlespace of the Indian Ocean, from the underwater domain to the surface of the ocean, up to the troposphere. The utility of large aircraft carriers, at least three in number, as well as missile firing nuclear attack submarines become obvious. Fortunately, the Indian Navy has developed a spectacular ship and submarine building capacity. This capability needs to be given priority to achieve force levels that, in Beijing's perception, can compromise Beijing's Grand Strategy, if it pursues an unfriendly policy towards India.

NOTES

1 Currently in the Archaeological Museum, Naples

2 "Largest Religious Structure." Guinness World Records. https://www.guinnessworldrecords.com/world-records/largest-religious-structure

3 Mahadevan, Raman. "Fortune Seekers: A Business History of Nattukottai Chettiars." 2025.

4 "China, Pakistan, and the bomb." The National Security Archive, George Washington University. May 3, 2004. https://nsarchive2.gwu.edu/NSAEBB/NSAEBB114/

5 Menon, Raja. "Personal Reminiscences of International Events."

6 Menon, Raja. "Personal Reminiscences of International Events."

7 "Kashmir: Four Days That Took India and Pakistan to the Brink." BBC. May 18, 2025. https://www.bbc.com/news/articles/cvgvr4r5d2qo.

8 Popescu, Alba Iulia Catrinel. "The 'China's Dream' - the Grand Strategy of Transforming China into a Global Maritime Power." Cogent Social Sciences 10 (1). 2024. doi:10.1080/23311886.2024.2414873.

9 Ibid.

10 "China Strategic Ports Worldwide under Chinese Control." IMR Media. May 15, 2025. https://imrmedia.in/china-strategic-ports-worldwide-under-chinese-control/.

11 Wang, Dan. "Breakneck: China's Quest to Engineer the Future." Kalorama. 2025.

12 Yadav, Tanya S., and Tuckfield, Hugh. "From SAGAR to MAHASAGAR: India's Strategic Evolution in the Indian Ocean Region." The Indo-Pacific Studies Center. April 28, 2025. https://www.indo-pacificstudiescenter.org/commentaries/india-MAHASAGAR-initiative.

13 "Africa India Key Maritime Engagement 2025." PIB, Ministry of Defence. December 4, 2025. https://www.pib.gov.in/PressReleasePage.aspx?PRID=2121218.

2

India and the Sea: A Civilisational Maritime Legacy

Saudiptendu Ray

Introduction

India's maritime history represents one of the world's oldest and most continuous traditions of seafaring. From the tidal dockyards of the Indus Valley to the export of Buddhist thought on merchant ships. From draining the Roman treasury through the pepper trade to the powerful naval expeditions of the Cholas, the Indian Ocean has served not as a frontier but as a connective highway—linking India directly with Africa, Arabia, and Southeast Asia, and indirectly with Europe. This vast maritime arena became the stage upon which India's economic prosperity, cultural diffusion, and spiritual imagination flourished for millennia. Maritime activity was integral to the evolution of India's cultural landscape and the spread of its religious geography. Ancient Indian civilisations also perceived the sea as a source of material wealth. Through archaeology, textual study, and cultural memory, India's maritime legacy reveals itself not merely as a chronicle of trade but as a civilisational continuum.

The Indus Valley and the Origins of Seafaring

The earliest evidence of organised maritime enterprise in the Indian subcontinent dates to the Indus Valley Civilisation (c. 3300– c. 1300 century BCE). Excavations at Lothal (covering an area of approximately 48,000 square metres), near the Gulf of Khambhat in Gujarat, uncovered what is widely regarded as the world's earliest known tidal dockyard.[1] Founded during the mature phase of the Indus Valley Civilisation around 2200 BCE,[2] Lothal demonstrates an advanced understanding of hydraulic engineering. The dockyard of Lothal measured about 215×37 meters, and was constructed with baked bricks and equipped with wharves. It had an inlet channel that connected it to the ancient course of the Sabarmati River.[3] It's hard-walled basin had two openings, likely functioning as sluice gates to control tidal flow.[4] The dockyard's sophisticated hydraulic engineering indicates precise knowledge of tidal movements and sedimentation—suggesting a sustained maritime economy rather than sporadic riverine activity.[5] Four large round stones with central perforations found at the bottom of the basin are believed to have served as anchors for ships that used the dockyard.[6] Similarly, *Dholavira*, now lying deep within the Rann of Kutch, was also a seaport during the Bronze Age.[7] Unfortunately, no remains of actual boats have been found from Lothal, but their shape can be inferred from excavated artefacts like clay models of boats and paintings on potsherds.[8] Similar clay models and depictions of boats have also been found at Harappa and Mohenjo-daro.[9]

Artefacts such as seals, carnelian beads, shell inlays, gold, cotton, lapis lazuli, wood, pearls and ivory were exported from the Indus Valley to Mesopotamia via the Persian Gulf.[10] Sumerian and Akkadian cuneiform tablets record extensive trade between Mesopotamia and the land known as *Meluhha*, generally identified with the Indus region.[11] Excavations at Harappa and Mohenjo-daro have also yielded Mesopotamian weights, attesting to commercial contact.[12] Conversely, Harappan traders imported copper, tin, and luxury goods from ancient Iran and Oman.[13] Indus seals discovered in Ur, Tell Asmar, Umma, and Kish further confirm that the Indus civilisation participated in a sophisticated trans-regional maritime network as early as the 3rd millennium BCE.[14] The Harappans' mastery of metallurgy, weights, and navigation made them pioneers of systematic seaborne commerce. These early contacts outside the Indian subcontinent were not isolated ventures; they were the initial stages in the cultural integration of the Indian Ocean. This foundation of maritime experience would shape India's coastal settlements for millennia.

The Vedic Age

In the Vedic corpus (c. 1500–500 BCE), maritime imagery assumes both practical and cosmic significance. In *Rigveda* Mandal 1, Verse (*Sukta*) 116, Hymn 3, there is a reference to a sea voyage with the help of a vessel called "*samudra-yana*", implying the exploration of sea and active navigation. Here, the vessel mentioned, was powered by a hundred oars.

तुग्रो ह भुज्युमश्विनोदमेघे रयिं न कश्चिन्ममृवाँ अवाहाः।
तमूहथुर्नौभिरात्मन्वतीभिरन्तरिक्षप्रुद्भिरपोदकाभिः॥[15]

Rigveda Mandal 9, Verse (*Sukta*) 33, Hymn 6, talks about ownership over the wealth of the ocean (*samudra*).

रायः समुद्राँश्चतुरोऽस्मभ्यं सोम विश्वतः ।
आ पवस्व सहस्रिणः॥[16]

Rigveda Mandal 1, Verse (*Sukta*) 25, Hymn 7, talks speak of Varuna "who knows the path of ships on the sea," indicating awareness of organised navigation.

वेदा यो वीनां पदमन्तरिक्षेण पतताम्।
वेद नावः समुद्रियः॥[17]

Rigveda Mandal 7, Verse (*Sukta*) 88, Hymn 3 mentions "crossing the wide rivers and the sea," which points to inland and possibly coastal voyages.

आ यद्रुहाव वरुणश्च नावं प्र यत्समुद्रमीरयाव मध्यम्।
अधि यदपां स्नुभिश्चराव प्र प्रेङ्ख ईङ्खयावहै शुभे कम्॥[18]

These references collectively show that **shipbuilding and navigation were sufficiently developed** to become metaphors for safety, salvation, and exploration in Vedic thought. The *Aitareya Brahmana*[19] and *Satapatha Brahmana*[20] also mention shipbuilding and trade by water, suggesting that the Vedic peoples were not confined to the inland plains. Beyond commerce, the sea (*samudra*) acquired sacred overtones—portrayed as a cosmic reservoir, the "gatherer of waters" that mirrors the universe.

Ramayana and Mahabharata

In the *Ramayana,* the term *suvarna rupyakam dvipam* (island of gold and silver) and *yava dvipam* (the island of Yava, possibly Java) is mentioned in *Kishkindha Kanda*, Sarga 40, where Sugriva instructs the southern search party led by Angad and Hanuman to explore all regions across the southern sea to search for the traces of Mother Sita.[21] The word *dvipa* is mentioned seven times and *samudra* is mentioned three times in the *Kishkinda Kanda*. These references from the *Ramayana* highlight the awareness of geography of distant islands, maritime routes to Southeast Asia and the presence of long-distance sea travel.

Similarly, the *Mahabharata* refers to words like *naubandhana* (habour) and *nau* (boat) multiple times. It also uses the term "shipwrecked merchants" as a simile at several instances. In *Sabha Parva*, during Yudhishthira's *Rajasuya* campaign, Sahadeva travels to "islands in the sea" (*samudra-dvesa*) and subdues their kings.[22] During the same *Rajasuya* campaign, Bhima was sent to conquer the eastern part of India (Bengal). After conquering the entire east, Bhima reached the port of Tamralipti. From there he proceeded towards *Sagaradvipa* (Sumatra) and subjugated the local ruler.[23] These are some of the instances of overseas expedition or island contact mentioned in the *Mahabharata*.

Mauryan Period

The Mauryan Empire (321–185 BCE) institutionalised maritime administration at the state level. Kautilya's *Arthashastra* details the office of the *Navadhyaksha* (Superintendent of Ships), who was responsible for overseeing all matters related to water transport and navigation, across canals, lakes, rivers, and oceans in the Mauryan Empire. The *Navadhyaksha's* duties included managing river and coastal trade operations, collecting taxes, monitoring fishing activities, enforcing port rules, ensuring adherence to local maritime customs, and maintaining ships in need of repair.[24] These administrative frameworks highlighted the Mauryan state's sophisticated knowledge of maritime administration, trade facilitation and security. It also highlighted a highly organised and state-supervised system of water transport.

The Mauryans achieved a high rate of vessels production in 3rd century BCE. The ship-building industry flourished under stringent state control. The artisans building those ships were public servants and were under the payroll of the state. These artisans were prohibited from building ships for private entities and individual traders. The state-owned ships were rented out to individuals for a time period for voyages and trade.[25] The Mauryans built ships of different classes for riverine, coastal and seaborne purpose. Teak wood and other hardwood were used for the construction of the hulls of the ships. The sophisticated designs and durability of the ships reflected their ability to undertake open-sea voyages.

Tamralipti (in West Bengal), Bharuch (Barygaza) and Sopara (Supparaka) were some of the major ports under the Mauryans. Tamralipti, which was the principal port on the eastern coast of India, was used as a primary port by Indian ships to and from Ceylon (Sri Lanka).[26] Goods from the Ganges plain were transported by river to Tamralipti, from where they were shipped to Sri Lanka and Southeast Asia. Bharuch, in Gujarat on the western coast of India was used for trade with Arabia.[27] Sopara in Thane, Maharashtra, which also has an Asokan rock edict, was an important commercial centre under the Mauryans.[28] These ports became nodal points linking the Indian subcontinent with Egypt, Arabia, Syria and Southeast Asia.[29] Buddhist missionaries used these trade routes to spread Buddhism in Southeast Asia. Ashoka's children Mahendra and Sanghamitra, in order to spread Buddhism, used the Tamralipti port to reach Sri Lanka.[30]

The Roman Trade Deficit

The *Periplus of the Erythraean Sea* (1st century CE) is an ancient Greek manuscript that provides a vivid Greek account describing the navigation and trading opportunities for Roman ports on the Egyptian coast and Horn of Africa with western Indian ports. The manuscript is a logbook recording sailing itineraries that provides a unique Hellenic view of India and the trade taking place in the Indian Ocean. It mentions Bharuch (Barygaza) port, a prominent centre for commerce on India's west. Bharuch exported agate, carnelian, muslins, silk, mallow cloth, ivory and gemstones, and imported wine, silver, copper, tin, lead, coral, topaz, glass, and metals.[31] Muziris, on the Malabar Coast, was flooded with Roman coins for pepper that was in high demand in Roman Empire.[32] Ancient Tamil poetry talks about these Roman cravings for pepper, *"Rich Muziris, the place where the large and well-crafted ships of the Yavanas come with gold and leave carrying pepper.*"[33]

The value of Indian trade may be estimated from a passage of Pliny, in which he recorded that India drained the Roman Empire of 50 million *sesterces* (ancient Roman coin) every year.[34] Thousands of Roman coins were also discovered in Tamil Nadu and Andhra Pradesh, which attest to thriving Indo-Roman trade.[35] William Dalrymple in his book 'The Golden Road', calls India "the sink of the world's precious metals". Indian merchants catered to Europe's unending appetite for luxury goods—diamonds and rubies, fine silks and cottons, sandalwood, spices such as cloves and pepper, rare medicinal substances, ivory, tortoiseshell, and even exotic animals.[36] A vivid example of this Roman opulence is Lollia Paulina, the wife of Emperor Caligula, who was said to have adorned herself with Indian emeralds and pearls valued at an astonishing 40 million *sesterces*.[37]

The seasonal monsoon winds, described by the Greek navigator Hippalus[38] but known earlier to Indian sailors, enabled predictable round-trip voyages between the Red Sea and western India. This phase marked the crystallisation of an Indian Ocean commercial system driven by indigenous knowledge and technology. The ports were not isolated entrepots but urban hubs integrated with inland markets and political authorities, reflecting a holistic economic geography.

Buddhism and Trade

A striking feature of India's maritime history is the integration of religion and commerce. Maritime and overland trade routes were the primary means by which Buddhist thought and imagery reached various parts of Asia from India. Archaeological evidences and literary sources highlight the important role played by the maritime trade routes in the exchange of Buddhist religious thoughts from India to Sri Lanka, Myanmar, Thailand, Indonesia, Vietnam, China, Korea and other parts of Asia.[39]

The trading ports provided the platform for interaction between missionaries, religious pilgrims and traders. Buddhist travellers from different parts of the world extensively used the Tamralipti seaport to visit the most important centres of Buddhism, such as Bodh Gaya, Pataliputra, Nalanda, Rajgir, Sarnath etc., in the Gangetic basin. *Mahavamsa*, the Sri Lankan Chronicle, mentions that the sapling of the great Bodhi tree from Bodh Gaya was brought to Sri Lanka by Sanghamitra via Tamralipti port.[40]

A majority of the Buddhist sites in western India, were connected with any one of the various seaports on the Arabian coast. These western seaports included Bharuch, Sopara, Semylla (Chaul), and Calliena (Kalyan).[41] These ports were also important centres of Buddhism and received donations from local and foreign merchant communities.[42] The prosperity of the Buddhist monasteries in the coastal region was dependent on the commercial ventures by sea. Inscriptions from Sanchi and Bharhut record donations by *setthis* (merchant-bankers) for the maintenance of monastic institutions and the construction of ships.[43] From the 3rd century BCE onward, Buddhist monasteries along the western coast—at Sopara, Kalyan, Bharuch, and later Amaravati in the east—served as rest-houses, warehouses, and moral anchors for merchants.[44]

These networks reveal a moralised economy in which trade was regarded as a field of merit (*punya*). Monks offered blessings for safe voyages, while merchants endowed stupas in gratitude for successful expeditions. This synergy of faith and enterprise transformed the Indian Ocean into a space of spiritual as well as material exchange.

Cultural Links with Southeast Asia

Between the 1st century BCE and the 7th century CE, Indian maritime networks expanded eastward across the Bay of Bengal into Southeast Asia, known in ancient sources as *Suvarnabhumi* (Land of Gold).[45] Merchants, Buddhist missionaries, and Brahmin scholars sailed from ports such as Kaveripattinam (in Kaveri Delta), Podouke (Pondicherry), Tamralipti, and Nagapattinam to regions that would become Funan (Cambodia), Dvaravati (Thailand), Srivijaya (Sumatra), Java and Champa (Vietnam).[46] These maritime exchanges carried not just goods but also Sanskrit language, literary epics, political models, and religious iconography.[47]

Inscriptions written in Pallava-Grantha and Kawi scripts appear throughout Southeast Asia,[48] while local adaptations of the *Ramayana*—the *Ramakien*[49] in Thailand and the *Reamker*[50] in Cambodia—demonstrate the cultural reach of Indian narratives.[51] *Kakawin Ramayana* emerged in the island of Java in Indonesia in the 9th century CE. *Wayang Kulit*, a shadow puppetry version of *Ramayana* evolved in the island of Bali. Similarly, other versions of *Ramayana* emerged in different parts of Southeast Asia like *Phra Lak Phra Lam* (Laos), *Yama Zatdaw* (Myanmar), *Hikayat Seri Rama* (Malaysia) and *Phra Ram* (Vietnam).

The Indic traditions that seeped into Southeast Asia through the maritime trade link underwent a gradual process of cultural assimilation with the native animist practices present in Southeast Asia. Shaivism and Vaishnavism also formed syncretic relationships with Buddhism in Southeast Asia.[52] The indigenous fertility cults and *Devaraja* cult merged with lingam worship practices of Shaivism. Similarly, Vishnu's divine forms merged with native rulers throughout Southeast Asia. In the *Devaraja* (God-King) cult in Southeast Asia, the king is considered to be Shiva's physical presence on earth.[53] Empires and kingdoms like Khmer in Cambodia; Mon and Ayutthaya in Thailand; Sailendra and Mataram in Indonesia and Lan Xang in Laos showed signs of the presence of the Hindu politico-religious institution of *Devaraja*. The sea was the great highway of cultural and religious intercourse, and not merely of commerce.

The Pallavas, Cholas, and the Zenith of Indian Naval Power

The Pallavas (3rd–9th century CE) were able to establish themselves as a strong maritime power in the early medieval period. They used the coastal cities of Nagapattinam and Mamallapuram to project their power and influence across the Indian Ocean, fostering diplomatic, commercial, and cultural connections with Sri Lanka and Southeast Asia. Nagapattinam became a hub for trade and maritime activity. The Pallavas nurtured vigorous maritime links with China and Southeast Asia. Archaeological finds of Chinese ceramics and Roman coins in Pallava port sites suggest continuity of long-distance trade traditions dating back to the Sangam period.

Inscriptions from the reign of Narasimhavarman mention embassies to the Tang court, underscoring the diplomatic dimension of seafaring.[54] Under Narasimhavarman's rule, a Buddhist monk named Vajrabodhi was sent to multiple regions including Sri Lanka, Srivijaya (in Indonesia) and China on a religious mission.[55] A Buddhist temple was constructed at Nagapattinam under Narasimhavarman's rule, reportedly under the orders of a Chinese king for the sake of Chinese Buddhists who came to Nagapattinam from China for trade.[56]

The Cholas (9th–13th century CE), however, epitomised the zenith of India's naval power. Under Rajaraja I and Rajendra I, the Cholas constructed formidable fleets that projected power across the Bay of Bengal. Rajendra's naval expedition against the Srivijaya Empire in Sumatra, Java and Malaysia (c. 1025 CE) demonstrated India's capacity to secure trade routes and assert influence throughout maritime Southeast Asia.[57] Chinese records (*Song Shi*) describe Chola envoys arriving at the imperial court, while inscriptions at Thanjavur and Gangaikonda Cholapuram celebrate naval conquests and overseas tribute.[58] The Chola navy ensured safe passage for traders, strengthened economic alliances, and symbolised India's civilisational confidence on the high seas. Their achievement represents not a sudden militarisation but the culmination of two millennia of maritime continuity reaching back to Harappan ports and Mauryan administration.

Indigenous Shipbuilding and Navigation

India's maritime achievements were underpinned by sophisticated indigenous technologies. Texts such as the *Yukti-kalpataru*[59] (11th century CE) and *Brihat Samhita* describe ship types, hull proportions, and auspicious measurements.[60] The *Yukti-kalpataru* classifies vessels into different categories based on size, quality of material used and purpose of use. The ships were generally divided into two broad categories: Ordinary (*Samanya*) and Special (*Visesa*) vessels. The special type (*Visesa*) was meant for sea voyages and was further subdivided into two: *Dirgha* (based on length of the vessel) and *Unnata* (based on height of the vessel).[61]

Archaeological evidence from Bet Dwarka and other coastal sites reveals the use of stitched-plank construction, in which wooden planks were sewn with coir cordage—a flexible and seaworthy design still visible in traditional dhows of Gujarat and Kerala.[62] Indian mariners also possessed advanced navigational knowledge. Instruments such as the *ghatika-yantra* (water clock) and *kamal* (celestial board) were employed to determine latitude. Mariners timed their departures with the southwest and northeast monsoons, knowledge that later Arab and European sailors would adopt.[63] As S. Balakrishna notes, the Indian contribution to navigation lay not in isolated invention but in the systematisation of oceanic science—a fusion of empirical observation and cosmological understanding.[64]

Merchant Guilds and the Organisation of Overseas Trade

By the early medieval period, maritime commerce was dominated by powerful guilds such as the Manigramam, the Five Hundred Lords of Ayyavole (*Ainurruvar*), and the Nanadesis. These associations transcended regional boundaries, operating across the Indian Ocean from Sri Lanka to Sumatra.[65] The Ayyavole 500 styled themselves as "lords of the markets and protectors of the ocean-crossing trade routes."[66]

Guild inscriptions from South India and Southeast Asia reveal their corporate character: they standardised trade practices, provided mutual insurance, and endowed temples and rest houses abroad. In Takuapa (Thailand) and Barus (Sumatra), Tamil inscriptions commemorate merchant donations to local shrines, confirming the diasporic presence of Indian trading communities.[67] These guilds exemplified a form of socially embedded capitalism, where profit was balanced by religious duty and collective ethics—an economic model that sustained maritime commerce for centuries.

The Ocean as Sacred Space

Beyond its material functions, the sea occupied a central place in Indian spiritual thought. The *Samudra Manthan* myth in the *Puranas*—the churning of the ocean to obtain *amrita* (nectar of immortality)—symbolised the creative tension between chaos and order. Rituals such as *Samudra Snan* (sea bathing) during *Magha Purnima* and pilgrimages to coastal tirthas express reverence for the ocean's purifying power.

Philosophically, the sea embodies both danger and deliverance. The concept of *bhava-sagara*—the ocean of worldly existence—frames human life as a voyage toward liberation. In literature, crossing the sea (*sagara-langhana*) becomes a metaphor for transcendence.[68] Thus, maritime imagery permeated India's metaphysics, linking physical navigation to spiritual aspiration.

This sacralisation of the sea explains why India's maritime enterprise was marked not by conquest but by cultural dialogue—the ocean was not to be conquered, but understood.

Decline, Continuity, and Transformation

India's maritime prominence waned after the 13th century CE due to political fragmentation, the rise of new Islamic polities, and the redirection of global trade through West Asia and, later, Europe. Yet coastal commerce remained resilient. Ports such as Calicut, Cochin, and Surat continued to flourish as hubs of the spice trade.[69] Even under shifting empires, India's coastal communities—Arab-Indian traders, Gujarati shipbuilders, and Tamil guilds—maintained transoceanic links.

When Portuguese and Dutch fleets entered the Indian Ocean in the 16th century, they encountered a maritime world already structured by Indian precedent. As historian Sanjay Subrahmanyam has shown, the Indian Ocean functioned as a single economic and cultural zone "long before the rise of modern empires."[70] The continuity of indigenous maritime institutions underlines the adaptability of India's oceanic civilisation.

Conclusion: Legacy and Contemporary Revival

India's ancient maritime heritage embodies a civilisational consciousness that fused material skill with spiritual depth. From the dockyards of Lothal to the naval armadas of the Cholas, from the Buddhist monasteries of the western coast to the temples of Angkor and Borobudur, the sea served as India's most profound metaphor and medium of connection.

In recent decades, India has sought to rediscover and preserve this heritage. The *Sagarmala* Project, aimed at modernising ports and coastal infrastructure, consciously invokes the spirit of ancient maritime connectivity. The proposed Lothal Maritime Heritage Complex will memorialise the Indus Valley's seafaring legacy through museum displays and archaeological conservation. Excavations at *Muziris*, *Arikamedu*, and *Bhitthargaon* continue to reveal the depth of India's oceanic engagement.

Beyond heritage, India's maritime history offers a philosophical blueprint for its role in the Indo-Pacific: a vision of connectivity rooted in exchange, not expansion. The idea of the Indian Ocean as a "shared cultural space" informs India's modern diplomacy through initiatives like Project Mausam, which seeks to revive ancient cultural linkages across littoral Asia. This revival affirms that maritime history is not simply a record of trade routes but a civilisational narrative of unity through diversity, echoing the timeless dictum *Vasudhaiva Kutumbakam*—"the world is one family."

NOTES

1 Habib, Irfan. "A People's History of India 2- The Indus Civilization". Tulika Books, Aligarh, p 44. 2002.

2 Kulke, Herman and Dietmar Rothermund. "A History of India", Fourth Edition. p 26.

3 Rao, S. R. "Lothal and the Indus Civilization", Asia Publishing House, 85–90. 1973.

4 Rao, S. R. "*Lothal: A Harappan Port Town*", Archaeological Survey of India. Vol. 1, pp 52–54. 1955–62.

5 Leshnik, Lawrence S. "The 'Harappan 'Port' at Lothal: Another View." *American Anthropologist*, New Series, 70, no. 5, 911–922. October 1968.

6 Op. cit. note no. 2.

7 Ibid. p 4.

8 Rao, S. R. "Shipping and Maritime Trade of the Indus People". Penn Museum, Expedition Magazine. 1965. https://www.penn.museum/sites/expedition/shipping-and-maritime-trade-of-the-indus-people/

9 "Harappa and the Erythraean Sea, The Maritime History Podcast, Episode 11. https://maritimehistorypodcast.com/wp-content/uploads/2022/01/011-Transcript-File.pdf?utm

10 Ratnagar, Shereen. "Encounters- The Westerly Trade of Harrappa Civilization". Oxford

University Press, pp 68-71. 1981.

11 Wheeler, Mortimer. "The Indus Civilization: Supplementary vplume to the Cambridge History of India", Third Edition, Cambridge University Press, 81. 1968.

12 Op. cit. note no. 10. p 227.

13 Ibid. p 97.

14 Possehl, Gregory L. "Ancient Cities of the Indus", Vikas Publishing House Pvt Ltd, New Delhi, 130-134. 1979.

15 *Rigveda* 1.116.3.

16 *Rigveda* 9.33.6.

17 *Rigveda* 1.25.7.

18 *Rigveda* 7.88.3.

19 Haug, Martin (ed. & tr.), "*The Aitareya Brahmanam of the Rgveda*", Vol. I. p 26 and 195.

20 *Satapatha Brahmanam*, Kanda I, Adhyaya 8, Brahmana 1

21 "Kishkindha Kanda - The Empire of Holy Monkeys Chapter" [Sarga] 40. (4-40-30, 4-40-31, 4-40-32) https://www.valmikiramayan.net/utf8/kish/sarga40/kishkindharoman40.htm

22 Kisari Mohan Ganguli (tr.). "Vyasa *Mahabharata*". Book 2, *Sabha-Parvan*, Section XXX (2.30.26–28).

23 Tripati, S. and S. R. Rao, "Tamralipti: The Ancient Port of India", *Studies in History and Culture*, Volume 2 No. 1. 1994.

24 Shamasastry, R. "The Duties of Government Superintendents (Book II, Chapter 28)" in Kautilya's Arthashastra, p 179.

25 Mookerji, Radhakumud. "*Indian Shipping: A History of the Sea-Borne Trade and Maritime Activity of the Indians from the Earliest Times*". London: Longmans, Green and Co., 1912, pp 102-103.

26 Thapar, Romila. "Asoka and the Decline of the Mauryas". Oxford University Press, 1961, p 131.

27 Ibid. p 81.

28 Ibid. p 236.

29 Mookerji, Radhakumud. "*Indian Shipping: A History of the Sea-Borne Trade and Maritime Activity of the Indians from the Earliest Times*". Longmans, Green and Co., 1912, p 113.

30 Geiger, Wilhelm (tr.). "The Mahavamsa: The Great Chronicle of Ceylon". Pali Text Society, Oxford University Press, p 128. 1912.

31 Schoff, Wilfred H. "The Periplus of the Erythraean Sea: Travel and Trade in the Indian Ocean by a Merchant of the First Century", Longmans, Green and Co., pp 41–48. 1912.

32 Ibid. p 287.

33 McLaughlin, Raoul. "*Rome and the Distant East: Trade Routes to the Ancient Lands of Arabia, India and China.*" Continuum, pp 48-49. 2010.

34 Majumdar, R. C. "Ancient India", Delhi Motilal Banarsidass, p 213. 1960.

35 Ibid. pp 210–14.

36 Saini, Ajay. "Review Of 'The Golden Road': How Ancient India Transformed the World." Outlook, December 7 2024. https://www.outlookindia.com/amp/story/books/review-of-the-golden-road-how-ancient-india-transformed-the-world?utm_source=chatgpt.com

37 Gori, Rachele. Mining and Minerals Trade on the Silk Road: Scientific and Archaeological Analyses of Gems, Gold, and Other Luxury Materials from the 1st Millennium BCE to

the 1st Millennium CE. PhD diss., Durham University, p 146. 2012.

38 Bostock, John and H. T. Riley. "The Natural History of Pliny", Vol. II, London, p 65.

39 Dayalan, D. "Digitalization of Buddhist Sites in India." In *Buddhism and the Fourth Industrial Revolution*, Hong Duc Publishing House, Hanoi, pp 171-184.

40 Ibid. pp 178-179.

41 Ray, Himanshu Prabha. "Monastery and Guild: Commerce under the Satavahanas", Oxford University Press, pp 57-65. 1986.

42 Ibid. pp 158-159.

43 Luders, Heinrich, revised by Ernst Waldschmidt and M.A. Mehendale. "*Corpus Inscriptionum Indicarum". Vol. II, Part II: Brahmi Inscriptions from Bharhut.* Archaeological Survey of India. 1963.

44 Ray, Himanshu Prabha. "*The Archaeology of Seafaring in Ancient South Asia"*. Cambridge University Press, pp 98-102. 2003.

45 Coedès, George. "*The Indianized States of Southeast Asia"*. Translated by Susan Brown Cowing. Honolulu: University of Hawai'i Press, p 29. 1968.

46 Ibid. pp 27-33.

47 Pollock, Sheldon I. "*The Language of the Gods in the World of Men: Sanskrit, Culture, and Power in Premodern India"*. University of California Press, pp 12–26. 2006.

48 Griffiths, Arlo. "Early Indic Inscriptions of Southeast Asia." In *Lost Kingdoms: Hindu-Buddhist Sculpture of Early Southeast Asia*, edited by John Guy, New York: Metropolitan Museum of Art; New Haven: Yale University Press, pp 47-55. 2014.

49 Shastri, Satya Vrat. "*Ramayana in Southeast Asia", Vol. 1: Ramakien (Thai Ramayana)*, New Delhi: Sahitya Akademi, pp 1–20. 2021.

50 Jacob, Judith M. (tr. & ed.), "*Reamker (Ramakerti): The Cambodian Version of the Ramayana"*, Oriental Translation Fund / Royal Asiatic Society, Psychology Press, pp 1-10. 1986.

51 Puri, B. N. "The Cult of Devaraja in Kambuja and in India," Proceedings of the Indian History Congress 18, pp 114–120. 1955.

52 Acri, Andrea. "Modern Hindu Intellectuals and Ancient Texts: Reforming Saiva Yoga in Bali." Bijdragen tot de Taal-, Land- enVolkenkunde 169, no. 1, pp 68–103. 2013.

53 Op. cit. note no. 45. pp 97-103.

54 Sastri, K. A. Nilakanta. "A History of South India", Oxford University Press. 1958.

55 Ray, Himanshu Prabha, and Susan Mishra, eds. "Sailing to Suvarnabhumi: Cultural Routes and Maritime Landscapes". Aryan Books International, p 39. 2013.

56 Sridhar, T.S. et al. "Foreign Coins in the collection of Government Museum", Chennai (Chinese, Roman & Venetian Coins), Bulletin of the Government Museum, Chennai, The Principal Secretary / Commissioner of Museums, Government Museum, p 6. 2011.

57 Sakhuja, Vijay and Sangeeta Sakhuja. "Rajendra Chola I's Naval Expedition to Southeast Asia: A Nautical Perspective," in Nagapattinam to Suvarnadwipa: Reflections on the Chola Naval Expeditions to Southeast Asia, ed. Hermann Kulke, K. Kesavapany, and Vijay Sakhuja, ISEAS, p 76. 2009.

58 Karashima, Noboru, and Tansen Sen. "Chinese Texts Describing or Referring to the Chola Kingdom as Zhu-nian." In Nagapattinam to Suvarnadwipa: Reflections on the Chola Naval Expeditions to Southeast Asia, edited by Hermann Kulke, K. Kesavapany, and Vijay Sakhuja, Appendix II, Singapore: ISEAS/Manohar, pp 292–316. 2009.

59 Bhoja, King. "Yukti-Kalpataru". Sitaram Ghosh Trust, Darshan Vidyalaya, Kolkata.

60 Kaye, G. R. "Indian Mathematics," Journal of the Asiatic Society of Bengal 73, pp 1–48. 1904.

61 Banger, M. K. "Ancient Shipbuilding in India." Journal of Naval Engineering 34, no. 1. pp 228-236. December 1992.

62 Hornell, James. "Maritime Activity in Ancient India", Marine Department, pp 45–52. 1920.

63 Balakrishna, S. "The Indian Contribution to Navigation", Bharatiya Vidya Bhavan, pp 19–25. 1961.

64 Ibid. p 40.

65 Raman, K.V. "Merchant Guilds of South India," Journal of the Economic and Social History of the Orient 12, no. 2, pp 155–162. 1969.

66 Karashima, Noboru. "A Concise History of South India", Oxford University Press, p 91. 2014.

67 Manguin, Pierre-Yves. "The Merchant and the King: Political Myths of Southeast Asian Coastal Polities," in Southeast Asia in the 9th to 14th Centuries, ed. Marr and Milner, ISEAS, pp 96–98. 1986.

68 Kramrisch, Stella. "The Hindu Temple", Motilal Banarsidass, pp 22–26. 1946.

69 Chaudhuri, K.N. "Trade and Civilization in the Indian Ocean", Cambridge University Press, pp 108–115. 1985.

70 Subrahmanyam, Sanjay. "The Political Economy of Commerce: Southern India, 1500–1650", Cambridge University Press, p 12. 1990.

3

The Outreach of India's Maritime Heritage

Raghvendra Singh

The Indian subcontinent juts out for a thousand miles, tapering off at Kanyakumari within the Indian Ocean. India and Indian Ocean have been inseparably connected by geography and history. The sphere of Indian Ocean extends from East Africa to Tasmania and from Asia to Antarctica, the Persian Gulf, the Red Sea, the Arabian Sea, the Bay of Bengal and several islands, are all part of its extension. This region has been a cradle of civilisations, major religions and faiths of the world, *Sanatan Dharma* and by extension Buddhism and Jainism, Judaism, Christianity and Islam—are all represented in the littoral and island nations of the Indian Ocean.

We know how geography exerts great influence on politics and security, particularly in matters 'maritime'. It is in this context that the Indian Ocean acquires importance. On its waters are carried half of the world's container shipments, one-third of bulk cargo traffic and two-thirds of oil shipments. Among its geographical features are the Cape of Good Hope, the Strait of *Bab-el-Mandeb* (entrance to Red Sea), the Straits of Hormuz, Malacca and Sunda. About one-third of the world's population inhabits the littoral straits and islands of the Indian Ocean. Four of these countries have populations in excess of 140 million people, namely, India, Pakistan, Indonesia and Bangladesh.

Millenniums before Columbus sailed the Atlantic and Magellan crossed the Pacific; the Indian Ocean was an active thoroughfare of cultural and commercial traffic. It was around 45 CE that discovery was made of how to use the monsoon winds to directly cross the Arabian sea instead of hugging the coast. The Indian navigators though had already sailed and discovered

Socotra long before first century CE. They had navigated the Red Sea using the magnetic needle, *matsya yantra,* for determining direction. The existence of prosperous Hindu colonies in Malaya, Sumatra, Java, Cambodia and modern-day Vietnam clearly indicates that the Bay of Bengal had been mastered long before 1st century CE. That peninsular India was maritime in its tradition is borne out by the writings of *Fa Hien*, a Chinese visitor to India between 400 CE and 410 CE. He was transported through sea from Sri Lanka to Sri Vijaya along with 200 merchants, all of whom professed the Sanatan Dharma. There are numerous other references to the *Mauryas* and the Andhras with regard to the Eastern Seas. The Chinese had an extensive sea trade along the Malabar Coast, this trade being there during the Tang dynasty period with Calicut. *Hiuen Tsang* who visited India in the 7th century CE describes the vast overseas trade during the Gupta period. There are numerous mentions of the Chola emperors and their powerful sea-faring capacity.

Using biannual monsoons, the east-bound shipping from the Red Sea and Persian Gulf regularly visited South India. During summer months, the prevailing wind system of Indian Ocean blows from South West. As a result, sailing used to be suspended from May until September along the West Coast of India as well as the South Arabian coast. A reversal takes place around October. The North-East monsoon dominated between November and April. The Red Sea has its own pattern of wind system which does not coincide with the monsoon. The ancient vessels that left the Red Sea ports in July attempted to reach the Indian ports before September. The return voyage took place between November and April with the beginning of North-East monsoon. The Roman ships, however, made the passage to India during the monsoons, when all other shipping was closed, perhaps due to the sturdy construction of Roman crafts.

A vibrant trade route through sea linked the east with the west, which stretches from the west coast of Japan, through islands of Indonesia, India and to the land of the Middle East; and from there across the Mediterranean to Europe. The links were formed by traders through buying and selling from port to port. They traded majorly in spices. The use of monsoon winds in the Indian Ocean was a boon to sailing ships. It helped them in their travels to and from India.

Artefacts of Saraswati-Sindhu Civilisation have been found in the Middle-East and Egypt dating back to 5000 years. Large colonies of Romans lived in the port cities of India, especially on the eastern coast in Tamil Nadu in the first millennium. Some of the earliest sea-faring ships plied between the coast of Kerala and the Middle East. The second oldest mosque in the world was constructed in *Kodungallur* in Kerala in 629 CE. Buddhism spread to all corners of Asia through sea and land routes. Centres like Sukhothai, Ayodhya, Angkor Wat in the East, or Swat, Bamiyan, or *Dun Hwang*, are manifestations of vibrant cultural links of India with the regions around the Indian Ocean. *Ramayan* was the most popular story told in this region. The Hindu and Buddhist traditions provide some of the finest paintings, sculptures and reliefs across Asia.

The historians and archaeologists in this region have focused largely on land-based concerns. Consequently, the cultural heritage that drove maritime connectivity and which related to the large rubric of geo-politics has been ignored. There is a need therefore to create a universally accepted and understood historical narrative of maritime connectivity. The answer lies in utilising the UNESCO's world heritage platform. A large number of world heritage sites are located on the coasts across the Western Indian Ocean.

How does one bring them into dialogue with each other and build partnerships on the basis of shared maritime heritage?

Some examples of commonality could be based on the *Dhow* culture of the Indian Ocean, rigorous research and analysis of sea stories circulating in the Western Indian Ocean in different languages, the great body of literature on the origin of major crops, the archaeological remains of which suggest contacts across the Western Indian Ocean, transportation of food on account of shortage, trade in spices, the language sea-farers communicated in. They could all result in building partnerships. Archaeological exploration in *Socotra* at the mouth of the Red Sea led to the discovery of more than 200 drawings dating from the second to fourth century CE. Of these, 192 are in Brahmi script, one in Kharoshti, one in Bactrian, three in Greek, and one in Aramaic. *Socotra* was inscribed on the world heritage list as a natural site in 2008.

But the building of transnational maritime network has received little attention from academics or policy makers. *Socotra* hardly finds any mention, as also several other coastal world heritage sites across the Western Indian ocean that show evidence of maritime activity. In Ajanta Caves the narrative of *Simhala*, a sea-faring merchant is prominently depicted. *Simhala* was an incarnation of *Siddhartha Gautama*. He, along with 500 merchants, had landed in *Tamradweep* (Sri Lanka). This is an interesting story which finds connect with Sri Lanka. There is great scope for collaboration amongst maritime museums. Several countries in the Indian Ocean region have already established links. A collaboration with the maritime museum, currently being set up at Lothal in Gujarat, India would prove very useful.

India has yet to bring to the fore its historical connections across Africa, the Middle East, and Southern Europe. India should aim to revive its maritime ties, among the Indian Ocean ports of Kerala, Deccan and Gujarat with Sri Lanka and the Gulf Cooperation Council (GCC) countries such as Oman, Bahrain and Saudi Arabia. While inaugurating the Kochi metro in June 2017, Prime Minister Modi had called Kochi, "The Queen of the Arabian Sea", an important spice trading centre. Kerala should identify a specific role under this initiative. A major goal should be to revive the historical trade routes in a large geo-political and geo-economic context.

How can India launch a project to sustain its cross-national connectivity with East Africa, the Arabian Peninsula, the Indian subcontinent, Sri Lanka, and South East Asian archipelagos?

More than three dozen countries can be identified as partners under this Outreach Project. Trade should be a major concern, given the fact that the Gulf Cooperation countries are India's biggest trading partners. India's trade diversification as well as free-trade agreements have affected the export potential of spices from Kerala. The international market of spice has also witnessed new players. The Project may be used to revive Kerala's trade route. In fact, it should seek to re-establish Kerala's maritime connectivity with countries it had exchanges with. India has a vast human resource already in existence in many GCC countries. This is a major source of soft power which India should make use of.

India is a signatory to various UNESCO conventions. This initiative will provide a platform across the Indian Ocean world through cross-cultural transnational narrative. It will seek a trans-national nomination under World Heritage by highlighting links of the Indian Ocean Maritime route. This will provide visibility to connectivity, encourage research, tourism, and develop heritage. The program will navigate through coastal architecture, maritime heritage, artefacts, maritime museums, underwater cultural heritage, industrial heritage, ship building, intangible cultural heritage, trade routes, cultural products, pilgrimage, religious travel, oral traditions and literary traditions.

The idea is to formalise subjects based upon which this effort gets executed. A possible way forward would be to begin collecting data on historical exchanges in the field of both tangible and intangible maritime cultural heritage. This may include knowledge pathways related to art, philosophy, mathematics, geography and sciences. No project of this kind exists at the moment. Scholars and experts across the region should examine the data of these exchanges and its implications jointly. This research should feed into proposing a World Heritage nomination to the UNESCO. This will truly place the maritime cultural heritage of the Indian Ocean on a firm and independent footing.

The Project should also have both cultural and serious strategic dimensions. India should consider including Andaman and Nicobar Islands also within this ambit, given the island's location, close to the straits of Malacca and Thailand. The purpose behind this Project should be to remind the region as to why the ocean is called the Indian Ocean. The Project should be made more meaningful so that it does not lack teeth.

The Chinese Maritime Silk Route (MSR) initiative is already impacting the strategic balance in the Indian Ocean region. It is common knowledge that MSR strives for an influence in the Indian Ocean. The new geo-politics of the Indian Ocean region is defined by America's declining influence. The old geo-politics of the Indian Ocean Region (IOR) – characterised by US hegemony as a leading force from the Middle East to the Pacific – is giving way to a new geo-politics as America's focus shifts gradually from the Indian Ocean to the West Pacific region. India and Australia have a maritime presence in the Indian Ocean along with Iran, Saudi Arabia and Pakistan. But in this region, the geo-political competition is now shifting from land to sea. Maritime rivalry in this region may intensify.

If United States continues to diminish its influence in the Indian Ocean, which country can replace it?

The power vacuum left by America's retreat needs to be compensated by a concerted effort by various other countries to maintain a strategic balance in the Indian Ocean Region. Though India's economy is the biggest in the IOR, China is the biggest user of its sea lanes. The MSR initiative is an indication of increasing realisation of the growing salience of the Indian Ocean. MSR is aimed at allowing China's maritime military power to break free from the geographical constraints of the Western Pacific island chains.

Over 60 per cent of China's oil imports transit via the Indian Ocean. Even as China builds pipe lines through Myanmar and Pakistan, they would be quite inadequate to mitigate its energy insecurity. MSR is China's crucial element of grand strategy to carve out a Chinese sphere of influence in an area where the American presence is ebbing. Many countries in the Indian Ocean Region endorse the MSR idea, because it comes with economic incentives, thus softening China's maritime rise. The MSR tends to also negate the anxiety caused on account of rapid expansion of PLA navy and also the String of Pearls theory.

Nearly all of India's merchandise trade transit via the sea. Land based trade routes are unlikely to come up in the near future. India would necessarily have to rely on international shipping lanes. Security and safety of the shipping would remain a paramount concern for many years to come. The critical question is whether MSR shall impair this safety? In what way could MSR harm India's freedom of navigation in this region? The ultimate goal of China is to acquire maritime hegemony in the Indian Ocean, thus raising its global image and ensuring energy security. The MSR belongs only to China. MSR has a potentiality of turning into a battlefield for maritime hegemony as China possesses the power to claim it.

China uses debt diplomacy to expand its global foot-print. India has been apprehensive of China's role in building outposts around its periphery. MSR highlights Sri Lanka's position on the East-West Sea route wherein China's economic and military interests' fuse. Gwadar, Hambantota, Kyaukpyu and Chittagong validate this argument.

The Belt and Road Initiative (BRI) and the Maritime Silk Road (MSR) have on boarded approximately 65 countries. The initiatives of China were first converted into strategy and thereafter put into action. China has used its full diplomatic abilities to bring the academia, media, museums and government apparatus to ensure the successful implementation of BRI and MSR initiatives. The Chinese initiative is a comprehensive one.

BRI and MSR offer thousands of scholarships, hold art and film festivals, book fairs, make it more convenient to apply for tourist visas, cooperate on epidemic information, treatment technologies, public health emergencies, technology transfer, maritime cooperation, cooperation among cities, and among non-governmental organisations. India is yet to implement an initiative that may promote understanding on common heritage and multiple identities.

We are yet to revive lost linkages, provide cross-cultural transnational narrative and evolve a relationship between natural and cultural heritage.[1]

NOTES

1 The following text is based on the Keynote Address delivered by the author at a webinar titled *"Roads, Winds, Spices in the Western Indian Ocean: The Memory and Geopolitics of Maritime Heritage"*, organised by the Indian Council of World Affairs (ICWA) on 6 July 2020. https://icwa.in/show_content.php?lang=1&level=1&ls_id=5709&lid=4033

4

India's Evolving Approach to Maritime Governance: Balancing Security, Prosperity, and Sustainability

Commodore Abhay Kumar Singh (Retd)

In the early decades of the twenty-first century, the seas surrounding India have assumed a central place in its national strategy. Bounded by more than 11,098 kilometres of coastline and flanked by the Arabian Sea, the Bay of Bengal and the broader Indian Ocean, India occupies a maritime space where economic, security and environmental imperatives converge.[1] The country's rising trade volumes, deeper dependence on sea-lines of communication and the evolving geo-strategic dynamics of the Indian Ocean Region (IOR) have prompted New Delhi to reconceive its maritime governance: no longer purely a matter of naval deterrence, but increasingly an integrated project that seeks to balance security, economic prosperity and sustainable ocean stewardship.[2]

This reorientation reflects three concurrent trends. First, India's economic growth and integration into global value chains have made its maritime lifelines increasingly vital: energy imports, export-led manufacturing, and maritime logistics now depend on both the quantity and quality of sea connectivity.[3] Second, the shifting power dynamics of the Indian Ocean Region (IOR), including China's expanding influence, the resurgence of littoral states, the proliferation of non-traditional threats (piracy, trafficking, IUU fishing), and the entry of extra-regional actors, have heightened the need for an effective maritime governance framework.[4] Third, the oceans themselves have become arenas for sustainable development: the "blue economy", marine biodiversity conservation, seabed resources, and climate resilience are now central to national interests rather than secondary concerns.[5]

Against this backdrop, the traditional Indian maritime paradigm, which emphasised territorial seas, naval defence and capacity-building, is evolving into a more holistic framework. New Delhi is shifting from an emphasis on being a "net security provider" in the IOR towards a broader conception of cooperative maritime governance that deliberately links security, economic opportunity and environmental sustainability as a 'preferred security partner'.[6] This conceptual evolution does not abandon hard security; rather it acknowledges that influence at sea requires a combination of naval capability, infrastructure, normative leadership, institutional cooperation and environmental stewardship.

This chapter examines how India's approach to maritime governance has developed over time. It explores India's strategic interests in the Indian Ocean, evaluates existing governance structures, and tracks the evolution of Indian maritime doctrine—including the expansion beyond the initial Security and Growth for All in the Region (SAGAR) framework toward more comprehensive strategies. The analysis considers India's participation in regional forums, particularly the Indian Ocean Rim Association (IORA), and their role in advancing sustainable ocean governance. Finally, the chapter outlines recommendations for building a resilient, inclusive, and sustainable regional maritime order that integrates security concerns with economic development and environmental protection.

Why the Indian Ocean Matters to India

For India, the Indian Ocean is not merely a geographical expanse; it constitutes the country's principal strategic and economic frontier. It shapes India's geopolitical environment, sustains its trade and energy security, and provides the stage upon which its regional and global aspirations unfold. The ocean's centrality to Indian statecraft stems from both geography and dependence: nearly 95 per cent of India's trade by volume and around 70 per cent by value traverse maritime routes, while more than 80 per cent of its crude oil imports pass through vulnerable chokepoints such as the Strait of Hormuz and the Strait of Malacca.[7] Maritime stability is, therefore, directly synonymous with India's economic vitality and national resilience.

Geopolitically, the Indian Ocean constitutes the connective tissue between the Indo-Pacific's two extremities, linking the Pacific economies to the energy producers of West Asia and Africa.[8] India's peninsular position, projecting deep into the ocean, grants it both opportunity and responsibility: it can shape maritime order, but must also guard against the volatility that characterises this semi-enclosed and contested sea space. It has been argued that the Indian Ocean has re-emerged as a "theatre of strategic competition", with regional rivalries intersecting global contestations.[9] India, thus, views maritime security as both a defensive necessity and a means of asserting strategic autonomy in a multipolar regional order.

Historically, Indian policymakers approached maritime affairs through a continental prism, prioritising land borders and territorial defence.[10] However, the post-1991 economic reforms, the expanding blue-water capability of the Indian Navy, and the emergence of globalisation redirected strategic attention seaward. The 2004 Indian Ocean tsunami marked a turning point: India's rapid humanitarian assistance and disaster relief operations underscored its capacity to act as a regional stabiliser. Since then, maritime cooperation has become a principal avenue for diplomatic engagement—whether through joint exercises, white-shipping agreements, or capacity-building initiatives with smaller littoral states.

Economically, the Indian Ocean functions as the engine of India's trade connectivity and energy security. Major ports such as Mumbai, Kochi, Chennai, and Visakhapatnam serve as commercial gateways linking the subcontinent to East Asia, Africa, and Europe.[11] India's maritime economy—encompassing shipping, fisheries, offshore energy, tourism, and marine biotechnology—contributes nearly 4 per cent of national GDP, and the government's blue economy initiative framework viz. "Maritime Amrit Kaal Vision 2047" framework envisions expanding this share through sustainable practices.[12] Yet, vulnerabilities persist: piracy in the western Indian Ocean, illegal fishing, marine pollution, and climate-driven disasters threaten not only livelihoods but also the integrity of sea-lines of communication vital to global trade.

The strategic salience of the Indian Ocean has also been heightened by China's Belt and Road Initiative (BRI) and its "String of Pearls" network of dual-use ports from Gwadar to Hambantota. India interprets these developments as challenges to its primacy in the region and has responded through a calibrated combination of partnerships and presence, by developing the Andaman and Nicobar Command, investing in the Chabahar Port project in Iran, and strengthening ties with maritime democracies through frameworks such as the Quadrilateral Security Dialogue (QUAD).[13] At the same time, New Delhi recognises that sustained influence cannot rely solely on military posturing. Its emphasis on the doctrine of SAGAR signals a cooperative approach grounded in inclusivity and shared prosperity.[14]

Beyond strategy and commerce, the Indian Ocean also holds ecological and humanitarian importance. Climate change, sea-level rise, and extreme weather events disproportionately affect the densely populated littorals of South Asia. India's growing participation in regional mechanisms, including the IORA and the Indian Ocean Naval Symposium (IONS), reflects a recognition that maritime governance must encompass sustainable development, disaster risk reduction, and environmental protection.[15] Consequently, the Indian Ocean matters to India not only as an arena of competition and connectivity but also as a shared ecological commons that demands stewardship.

Assessment of Maritime Governance in the Indian Ocean

Maritime governance in the Indian Ocean is characterised by legal pluralism, institutional fragmentation, and uneven capacities across states. The region's governance landscape is built upon the United Nations Convention on the Law of the Sea (UNCLOS), which codifies the legal order of the oceans by defining maritime zones, rights, and obligations.[16] While UNCLOS provides a universal normative foundation, it leaves implementation and enforcement largely to coastal states and regional institutions. Consequently, maritime governance in the Indian Ocean has evolved through overlapping national jurisdictions, informal networks, and multilateral initiatives rather than a single, coherent institutional design.

Within this complex environment, the principle of "Good Order at Sea" offers a conceptual framework for linking legal, economic, environmental, and security concerns. The concept refers to a condition in which the maritime domain is governed by law, enabling legitimate economic and developmental activities to be carried out freely and safely.[17] It implies not merely the absence of disorder or conflict but the presence of a stable and predictable system of norms, institutions, and practices that safeguard the collective interests of states and other maritime users.[18]

In contemporary strategic literature, "Good Order at Sea" has evolved from a naval operational concern to a comprehensive governance ideal. It encompasses both hard security, preventing piracy, terrorism, trafficking, or armed conflict at sea, and soft security, including regulation of marine pollution, fisheries management, search and rescue, and disaster response.[19] It also integrates economic and environmental stewardship, recognising that the seas constitute a global commons whose security depends on sustainable and equitable use.[20] The idea aligns with the broader principles of the "Blue Economy," the Sustainable Development Goals (especially SDG 14), and the rule-based maritime order envisioned under UNCLOS.

Good Order as a Normative Basis for Cooperation

In the Indian Ocean context, the pursuit of "good order" has significant strategic and normative implications. It provides a means for reconciling the diverse priorities of regional actors, from naval deterrence to economic development, under a shared commitment to lawful and responsible ocean use.[21] For India, this framework reinforces its broader vision of SAGAR, which conceptualises maritime security and prosperity as mutually reinforcing rather than competing objectives. The emphasis on law-based order and cooperative security also complements the approaches of partners such as Japan and Australia, which advocate freedom of navigation, sustainable resource utilisation, and inclusive regional governance.

India has endeavoured to operationalise collaborative approach to enhance "good order at sea" through maritime dialogue, capacity-building, and coordinated action. The principle encourages collaborative Maritime Domain Awareness (MDA), coordinated patrols, information sharing, and harmonisation of domestic legal frameworks.[22] It also promotes a non-hegemonic form of maritime governance that respects sovereignty while fostering collective security. This multidimensional understanding has informed several initiatives, from India's anti-piracy patrols in the western Indian Ocean to joint exercises under the IONS and capacity-building projects supported through the IORA.[23]

Persistent Challenges to Good Order

Despite its conceptual utility, "good order at sea" remains difficult to achieve in practice. Governance in the Indian Ocean continues to suffer from fragmentation. Regional institutions such as IORA, IONS, and the Colombo Security Conclave address discrete aspects of governance, economic cooperation, naval dialogue, and maritime security respectively, but lack integration or central coordination.[24] Overlapping jurisdictions and mandates produce duplication of effort, while the absence of binding enforcement mechanisms limits their operational impact.

Another constraint lies in capacity asymmetry. While some states have developed advanced surveillance and enforcement capabilities, others, particularly small island and East African littoral states, face acute resource and technological deficits.[25] This imbalance weakens collective enforcement of maritime laws and leaves significant areas vulnerable to illegal activities such as IUU fishing, trafficking, and pollution. The sustainability of "good order" depends on narrowing these capability gaps through regionally owned capacity-building and knowledge-sharing arrangements.[26]

A further obstacle arises from politicisation. Governance efforts are frequently shaped by strategic rivalries among major powers. Competing visions, such as the Belt and Road Initiative (BRI) and the Indo-Pacific framework, have produced parallel initiatives that risk fragmenting the maritime order rather than reinforcing it.[27] The securitisation of regional politics can overshadow cooperative agendas for environmental protection and blue economy development. Preserving "good order" under such conditions demands political restraint and adherence to international law as a neutral reference point for cooperation.

Towards an Integrated Maritime Governance Framework

Despite these challenges, the Indian Ocean has witnessed gradual consolidation of governance practices. IORA's *Outlook on the Indo-Pacific* articulates a broad political consensus on sustainable development, disaster resilience, and blue economy growth.[28] IONS has strengthened habits of naval cooperation, building interoperability through humanitarian assistance and disaster relief (HADR) exercises. Complementary arrangements such as *Regional Cooperation Agreement on Combating Piracy and Armed Robbery against Ships in Asia* (ReCAAP) and the Djibouti Code of Conduct have improved information sharing and standardised responses to piracy and armed robbery.[29]

Yet, two policy gaps remain critical. The first is institutional integration: maritime governance remains compartmentalised among legal, environmental, and security institutions. Effective implementation of "good order" requires a holistic architecture that brings together maritime law enforcement, environmental management, and trade facilitation.[30] The second is sustainability of capacity-building: many regional initiatives are donor-driven and episodic, limiting long-term impact. Without autonomous regional financing and governance ownership, the pursuit of "good order" will remain externally dependent.[31]

In essence, the governance of the Indian Ocean stands at a crossroads. The region possesses strong normative foundations but weak institutional cohesion. The concept of "good order at sea" offers a unifying framework capable of balancing competing imperatives, security, prosperity, and sustainability, under a rules-based and inclusive order. Advancing this vision requires not only strengthening legal and institutional frameworks but also fostering shared responsibility among coastal states to manage the ocean as a collective public good.

India's Evolving Approach towards Maritime Governance

India's approach to maritime governance has evolved significantly over the past decade, reflecting the country's recognition that maritime security, economic prosperity, and sustainable ocean management are deeply interconnected. From the articulation of the *Security and Growth for All in the Region* (SAGAR) vision in 2015 to the announcement of the *Mutual and Holistic Advancement for Security and Growth Across Regions* (MAHASAGAR) initiative in 2025, India has moved from a regionally focused to a globally inclusive maritime outlook. This evolution is visible not only in doctrine but also in the institutional and diplomatic mechanisms through which maritime governance is pursued.

Doctrinal Evolution: From SAGAR to MAHASAGAR

The SAGAR doctrine was first articulated by the Prime Minister of India during a visit to Mauritius in March 2015, marking the first comprehensive expression of India's maritime policy.[32] It sought to secure the Indian Ocean as a zone of peace and prosperity through collective action and shared security responsibilities. SAGAR rested on four key pillars: (a) safeguarding India's mainland and island territories; (b) deepening economic and security cooperation with maritime neighbours; (c) responding swiftly to regional crises and disasters; and (d) strengthening the capabilities of smaller littoral states through capacity-building and training.[33] The vision positioned India as a "Net Security Provider/Preferred Security Partner" and an advocate of cooperative rather than competitive regionalism.[34]

India's shift from the notion of a 'Net Security Provider' to that of a 'Preferred Security Partner' in the Indian Ocean marks a significant reorientation in its maritime strategy—from a unilateral and capacity-driven approach to one rooted in inclusivity and partnership. The earlier concept projected

India as an autonomous guarantor of regional stability, capable of independently ensuring security across the Indian Ocean littorals. However, limitations in resources, the growing complexity of transnational maritime challenges, and sensitivities among smaller littoral states to perceptions of dominance led to a conceptual recalibration. The newer framework of a *preferred security partner* reflects a more collaborative and trust-based model that emphasises joint responsibility, capacity building, and multilateralism through mechanisms such as the Colombo Security Conclave, IONS, and IORA. It also underscores reciprocity, positioning India not as a unilateral provider but as a partner chosen by regional states based on demonstrated reliability, unconditional security assistance, and a credible track record. Fundamentally, both terms denote a state possessing requisite military capabilities and political commitment to address common security challenges, but "*Preferred Security Partner*" better encapsulates India's inclusive, non-hegemonic vision while rendering its regional role less susceptible to politicization and misinterpretation.[35]

Over the following decade, the scope of India's maritime interests expanded. The Indo-Pacific emerged as the central theatre of global geopolitics; blue economy governance and climate resilience rose on international agendas; and the proliferation of extra-regional naval activity demanded a broader strategic perspective. To address these changes, PM Modi announced the MAHASAGAR initiative (Mutual and Holistic Advancement for Security and Growth Across Regions) in March 2025, again during a visit to Mauritius.[36]

Official government statements describe MAHASAGAR as an *evolution* rather than a replacement of SAGAR, one that seeks to apply the latter's principles beyond the Indian Ocean to a wider set of maritime partnerships across the Global South.[37] The Ministry of External Affairs (MEA) defined it as a framework "to advance mutual and holistic cooperation across regions in the maritime domain," encompassing security partnerships, blue economy development, and sustainable ocean governance.[38] The joint press statement issued by India and Mauritius elaborated on its operational content: maritime security assistance, exclusive economic zone surveillance, renewable-energy collaboration, and disaster resilience.[39]

Subsequent Parliamentary replies and press releases confirmed that MAHASAGAR is an official government initiative and a key component of India's maritime diplomacy. It has also characterised it as the "natural progression of India's maritime vision," extending cooperative security, capacity-building, and sustainable growth to new regions beyond the traditional Indian Ocean community.[40] The doctrine underscores an inclusive and rules-based maritime order where development and security reinforce one another rather than compete.

Balancing Security, Economic Prosperity and Sustainable Governance

India's maritime approach now rests on three interdependent pillars, viz. security, economic prosperity, and sustainability. The doctrinal transition from SAGAR to MAHASAGAR reflects an attempt to balance these imperatives within a coherent governance framework.

Security remains foundational. India's naval modernisation, coastal surveillance, and maritime domain awareness (MDA) initiatives are directed toward ensuring the security of sea lines of communication and deterring threats such as piracy, trafficking, and terrorism.[41] The Information Fusion Centre–Indian Ocean Region (IFC-IOR) serves as the focal point for real-time data sharing and cooperative surveillance with partner navies.[42] India has also expanded defence diplomacy through coordinated patrols, hydrographic cooperation, and humanitarian assistance missions with littoral states.

Economic prosperity constitutes the second pillar. The Maritime India Vision 2030, released by the Ministry of Ports, Shipping and Waterways, lays out plans for modernising port infrastructure, enhancing shipping capacity, and fostering coastal industrial clusters to harness India's blue economy.[43] Maritime logistics, renewable energy, and undersea resource exploration are increasingly integrated into India's external economic strategy. These initiatives also serve foreign-policy goals by positioning India as a source of infrastructure and connectivity alternatives for the wider Indo-Pacific.[44]

Sustainability forms the third and increasingly critical pillar. India's official policy documents, including *India's Blue Economy* by NITI Aayog, stress that maritime development must align with ecological stewardship.[45] Marine pollution control, biodiversity conservation, and climate-change adaptation have become integral to maritime cooperation. This aligns with the notion of "good order at sea," in which lawful, safe, and sustainable use of the oceans underpins both security and development.[46] MAHASAGAR's emphasis on holistic growth reflects the incorporation of this principle at the doctrinal level.

Together, these three dimensions signal India's effort to integrate strategic, economic, and environmental interests into a single maritime governance framework. The challenge lies in ensuring policy coherence across multiple ministries and converting strategic declarations into sustained institutional practice.

Regional and Bilateral Mechanisms for Implementation

India's evolving maritime vision is implemented through a layered network of regional and bilateral mechanisms. At the regional level, India plays an active role in the IORA and the IONS. These organisations have emerged as key venues for dialogue on blue economy cooperation, disaster management, and capacity-building.[47] India's chairmanship of IORA (2022–23) placed emphasis on the sustainable use of marine resources and gender equality in ocean industries, signalling a broader approach to maritime governance.

Sub-regional initiatives complement these efforts. The Colombo Security Conclave, bringing together India, Sri Lanka, Maldives, and Mauritius (with Bangladesh and Seychelles as observers), has expanded its agenda from counterterrorism and cyber security to include environmental and maritime safety cooperation.[48] The Djibouti Code of Conduct and ReCAAP further enhance India's participation in trans-regional mechanisms focused on piracy suppression and maritime information-sharing.

Bilateral engagements remain critical in translating doctrine into tangible action. India's partnerships with Mauritius, Seychelles, and Maldives exemplify this approach. These relationships feature a blend of security assistance (such as patrol vessels and radar systems), development cooperation (renewable-energy projects, undersea cables), and training programmes. The India–Mauritius package of agreements accompanying the MAHASAGAR announcement illustrates the integrated nature of contemporary partnerships, combining infrastructure investment, maritime security cooperation, and economic support.[49]

At the same time, India's engagement within minilateral frameworks such as the QUAD aligns with the broader MAHASAGAR ethos by promoting an open and inclusive Indo-Pacific. Through joint exercises, coordinated HADR operations, and collaboration on maritime domain awareness, these arrangements contribute to regional resilience while avoiding exclusionary alignments.

Strategic Assessment and Challenges

The doctrinal and operational evolution from SAGAR to MAHASAGAR indicates India's ambition to shape the maritime order through a balanced and inclusive governance model. However, several challenges remain.

First, institutional coherence is uneven. Coordination among the Ministries of External Affairs, Defence, Ports, Fisheries, and Environment remains limited, often resulting in fragmented implementation. Second, capacity asymmetry among regional partners constrains the scope of cooperative projects; many smaller states lack resources to sustain joint initiatives without external support. Third, geopolitical competition continues to colour regional perceptions, requiring India to balance leadership with reassurance to ensure that its initiatives are not viewed as hegemonic. Finally, the sustainability of capacity-building programmes and funding remains uncertain, raising questions about long-term impact.

Despite these challenges, the MAHASAGAR doctrine represents a significant conceptual advance. By embedding the principles of security, growth, and sustainability in a holistic framework, it signals India's readiness to act as both a responsible stakeholder and a system-shaper in maritime governance. The transition from SAGAR to MAHASAGAR thus marks not only a geographic expansion but also a qualitative deepening of India's maritime vision—from regional stewardship to global partnership.

India's Engagement with IORA in Strengthening Sustainable Ocean Governance

India's engagement with the IORA constitutes a central pillar of its maritime diplomacy and an institutional expression of its commitment to sustainable ocean governance. Since becoming a founding member in 1997, India has leveraged IORA as a platform to promote cooperative security, inclusive economic growth, and responsible management of marine resources. Over time, IORA has evolved from a modest trade-oriented grouping into a broad-based regional forum encompassing thirty-three members and twelve dialogue partners, addressing themes ranging from blue economy and disaster resilience to marine spatial planning and capacity building.

For India, IORA provides an institutional mechanism through which its maritime doctrines, first SAGAR and now MAHASAGAR, are operationalised in multilateral settings. IORA's inclusive membership and consensus-driven character align closely with India's advocacy of a rules-based, non-hegemonic regional order. The Association's thematic focus on the blue economy, safety and security, and sustainability resonates with India's national priorities, making it both a diplomatic and developmental anchor of India's Indian Ocean policy.[50]

IORA and India's Maritime Vision

India perceives IORA as the pre-eminent regional organisation of the Indian Ocean, linking its national maritime policies with broader regional priorities. IORA's six priority areas, maritime safety and security, trade and investment, fisheries management, disaster-risk management, academic exchange, and tourism, correspond directly with India's strategic and developmental objectives.[51]

During its tenure as IORA chair (2022–23), India played a central role in advancing the *IORA Blue Economy Handbook* (prepared with UNESCAP)[52] and the *IORA Outlook on the Indo-Pacific (2022)*, both of which articulate the need for inclusive and sustainable maritime governance. These documents reflect India's belief that ocean governance must balance prosperity and preservation through regional partnership. The Outlook, in particular, affirms the centrality of UNCLOS, transparency, and environmental responsibility as cornerstones of a stable Indo-Pacific order.[53]

Blue Economy and Sustainable Development

India has been pivotal in embedding the blue economy within IORA's policy framework. It recognises that economic activity in the ocean space must be aligned with sustainability, equity, and ecological balance. The *Jakarta Ministerial Declaration on the Blue Economy (2017)*, endorsed with India's strong advocacy, underscores the principle that the ocean is a shared resource whose long-term productivity depends on responsible stewardship.[54]

Through technical and institutional contributions, India has promoted sustainable fisheries, renewable ocean energy, and marine biodiversity protection. Its support to the IORA Fisheries Support Unit (Oman) and cooperation with the United Nations Environment Programme (UNEP) in implementing the *Regional Marine Litter Action Plan* which illustrate New Delhi's role in transforming normative commitments into practical cooperation.[55] India's domestic frameworks, including *Maritime India Vision 2030* and India's *Blue Economy* , serve as policy templates for regional engagement, combining growth with environmental safeguards.

Security and Environmental Resilience

India's engagement in IORA's Working Group on Maritime Safety and Security (WGMSS) has reinforced regional efforts against piracy, trafficking, and illegal fishing, while promoting maritime domain awareness and information sharing. The concept of "Good Order at Sea", understood as the maintenance of lawful, predictable, and sustainable maritime conditions, underpins India's advocacy within IORA.

India has also integrated disaster resilience into IORA's governance agenda. The *IORA Working Group on Disaster Risk Management Framework (WGDRM)* reflects Indian experience in humanitarian assistance and disaster relief (HADR) operations, providing models for coordinated early-warning systems and rapid response mechanisms.[56] This linkage between environmental governance and human security represents a key area of India's normative leadership.

India's Maritime Future: Strategic Priorities and Pathways

India's maritime governance approach stands at a critical juncture. The progression from SAGAR to MAHASAGAR has broadened its outlook from regional stability to global stewardship, embedding sustainability, inclusivity, and cooperative security at the heart of policy formulation. Yet, translating this normative vision into tangible outcomes requires sustained institutional capacity, policy coherence, and regional consensus. The coming decade will therefore determine how effectively India can align its strategic ambitions with the collective priorities of the Indian Ocean community.

Within this framework, the IORA remains the most significant multilateral platform through which India can shape the future maritime order. As it assumes the Association's presidency, India faces the dual challenge of revitalising IORA's institutional mechanisms and deepening engagement across its priority areas. The presidency offers an opportunity to set the long-term trajectory of ocean governance around five interrelated thrust areas:

1. **Maritime Safety and Domain Awareness:** Strengthening surveillance cooperation, information exchange, and capacity building through mechanisms such as the Information Fusion Centre–Indian Ocean Region (IFC-IOR) to ensure "good order at sea."
2. **Sustainable Blue Economy and Green Transition:** Encouraging eco-friendly maritime infrastructure, renewable ocean energy, and

sustainable fisheries that align growth with environmental protection.

3. **Climate and Environmental Resilience:** Integrating climate adaptation, marine ecosystem restoration, and disaster-risk reduction into regional governance frameworks, consistent with the *UN Decade of Ocean Science for Sustainable Development*.
4. **Capacity Building and Knowledge Exchange:** Establishing transnational academic and training networks linking maritime universities and research institutions to create a regional blue knowledge economy.
5. **Institutional Strengthening and Inclusivity:** Enhancing IORA's Secretariat, promoting equitable participation of small island developing states (SIDS), and improving the efficiency of project implementation and financing.

Together, these focus areas encapsulate the operational essence of the *MAHASAGAR* doctrine, a vision that seeks to harmonise national capability with regional partnership.

In strategic terms, India's future maritime governance must remain multi-layered: rooted in national resilience, advanced through regional cooperation, and legitimised by international law. Sustained investment in maritime infrastructure, technological innovation, and environmental protection will be vital to balancing the triad of security, prosperity, and sustainability.

Ultimately, India's leadership in maritime governance will be judged not merely by its naval reach or economic capacity, but by its ability to build a cooperative, rules-based, and sustainable order in the Indian Ocean and beyond. The IORA presidency offers a pivotal opportunity to advance that goal, transforming the Indian Ocean from a contested arena into a community of shared responsibility.

Conclusion

India's evolving approach to maritime governance, as traced through the doctrinal progression from SAGAR to MAHASAGAR, signifies a significant maturing of the country's strategic thinking about its role in the Indian Ocean and beyond. This development reflects India's realisation that maritime leadership in the twenty-first century requires more than naval power, it demands an integrated framework that aligns security imperatives, economic growth, and environmental sustainability within a rules-based, cooperative order.

The analysis shows that India has shifted from a mainly defence-focused maritime stance to adopt a comprehensive governance approach based on three interconnected pillars. Security remains essential, grounded in naval upgrades, maritime domain awareness, and anti-piracy efforts that establish India's credibility as a reliable first responder. Economic prosperity, expressed through the Maritime India Vision 2030 and blue economy programmes, makes maritime development key to national growth while providing infrastructure and connectivity options for regional partners. Sustainability, which is increasingly important in policy discussions, reflects India's view that long-term maritime influence relies on responsible ocean management, climate resilience, and adherence to international environmental commitments.

The MAHASAGAR initiative, announced in March 2025, signifies both a geographical expansion and a deeper conceptualisation of India's maritime vision. By broadening cooperative security principles beyond the Indian Ocean to include wider Global South partnerships, India indicates its readiness to act not just as a regional power but as a global player in maritime governance. However, the real test of MAHASAGAR lies not in its declaration but in its realisation, whether India can turn strategic statements into consistent institutional practices, coordinate effectively across divided domestic bureaucracies, and mobilise adequate resources to compete with alternative approaches, especially China's Belt and Road Initiative.

India's leadership of regional institutions, particularly the IORA during its 2025-27 chairmanship and its sustained engagement with the IONS, provides critical platforms for operationalising this vision. Yet institutional leadership alone is insufficient. The persistent challenges identified in this paper, capacity asymmetries among regional partners, geopolitical competition that risks fragmenting rather than consolidating maritime order, domestic political sensitivities in partner states, and the unresolved tensions between rapid economic development and environmental protection, require not only diplomatic finesse but also difficult trade-offs that Indian policymakers have yet to fully confront.

Perhaps most critically, the chapter reveals a gap between normative ambition and critical assessment. While India's commitment to "Good Order at Sea" and inclusive multilateralism is well-documented, the analysis would benefit from deeper engagement with implementation constraints and contradictions. How does India reconcile its coal-dependent economy with climate leadership? When naval expansion imperatives conflict with marine ecosystem protection, which prevails? How can capacity-building programs achieve sustainability without perpetual external funding? These questions deserve more than procedural answers, they require honest acknowledgment of the structural tensions inherent in pursuing security, prosperity, and sustainability simultaneously under resource constraints.

Looking forward, India's maritime governance approach faces three interrelated imperatives. First, it must demonstrate that MAHASAGAR represents genuine policy evolution rather than rhetorical rebranding, with measurable outcomes in security cooperation, economic integration, and environmental stewardship. Second, it must navigate the increasingly competitive geopolitics of the Indian Ocean without succumbing to either strategic overextension or reactive posturing that undermines its stated commitment to inclusive, rules-based order. Third, it must build domestic institutional coherence, coordinating the fragmented mandates of external affairs, defence, ports, fisheries, and environment ministries—to ensure policy consistency and implementation effectiveness.

Ultimately, India's success in maritime governance will be judged not by the sophistication of its doctrinal frameworks or the prominence of its institutional leadership, but by its capacity to deliver tangible security benefits to regional partners while adapting to evolving challenges. The progression from SAGAR to MAHASAGAR provides a promising conceptual foundation, but the transition from vision to reality requires sustained political commitment, adequate resource allocation, genuine multilateral collaboration, and, perhaps most importantly, the humility to acknowledge limitations while maintaining strategic ambition.

The Indian Ocean's transformation from a contested arena into a community of shared responsibility remains an aspirational goal rather than an achieved reality. India's maritime governance approach, with its emphasis on balancing security, prosperity, and sustainability, offers a principled pathway toward that goal. Whether this pathway leads to effective regional order or remains an unrealised vision will depend on choices made in the coming decade, choices that will shape not only India's maritime future but the broader architecture of Indo-Pacific security and governance.[57]

NOTES

1 Mukherjee, Anit. "India as a Net Security Provider: Concept and Impediments." RSIS, Nanyang Technological University. 2014. https://rsis.edu.sg/rsis-publication/gpo/india-as-a-net-security-provider-concept-and-impediments/.

2 Sahu, Priyadarsini. "India's Maritime Security: Strategy and Challenges." Research Review International Journal of Multidisciplinary 7, no. 10 (2022): 99–106. https://doi.org/10.31305/rrijm.2022.v07.i10.012.

3 "India's Growth Linked to Energy and Maritime Strength: Shri Hardeep Singh Puri." PIB, Ministry of Petroleum & Natural Gas. 2025. https://www.pib.gov.in/PressReleasePage.aspx?PRID=2183703.

4 Singh, Abhijit. "India's Evolving Maritime Posture in the Indian Ocean: Opportunities for the Gulf." Emirates Diplomatic Academy. 2020. https://www.agda.ac.ae/docs/default-source/Publications/eda-insight-aug-2020-eng-abhijit.pdf.

5 "Prime Minister Shares an Article on How the Blue Economy Is Central to India's Growth." PIB, Prime Minister's Office. 2025. https://www.pib.gov.in/PressReleasePage.aspx?PRID=2168414.

6 Roy-Chaudhury, Rahul. "From 'Net Security Provider' to 'Preferred Security Partnerships': The Rhetoric, Reality and Result of India's Maritime Security Cooperation." Journal of the Indian Ocean Region 18, no. 2, 87–98. 2022. https://doi.org/10.1080/19480881.2022.2118191.

7 Abhijit Singh. "Securing Sea Lines of Communication in Asia." Observer Research Foundation. July 17, 2023. https://www.orfonline.org/research/securing-sea-lines-of-communication-in-asia.

8 Brewster, David. "India's Ocean: The Story of India's Bid for Regional Leadership: The Story of India's Bid for Regional Leadership." Routledge. 2014.

9 Baruah, Darshana M. The Contest for the Indian Ocean: And the Making of a New World Order. New Haven, CT: Yale University Press. 2024.

10 Singh, Abhay K. "Emerging Contours of Maritime Security Architecture under the Belt and Road Initiative." Journal of Defence Studies 12, no. 4, 47–49. 2018. https://www.idsa.in/publisher/journal-of-defence-studies/emerging-contours-of-maritime-security-architecture-under-the-belt-and-road-initiative.

11 "Maritime India Vision 2030." Ministry of Ports, Shipping and Waterways. 2021. https://sagarmala.gov.in/sites/default/files/MIV%202030%20Report.pdf.

12 "Navigating India's Blue Economy Landscape." KPMG. 2025. https://assets.kpmg.com/content/dam/kpmgsites/in/pdf/2025/07/navigating-indias-blue-economy-landscape.pdf.

13 Malhotra, Aditi. "Engagement, Not Entanglement: India's Relationship with the Quad." Georgetown Journal of International Affairs. May 1, 2023. https://gjia.georgetown.edu/2023/05/01/engagement-not-entanglement-indias-relationship-with-the-quad/.

14 Singh, Abhay Kumar. "India as a Net Security Provider in the Indian Ocean Region: The Strategic Approach of a Responsible Stakeholder." In Maritime Governance and South Asia, 63–78. World Scientific. 2018.

15 Roy-Chaudhury, Rahul. "From 'Net Security Provider' to 'Preferred Security Partnerships': The Rhetoric, Reality and Result of India's Maritime Security Cooperation." Journal of the Indian Ocean Region 18, no. 2, 87–98. 2022. https://doi.org/10.1080/19480881.20

22.2118191.

16 "United Nations Convention on the Law of the Sea". United Nations. December 10, 1982. https://www.un.org/Depts/los/convention_agreements/texts/unclos/unclos_e.pdf

17 Abhay K Singh. "India-Japan Strategic Partnership: Imperatives for Ensuring 'Good Order at Sea' in the Indo-Pacific." In Scaling India-Japan Cooperation in Indo-Pacific and beyond 2025: Corridors, Connectivity and Contours, edited by Jagannath P. Panda, 243–263. KW Publishers Pvt Ltd. 2020. https://www.idsa.in/system/files/book/book-scaling-india-japan-cooperation.pdf.

18 Ibid. 15–17.

19 Singh, Abhay Kumar. "Emerging Contours of Maritime Security Architecture under the Belt and Road Initiative." Journal of Defence Studies 12, no. 4, 35–55. 2018.

20 Weiand, Laura, Sebastian Unger, Julien Rochette, Alexander Müller, and Barbara Neumann. "Advancing Ocean Governance in Marine Regions through Stakeholder Dialogue Processes." Frontiers in Marine Science 8. 2021. https://doi.org/10.3389/fmars.2021.645576.

21 Op. cit. note no.17.

22 Ibid. 20–22.

23 "Outlook on the Indo-Pacific." Indian Ocean Rim Association (IORA). 2022. https://www.iora.int/sites/default/files/2024-03/indo-pacific-outlook.pdf.

24 Bateman, Sam. "Maritime Security Governance in the Indian Ocean Region." Journal of the Indian Ocean Region 12, no. 1, 5–23. 2016. https://doi.org/10.1080/19480881.2016.1138709.

25 Pant, Harsh V., and Ivan Lidarev. "India and Maritime Governance." In India and Global Governance, 166–200. London: Routledge India. 2022.

26 Op. cit. note no.17.

27 Baruah, Darshana M. "India in the Indian Ocean: The Significance of the Maritime Domain." Carnegie Endowment for International Peace. 2020. https://carnegieendowment.org/2020/11/30/india-in-indian-ocean-significance-of-maritime-domain-pub-83398.

28 Op. cit. note no.23.

29 "ReCAAP Information Sharing Centre Annual Report 2023." 2023. https://www.recaap.org/resources/ck/files/reports/annual/ReCAAP%20ISC%20Annual%20Report%202023.pdf.

30 Nunan, Fiona, Marlyna Omondi, Azizay Nchimbi, Mwitam Mangora, Jamesg Kairo, Mwanahijas Shalli, and Narrimans Jiddawi. "The Silos of Natural Resource Governance: Implications of Sector-Led Coastal Management at the Village Level in Kenya and Zanzibar-Tanzania." Conservation & Society 18 (2): 148. 2020. https://doi.org/10.4103/cs.cs_18_116.

31 Op. cit. note no.17. Pg 253-254.

32 "Prime Minister's Remarks at the Commissioning of Offshore Patrol Vessel (OPV) Barracuda in Mauritius," Ministry of External Affairs, Government of India. 2015. https://www.mea.gov.in/Speeches-Statements.htm?dtl/24912/Prime_Ministers_Remarks_at_the_Commissioning_of_Offshore_Patrol_Vessel_OPV_Barracuda_in_Mauritius_March_12_2015.

33 Padmaja, G. "Revisiting 'SAGAR' – India's Template For Cooperation In The Indian Ocean Region." National Maritime Foundation. 2018. https://maritimeindia.org/revisiting-

sagar-indias-template-for-cooperation-in-the-indian-ocean-region/.

34 Op. cit. note no.14.

35 Op. cit. note no.15.

36 "Prime Minister Shri Narendra Modi Announced Vision MAHASAGAR- 'Mutual and Holistic Advancement for Security and Growth Across Regions' for the Global South in Mauritius," Ministry of External Affairs. 2025. https://www.mea.gov.in/newsdetail1.htm?13355/.

37 "Press Statement by Prime Minister during the India - Mauritius Joint Press Statement." PIB, Prime Minister's Office. 2025. https://www.pib.gov.in/PressReleseDetail.aspx?PRID=2110746.

38 Durai, Suchitra. "India's Maritime Vision: From SAGAR to Indo-Pacific to MAHASAGAR." Embassy of India, Timor Leste. https://www.indembassydili.gov.in/section/articles-commissioned-by-xpd-division/india-s-maritime-vision-from-sagar-to-indo-pacific-to-mahasagar-by-amb-suchitra-durai/?utm_source=chatgpt.com.

39 "Press Statement by Prime Minister during the India - Mauritius Joint Press Statement," Ministry of External Affairs. 2025. https://www.mea.gov.in/Speeches-Statements.htm?dtl/39157/English_translation_of_Press_Statement_by_Prime_Minister_during_the_India__Mauritius_Joint_Press_Statement_March_12_2025.

40 "Question No- 3101 India's Strategic Partnerships to Address Emerging Geopolitical Challenges," Ministry of External Affairs. 2025. https://www.mea.gov.in/rajya-sabha.htm?dtl/39265/QUESTION+NO+3101+INDIAS+STRATEGIC+PARTNERSHIPS+TO+ADDRESS+EMERGING+GEOPOLITICAL+CHALLENGES.

41 "Evaluation India's Indian Ocean Strategy," Ministry of External Affairs. 2025. https://sansad.in/getFile/lsscommittee/External%20Affairs/18_External_Affairs_8.pdf?source=loksabhadocs.

42 "Annual Report 2024," Information Fusion Centre–Indian Ocean Region (IFC-IOR). 2024. https://ifcior.indiannavy.gov.in/themes/custom/ifc_ior/static/img/2025/Annual_report.pdf.

43 "Maritime India Vision 2030". Ministry of Ports, Shipping & Waterways," Government of India. 2021. https://sagarmala.gov.in/sites/default/files/MIV%202030%20Report.pdf.

44 Singh, Anil Jai. "India's Maritime Economy: Driving India's Growth." India Foundation. February 27, 2021. https://indiafoundation.in/articles-and-commentaries/indias-maritime-economy-driving-indias-growth/.

45 Patel, Neelam, Pavan Raj G.H, Namrata Thapa, and Sambuddha Goswami. "Indias Blue Economy: Strategy for Harnessing Deep Sea and Offshore Fisheries." NITI Aayog. 2025. https://niti.gov.in/sites/default/files/2025-10/Indias-Blue-Economy-Strategy-For-Harnessing-Deep-Sea-And-Offshore-Fisheries.pdf.

46 Op. cit. note no.17. Pg 250-255.

47 Op. cit. note no.23

48 "Joint Press Statement on Colombo Security Conclave," Ministry of External Affairs. 2024. https://www.mea.gov.in/press-releases.htm?dtl/38242/Joint+Press+Statement+on+Colombo+Security+Conclave.

49 Op. cit. note no.37.

50 Op. cit. note no.23.

51 "Charter of the Indian Ocean Rim Association." IORA Secretariat. 2022. https://www.iora.int/sites/default/files/2024-03/iora_charter.pdf

52 Attri, Vishva Nath, and Narnia Bohler-Muller, eds. "The Blue Economy Handbook of the Indian Ocean Region". Africa Institute of South Africa. 2018. http://www.jstor.org/stable/j.ctvgc60f0.

53 Op. cit. note no.23.

54 "Jakarta Ministerial Declaration on the Blue Economy," Indian Ocean Rim Association (IORA). 2017. https://www.iora.int/sites/default/files/2024-04/jakarta-declaration-on-blue-economy-final.pdf.

55 "Strategic Framework of Action on Marine Debris in the Indian Ocean," Indian Ocean Rim Association (IORA). 2022. https://www.iora.int/sites/default/files/2024-12/IORA%20Strategic%20Framework%20on%20Marine%20Debris.pdf.

56 "Disaster Risk Management Framework for the Indian Ocean Region," Indian Ocean Rim Association (IORA). 2022.

5

Reframing India's Maritime Vision: Aligning MAHASAGAR with Regional Architectures in the Indian Ocean

Rear Admiral Monty Khanna (Retd)

Since the end of World War II, the Indian Ocean has, fortunately and to a large extent, been a zone of peace. While there have been disputes that at times have morphed into conflicts amongst littoral states, these have been short and swift, and have not manifested into prolonged security challenges that have impacted the vast majority of users of this ocean space. More importantly, disputes related to maritime boundaries have been amicably settled by resorting to international arbitration. This has been amply demonstrated by three telling examples. The first, relating to the dispute between Bangladesh and Myanmar, was resolved in March 2012 by the International Tribunal for the Law of the Sea (ITLOS).[1] The second, between Bangladesh and India, was resolved in 2014 by a tribunal of the Permanent Court of Arbitration (PCA) in The Hague.[2] While this ruling has created the complexity of a 'Grey Area' within which seabed rights have been allocated to Bangladesh while rights to the superjacent water column remain with India, it is hoped that this issue too will be amicably resolved as political relations between the two countries improve. The third and last issue relevant to this ocean is the reversion of sovereignty of the Chagos archipelago to Mauritius. Given the geo-strategic complexities associated with the United States base in Diego Garcia, unsurprisingly, the resolution of this issue has been complex. It is, however, to India's credit that viewing this issue through the prism of the unfinished agenda of colonialism, support to Mauritius has been unwavering. It is after several decades of sustained effort that the United Kingdom finally agreed to sign a GBP 3.4 billion (USD 4.6 billion) deal to hand over sovereignty of the Chagos Islands to Mauritius, while leasing the UK-US military base on Diego Garcia for which an annuity of GBP 101 million will be payable.[3]

It can thus be seen that that unlike other parts of the globe, particularly the Western Pacific, respect for the principles of international law through adherence to a rules-based order has been the default position adopted by littoral nations of the Indian Ocean Region (IOR). That being said, it would be complacent for nations in the region to rest on their laurels and assume that this path of reconciliation is irreversible. The challenges in the IOR are steadily increasing across the entire spectrum of geopolitical and geoeconomic issues and it is imperative for us to address them both bilaterally as well as multilaterally in an increasingly complex world.

One of the factors that is characteristic of the region is the lack of capacities. The Indian Ocean itself is an expanse of 70 million square km and encompasses several littoral states whose capacity to effectively monitor and police their vast Exclusive Economic Zones and extended continental shelves is weak. Mauritius for example, with a population of slightly above 1.2 million has an EEZ of 2.3 million square km[4], roughly equivalent to that of India. For Seychelles, the comparison is even more stark. The nation has a population of 1,33,000 but an EEZ of 1.35 million square km.[5] The situation with Maldives and Sri Lanka is only marginally better. Given the shortfalls in capacity, there is a pressing need for external assistance in the form of capability building and capacity enhancement to fulfil maritime security requirements. India, to an extent, has tried to fulfil this requirement. However, there are challenges related to the tyranny of geography, as the distances involved are large, particularly when it comes to nations located in the South West Indian Ocean, East Africa and the Horn of Africa. In addition is the issue related to resources for which, given our focus on development, there are competing requirements. It is therefore imperative to craft a viable policy that provides greater visibility to stakeholders on the quantum of resources available and to devise the most efficient means for translation of these resources into deliverables. A robust policy of this nature would address the long-standing complaint of nations in the region that India tends to be tall on promises but short on deliveries.

What then would be the correct approach to follow in terms of rolling out a policy? We have several vision statements in this regard – *Act East*, *Security and Growth for All in the Region* (SAGAR) *and Mutual and Holistic*

Advancement for Security and Growth Across Regions (MAHASAGAR) being a few of them. Having more than one vision that forms the bedrock of our international engagement tends to dissipate effort. It would therefore be wise to select a single vision statement and focus all our effort and resources on providing it with substance.

The term MAHASAGAR was articulated in a speech by the Honourable Prime Minister on 12 March 2025 during his state visit to Mauritius.[6] It essentially makes a pitch for expanding the geostrategic framework of the earlier concept of SAGAR to include the wider 'Global South' meaning developing countries across the globe and not limited to the Indian Ocean (the original geostrategic reach of SAGAR). As things stand today, the parameters of MAHASAGAR are somewhat amorphous and need much greater conceptual clarity.

Hitherto, the vehicle used by the MEA for providing greater specificity to the SAGAR vision has been the Indo-Pacific Oceans Initiative (IPOI), which is essentially a track 1.5 level initiative executed in conjunction with the National Maritime Foundation (NMF). The IPOI has identified seven pillars for collaboration, each of which is led by two nations which have signed on to the initiative. It involves the conduct of a conference on an annual basis and possibly some pillar-focused sub-group meetings. It is opined that this is insufficient to take forward a key policy initiative articulated at the apex level. If our ambition is to elevate MAHASAGAR as the primary vehicle for governing the entire spectrum of our assistance effort to the Global South in a coordinated and coherent manner, in some ways akin to China's Belt and Road Initiative (BRI), then the effort will have to be led, resourced and executed by a robust framework at the Track 1 level. Towards this end, the following are proposed:

(a) Develop a well-articulated MAHASAGAR policy document that clearly outlines the outcomes desired, the methodology for allocating resources, and the broad contours of an implementation and monitoring structure to efficiently convert the resources into outcomes.

(b) Create a suitable structure headed by an office/office of authority that will lay down priorities in the form of a roadmap (preferably classified) which will be periodically reviewed and updated. The structure should include members from all ministries, departments and agencies involved in capacity building and capability enhancement in Global

South nations. The roadmap should ensure that multiple lines of effort remain synchronised so as to optimise our conversion of resources into influence.

(c) The initial tasking of the MAHASAGAR implementation mechanism could also include mapping and stocktaking of the various facets of our engagement and re-branding all of them under its ambit. This would assist in enhancing coherence, visibility, and influence as aggregation of multiple lines of effort will generate a multiplier effect, making the outcome larger than a mere summation of each project.

(d) With time, MAHASAGAR may require the creation of a permanent secretariat headed by a CEO/Director General to ensure effective administrative control and oversight on a continual basis. The size and scope of this organisation will depend upon our ambition in making it an effective vehicle for the delivery of our assistance effort.

Given the scale and scope of our development assistance, it would be best if coordination under MAHASAGAR were executed under pillars which include domestic ministries, agencies and organisations with large overlaps. While doing so, aligning these pillars with those in an existing construct would be beneficial as it would allow the transition from building national capacities to international assistance with a greater degree of seamlessness. Towards this end, the best organisation to do so would be the Indian Ocean Regional Association (IORA), which has identified six priority areas as listed below:

- Maritime Safety and Security (MSS)
- Fisheries Management (FM)
- Academic, Science and Technology Co-operation (ASTC)
- Trade and Investment Facilitation (TIF)
- Disaster Risk Management (DRM)
- Tourism and Cultural Exchanges (TCE)

Creating a robust framework for converting the MAHASAGAR vision into a coherent delivery platform for steering our development assistance with the Global South would have the undermentioned advantages:

(a) Provide greater direction to the scope and scale of our development assistance to the Global South.

(b) Provide visibility to all stakeholders on projects underway thereby allowing them to identify and pursue efforts that are complementary in nature thus enabling greater self-synchronisation.

(c) Increase the visibility of India as a capable and committed partner through the mainstreaming of brand MAHASAGAR.
(d) Allow for a higher degree of supervision and oversight of projects underway.
(e) Provide greater agility in our development assistance by assessing outcomes with greater fidelity and making timely course corrections across all lines of effort.

Another element for turbocharging our development assistance is building capacities. As we increase the scale of support for our domestic programmes on shipbuilding, ship repair, ship dismantling, port operations, maritime services and training of mariners amongst others, efficiencies towards the translation of investment into capacities will rise hand in glove. The success of *Sagarmala* in all its dimensions is therefore critical. The recent focus on the shipping sector includes the modernisation and enactment of five bills related to the industry, these being—the Bills of Lading 2025, Carriage of Goods by Sea Bill 2025, Coastal Shipping Bill 2025, Indian Ports Bill 2025, and the Merchant Shipping Bill 2025[7]; reinforced by an allocation by the Union Cabinet of a package of INR 69,725 crore to revitalise the shipbuilding sector. The package extends shipbuilding financial assistance till 2036 with a corpus of INR 24,736 crore, sets up a INR 20,000 crore Maritime Development Fund, and launches an INR 19,989 crore Shipbuilding Development Scheme.[8] Thus while the groundwork for the policy push has been completed, its translation into capabilities will need constant monitoring and adjustments to remain synchronised with changing realities.

The next issue that comes up is that if *Sagarmala* were to align itself with IORA, what happens to be our bilateral regional engagement and other regional and subregional constructs such as the Indian Ocean Naval Symposium (IONS), Bay of Bengal Initiative for Multi-Sectoral Technical and Economic Cooperation (BIMSTEC), Colombo Security Conclave (CSC) and the Indian Ocean Commission (IOC) amongst others. The answer to this question is that each has its own place. Typically, when it comes to multilateral cooperation and collaboration, the lines of effort get restricted to the least common denominator. In that sense, the larger the construct, the less one can agree upon, particularly when it comes to hard security such as intelligence sharing, provision of assets and access to facilities. For such matters, bilateral discussions anchored in a robust multi-dimensional bilateral relationship will invariably be the best construct. However, when it comes to relatively low-end tasking related to maritime security issues such as coping with climate change, Illegal, Unreported, and Unregulated (IUU) fishing, smuggling and piracy amongst others, given the transnational nature of these threats, a regional organisation in which littoral nations participate as equal partners is ideally suited.

Putting IORA in the lead on all such issues has the potential to de-hyphenate regional geopolitics from undertaking collective action thereby encouraging participation. The added advantage of regional nations coming together to address their common concerns devoid of extra-regional baggage is a compelling argument that would resonate with littoral nations of the IOR. Other regional constructs such as IONS, BIMSTEC and IOC could strengthen this IORA led approach by focussing on other enablers that in due course, would assist IORA in achieving its long-term goals.

Where would parallel efforts of capacity building and capability enhancement by extra-regional players fit into such an architecture? Given the scale of the capacity shortfall and resources required to mitigate the deficit, it would be foolish to shun such efforts. What could, however be done is to make IORA a key stakeholder for all such initiatives. Capacity building efforts could therefore be undertaken in consultation with the IORA Secretariat through a transparent process that would provide full visibility to regional and extra-regional players alike on efforts underway and the timelines for their execution. This would result in reduced overlaps thereby enabling the better allocation of resources. It would also provide opportunities for undertaking collaborative initiatives with each party playing to its strengths.

It can thus be seen that aligning MAHASAGAR with the key priority areas of IORA has immense potential in streamlining our contribution towards collective maritime security in the region and in strengthening our position as a preferred security partner. Our forthcoming chairmanship of IORA provides an ideal setting for pursuing such an approach. On a broader perspective, a key component of such an initiative would be the building of internal capacities for which, the success of *Sagarmala* would be critical.[9]

NOTES

1 Rosen, M., and D. Jackson. "Bangladesh v. India: A Positive Step Forward in Public Order of the Seas," 2017. https://www.cna.org/archive/CNA_Files/pdf/dop-2017-u-016081-final.pdf.

2 Ibid

3 Chater, James. "What is the Chagos Islands deal between UK and Mauritius?," BBC News. May 23, 2025. https://www.bbc.com/news/articles/c9dqg3nqynlo

4 "Marine Resources," Ministry of Agro-Industry, Food Security, Blue Economy and Fisheries, Government of Seychelles. https://blueconomy.govmu.org/Pages/Marine-Resources.aspx

5 "Seychelles Marine Spatial Plan Initiative," https://seymsp.com/the-initiative/planning-scope/

6 "Press Statement by Prime Minister during the India - Mauritius Joint Press Statement," Press Information Bureau, Government of India. March 12, 2025. https://www.pib.gov.in/PressReleasePage.aspx?PRID=2110746

7 "Parliament passes 5 landmark maritime bills to boost Blue Economy, replace colonial era laws," Economic Times. August 22, 2025. https://infra.economictimes.indiatimes.com/news/ports-shipping/parliament-enacts-5-historic-maritime-bills-to-transform-indias-blue-economy/123449456

8 Ftakia, Hormaz. "Cabinet approves shipping and maritime reform schemes worth Rs 69,725 crores," CNBC TV18, September 24, 2025. https://www.cnbctv18.com/market/shipping-stocks-cabinet-meeting-announcements-impact-scheme-sci-grse-shares-19686396.htm

6

Operationalising India's Maritime Resurgence through MAHASAGAR

Captain Anurag Bisen (Retd)

The Maritime Consciousness of India

India's civilisational identity has always been defined by geography, *the Himalayas in the north and the ocean in the south.* In the *Vishnu Purana (2.3.1)*, this consciousness is articulated with remarkable clarity:

> उत्तरं यत् समुद्रस्य हिमाद्रेश्चैव दक्षिणम्।
> वर्षं तद् भारतं नाम भारती तत्र सन्ततिः ॥ (विष्णु पुराण २.३.१)
> *Uttaraṃ yat samudrasya himādreś caiva dakṣiṇam,*
> *varṣaṃ tad bhāratam nāma bhārataḥ tatra santatiḥ*

"The country that lies north of the ocean and south of the Himalayas is called *Bharatavarca*; and the people are known as *Bharati.*" The Indian Ocean, unique in world geography for bearing the name of a single nation, stands as a civilisational mirror reflecting millennia of Indian engagement with the sea, spanning the spiritual and economic domains.

The *Rigveda,* the world's oldest surviving text, speaks of the ocean (*samudra*) as a source of abundance and unity. The *Nadistuti Sukta* (Rigveda 10.75.5) lists the great rivers of northern India, culminating in the *Sindhu* (Indus), symbolising the natural flow of life from mountains to the sea:

> इमं मे गङ्गे यमुने सरस्वति शुतुद्रि स्तोमं सचता परुष्ण्या ।
> असिक्न्या मरुद्वृधे वितस्तयार्जीकीये शृणुह्या सुषोमया ॥
> *imam me gaṅge yamune sarasvati śutudri stomaṃ sacatā paruṣṇyā*
> *asiknyā marudvṛdhe vitastayārjīkīye śṛṇuhy ā suṣomayā*

"Accept this my praise, Ganga, Yamuna, Sarasvati, Sutudri, Parusni, Marudvrdha with Asikni, and Vitazsta; listen, Arjikiya with Susoms."

Indeed, the word *navigation* itself is often traced by Indian scholars to the Sanskrit *navgatih* (नवगतिh), "the movement or course of a ship." Likewise, the term *navy* is said to arise from nou (नौ), meaning "boat".[1]

Though Western etymology recognises a Latin link (*navis* + *agere*), both Latin and Sanskrit share the Indo-European root *nau*, signifying the common linguistic ancestry of seafaring cultures. Even a sextant was used for navigation and was called *Vruttashanga-Bhaga* and a contrived mariner's compass (*Matsya yantra*) was used by Indian navigators nearly 1500 to 2000 years ago[2].

Before the rise of Mediterranean Sea powers, the Indus Valley Civilisation (c. 2600–1900 BCE) maintained maritime links with Mesopotamia and the Persian Gulf. The dockyard at Lothal, excavated in Gujarat, remains one of the earliest known tidal ports in the world. Harappan seals found in Ur and Bahrain (Dilmun) prove a robust seaborne trade in textiles, beads, ivory, and precious stones[3].

Indian sailors mastered the monsoon winds, sailing westward during the southwest monsoon and returning home with the northeast monsoon, centuries before the Greek navigator *Hippalus* (45 CE) was credited with "discovering" them[4].

In the early historic period (2nd century BCE – 3rd century CE), India's southern and western coasts witnessed vibrant maritime activity. The *Satavahanas* of the Deccan controlled key western ports such as Kalyan, Bharuch, and Sopara, linking India with Rome and Arabia[5]. The *Chera* rulers of the Malabar coast encouraged trade through Muziris, a port so rich that the Roman author and military commander, Pliny the Elder, complained that Rome was losing its gold to India[6]. From these ports, traders exported pepper, pearls, silk, cotton, sandalwood, and other spices, while importing gold, silver, wine, and horses.

An ancient Greek text called *The Periplus of the Erythraean Sea* (written in the 1st century CE) describes Indian ports as lively trading hubs where merchants from Egypt and Arabia met Indian traders, proof that India had thriving global maritime links.[7]

India's naval strength reached its peak under the Chola dynasty between the 9th and 13th centuries CE. King Rajendra Chola I, who ruled from 1014 to

1044 CE, even led an overseas campaign in 1025 CE against the Srivijaya Empire in present-day Sumatra, Java, and the Malay Peninsula[8].

The Chola inscriptions from the *Tiruvalangadu* plates and *Kalingattuparani* commemorate these campaigns, while Southeast Asian inscriptions record Indian influence on art, language, and governance. Merchant guilds like *Manigramam*, *Ayyavole*, and *Nanadesi* maintained commercial outposts across the Bay of Bengal, forming a proto-global network linking Nagasaki to Aden[9]. Through trade and diplomacy, the Cholas and their contemporaries spread Indian ideas of law, temple architecture, and sanskritised governance across Southeast Asia, creating what modern scholars term the "Indian Ocean World."[10]

These examples underscore that India's maritime tradition is ancient, indigenous, and deeply ingrained in its language, culture, and imagination.

Colonisation from the Sea

After the 13th century, repeated invasions from Central Asia shifted India's political and cultural axis northward. Under the Delhi Sultanate and later the Mughal Empire, imperial energy turned inland, towards land campaigns. The oceans were neglected, the once busy shipyards decayed, and coastal polities like the Cholas and Cheras faded from power. This strategic turn inward had far-reaching consequences. When European powers entered the Indian Ocean, India's maritime frontier was undefended. Colonisation, when it came, came from the sea. The colonisers, using maritime control to seize territorial power, reversed the civilisational pattern that had once seen Indian traders sail outward as cultural ambassadors.

Shivaji and the Revival of Maritime Power

The 17th century witnessed a brief resurgence of indigenous maritime power under Chhatrapati Shivaji (1630–1680). Recognising that control of the Konkan coast was essential to sovereignty, Shivaji built India's first modern naval force and a chain of sea forts that still stand as engineering marvels[11].

Shivaji's navy included a diverse fleet, *ghurabs*[12] (gunboats), *pals*[13] (sloops), and *galbats*[14] (oared warships). He appointed Kanhoji Angre as Admiral (*Sarkhel*), who later became the terror of European traders.

Among Shivaji's most formidable sea forts were Sindhudurg Fort off the coast of Malvan, Padmadurg, constructed to counter the Siddi stronghold of Janjira, which also served as a shipyard and Vijaydurg Fort, which later became the headquarters of the Maratha navy. These forts, supported by inland bastions such as Raigad and Rajgad, created a layered defence system integrating land and sea.

Shivaji's fleet clashed with the Portuguese, the Siddis, and the English East India Company. Battles such as those at Kudal, Khanderi, and Kolaba demonstrated his strategic foresight: he realised that a state without a navy was vulnerable to seaborne invasion, a truth that had already cost India dearly.

Indian Shipbuilding Excellence

By the 18th century, Indian shipyards, especially those at Surat, Bombay, and Chittagong, were producing ships that astonished the world. The Wadia family of shipbuilders in Bombay constructed hundreds of vessels for the British East India Company and the Royal Navy, noted for their superior teak construction and longevity[15]. Several notable ships built in India during the late 18th and early 19th centuries highlight the region's exceptional shipbuilding heritage. HMS *Minden*, constructed at the Bombay Dockyard in 1810, is remembered as the vessel aboard which the American national anthem, *The Star-Spangled Banner*, was composed in 1814. Another ship, HMS *Trincomalee*, also built at the Bombay Dockyard in 1817, remains one of the world's oldest warships still afloat and now serves as a museum ship in the United Kingdom[16]. The *Thetis*, launched at Chittagong in 1794, made several voyages to England and was in operation until at least 1839, demonstrating the outstanding durability of Indian teak. Similarly, the *Daria Daulat*, built at Bhavnagar in the early 19th century, was noted to be seaworthy even after 87 years of service, a testament to the superior craftsmanship and materials of Indian shipbuilders[17]. These ships, often superior to their British counterparts, became a source of colonial anxiety.

Colonial Suppression of Indian Maritime Capability

As Indian built ships began to compete with British yards, London responded with restrictive legislation. The *East India Ships Registry Bill* (1815) barred most Indian built ships from registering as British, effectively excluding them from lucrative transoceanic trade[18]. Additional Navigation Acts required that only British built ships, with British crews, could carry goods to England[19]. Indian merchants were further penalised by double import duties on non-British vessels.

This single act crippled a proud heritage and ensured that British companies monopolised shipping. The decline was catastrophic. In 1857, India's ports recorded 34,286 Indian ships carrying more than 1.2 million tons of cargo. By 1900, that number had collapsed to just 1,676 ships, moving barely 100,000 tons, a stark illustration of how colonial policy devastated Indian shipping[20]. By the late 19th century, over 100 Indian shipping companies had been forced into liquidation[21].

At the beginning of World War II in 1939, as against the world tonnage of nearly 70 million Gross register tonnage (GRT), and that of Britain's over 17 million GRT, India possessed barely 132,000 GRT of shipping with ten shipping companies owning 63 vessels. Due to losses during the war, the tonnage was brought down to less than 100,000 GRT[22].

The same colonial government that had once depended on Indian shipbuilders to run its empire at sea later destroyed their industry, wiping out centuries of local shipbuilding skill and independence.

Consequences of Maritime Amnesia

India's long relationship with the sea shows a clear pattern. In ancient times, India was a sea-faring civilisation that traded and engaged across the Indian Ocean. But over the centuries, this outlook changed. During the medieval period, repeated invasions from the north shifted power inland. Under the Mughals, attention turned away from sea and towards land wars and empire building. As a result, the rich maritime traditions that once thrived in southern India slowly disappeared.

This loss of maritime focus had serious consequences. When European powers began arriving, India was unprepared. The Portuguese came first, followed by the Dutch, French, and finally the British, all using control of the sea to build their empires. The British East India Company did not conquer India from land but came as traders by sea and eventually ruled the country. By neglecting shipyards, ports, and seafaring traditions, India left an empty space that outsiders quickly occupied. The same ocean that had once carried Indian trade and culture became the conduit for the through which foreign rule entered.

This history offers an important lesson, that a land-focused India risks dependencies, while a maritime-oriented India achieves progress and prosperity. In a world where oceans once again decide wealth and power, India's security, growth, and influence depend on how it engages with the sea, just as its ancestors once did.

The Modern Maritime Resurgence

Thankfully, the wheels of India's maritime connection have turned full circle. In the 21st century, the country is rediscovering its maritime identity, and the Indian Ocean is once again central to its national vision. India is reclaiming its place as the natural leader of the Indian Ocean region. Through its vision of SAGAR (meaning sea in Hindi) (Security and Growth for All in the Region) and MAHASAGAR (meaning Ocean in Hindi) (Mutual and Holistic Advancement for Security and Growth Across Regions)[23] and initiatives such as the *Sagarmala*, and Maritime India Vision 2030, the country is turning its attention back to the seas, modernising ports, rebuilding its shipyards, boosting trade and the blue economy, and strengthening partnerships across the Indo-Pacific and beyond. They reflect a conscious effort to revive India's maritime legacy and heritage.

Maritime Civilisational Resurgence

India's renewed maritime focus is also a return to its civilisational roots. This revival can be seen in efforts that connect modern India with its ancient seafaring traditions.

One example is the *Kaundinya* Stitched Ship Project, jointly undertaken by the Ministry of Culture, the Indian Navy, and IIT Madras[24]. The project involved building an ancient type of wooden ship described in old texts like the *Yuktikalpataru* and shown in a 5th century mural at the Ajanta Caves. The entire ship was built without metal nails, its wooden planks were stitched together with hand-twisted coir rope, just as Indian shipbuilders did more than 2,000 years ago. Named *Kaundinya*, after the legendary sailor who undertook voyages to Suvarnabhumi (present day Southeast Asia), the vessel was launched at the Cochin Shipyard in December 2023[25].

This project is part of a wider effort to revive India's maritime memory. The Lothal Maritime Heritage Complex in Gujarat and the Muziris Heritage Project in Kerala honour India's ancient ports and seafaring history. They highlight India's early leadership in ship design, port building, and ocean trade, centuries before the Europeans began. Together, these projects form a national movement to link India's maritime past with its future.

India's maritime renewal is not simply about economic growth or maritime security. It is also about rediscovering the spirit that once shaped *Bharatavarsha*, a civilisation defined as much by the sea as by the land. The image of the stitched ship sailing again is a powerful symbol of India's return as a great maritime civilisation.

The SAGAR vision, announced by the Prime Minister in 2015, is built on five main goals: keeping India's mainland and islands safe, maintaining peace and stability in the Indian Ocean Region (IOR), deepening economic and security cooperation with maritime neighbours, promoting collective regional action, supporting sustainable and inclusive development, and strengthening India's maritime engagement. It is based on the idea that the stability and prosperity of the IOR should be shared by all the countries that border it[26].

On March 12, 2025, during a visit to Mauritius, Prime Minister Narendra Modi announced the launch of MAHASAGAR (meaning Ocean in Hindi) (Mutual and Holistic Advancement for Security and Growth Across Regions)[27]. Coming 10 years after SAGAR, the initiative upgrades the focus from a regional to a global vision with an emphasis on the global south[28]. The transformation of SAGAR to MAHASAGAR will propel India toward becoming a global leader in the maritime sector by 2047[29].

Maritime Connectivity Initiatives

India's maritime resurgence is also being shaped by its expanding connectivity architecture, designed to link the Indian Ocean with the Eurasian heartland and the wider Indo-Pacific. Around 95 per cent of India's external trade by volume and approximately 70 per cent by value is carried by maritime transport[30].

Through flagship initiatives such as the International North–South Transport Corridor (INSTC), the Chennai–Vladivostok Maritime Corridor (CVMC), the Kaladan Multi Modal Transit Transport Project, and the India–Middle East–Europe Corridor (IMEC), India is building strategic linkages that reduce dependence on narrow chokepoints and diversify trade routes. The INSTC, a 7,200 km multimodal corridor connecting Mumbai to St. Petersburg via Bandar Abbas, and the Caspian Sea, aims to cut freight time by 30–40 per cent compared to the Suez route. The CVMC, connecting Chennai with Vladivostok through the Malacca Straits and the Sea of Japan route, is expected to reduce transit distance by 40–45 per cent and significantly lower freight costs[31]. The Kaladan Project, linking Kolkata Port to Sittwe in Myanmar and onward to Mizoram through river and road networks, will open a vital alternative route to India's Northeast, enhancing connectivity with ASEAN and strengthening India's Act East policy[32]. The newly announced IMEC, launched during the G20 Summit in 2023, envisions an interlinked network of ports, railways, and energy corridors from India through the UAE and Saudi Arabia to Europe, symbolising India's centrality in future transcontinental trade[33]. Together, these initiatives are reflective of India's transition to a global maritime power. India's ports and logistics systems are now vying to be hubs in the Indo-Pacific and Eurasian economic corridors.

Blue Economy

The blue economy has now become a key component of India's national growth plan. A recent report by NITI Aayog, *"India's Blue Economy: Strategy for Harnessing Deep Sea and Offshore Fisheries,"* highlights India's huge potential in this sector. India is the world's second-largest fish producer, providing livelihood to nearly 30 million people and earning over INR 60,000 crore in exports in 2023–24. With an Exclusive Economic Zone (EEZ) of more than 2 million square kilometres, a deep-sea potential of over seven million tonnes, and a coastline stretching 11,098 kilometres, India has great scope to expand its deep-sea and offshore fishing[34]. The report lays out a step-by-step plan for 2025–2032 and beyond, focusing on better policies, improved infrastructure, local participation, and sustainable practices. The goal is to make the blue economy not only a source of growth but also a pillar of national security, jobs, and competitiveness.

Port Capacity

India's port infrastructure has grown rapidly over the last ten years. The total capacity of the country's major ports has more than doubled, from about 800 million tonnes per annum (MTPA) in 2014 to around 1,630 MTPA by March 2024[35]. This major expansion has greatly increased India's ability to handle rising cargo volumes and strengthen its role in global trade. Similarly, the cargo handled at major ports in the year 2024-25 reached approximately 853.6 million tonnes, up from 819 million tonnes in the previous year[36].

Inland Waterways

Inland waterways have also emerged as a key component of multimodal transport connectivity. Cargo traffic through National Waterways has grown from just 6.89 MTPA a decade ago to about 126 MTPA, reflecting nearly a twenty-fold increase. Recent reports indicate that in FY 2024–25, the cargo volume on inland waterways reached 145.5 million metric tonnes (MMT), underscoring their growing role in easing pressure on congested road and rail networks[37]. The operationalisation of major river systems, such as the Ganga under *Jal Marg Vikas Project*, the Brahmaputra (NW-2), and the Barak (NW-16), is enabling cheaper, cleaner, and more sustainable cargo transport across India's heartland.

Seafarers

The sharp rise in the number of Indian seafarers underscores the sector's expanding human capital and global relevance. Their pool has grown from about 1.17 lakh in 2014 to nearly 3 lakhs today, representing roughly 12 per cent of the world's seafaring workforce. This growth has made India one of the world's top three sources of seafarers and has opened up many new job opportunities in areas like navigation, ship operations, logistics, and related industries both in India and overseas[38]. This growth has been made possible through the expansion of maritime training institutes, improved certification systems, and aligned Indian training standards with international rules such as the **STCW (Standards of Training, Certification and Watchkeeping).**

Public–Private Partnerships (PPP)

Private investment in India's maritime infrastructure has grown sharply in recent years. The total value of PPP projects in the port sector has increased from about INR 16,000 crore in 2014 to nearly INR 40,000 crore in 2025. In the financial year 2024–25 alone, more than INR 2,500 crore worth of new PPP projects were launched, mainly focused on container terminals, port modernisation, and connectivity improvements. Since India opened up its port sector in the 1990s, total private investment in maritime and logistics projects has crossed INR 24.23 trillion (around USD 295 billion) and continues to increase. These partnerships have helped modernise port operations, introduce new technology, and bring in global best practices in efficiency and sustainability[39].

Renewable Energy

India's ports are also becoming greener. Renewable energy generation has become a major focus area, with installed wind and solar capacity at major ports growing from just 10 megawatts (MW) in 2014 to around 139 MW by 2024. Several new projects are underway at ports like **Kandla, Paradip, and Tuticorin** to further boost clean energy production and make ports more self-sufficient and environmentally friendly[40]. Self-sufficiency for all major ports has been targeted by 2030 through solar rooftops, onshore wind farms, and the electrification of cargo handling equipment, turning ports into exemplars of the *Green Ports & Shipping* initiative announced during India Maritime Week 2025[41].

Shipbuilding

India's shipbuilding and shipping capacity has also improved, albeit modestly compared with other parameters. The average ship carrying capacity of Indian flagged commercial vessels has grown from roughly 10,000 GRT in 2014 to about 14,000 GRT in 2025, reflecting gradual fleet modernisation. The ship recycling industry has simultaneously expanded its capacity from about 2.3–2.6 million gross tonnes (GT) in 2024 to 3.8–4.2 million GT in 2025, consolidating India's position as one of the world's largest ship recycling hubs, centred at Alang, Gujarat[42]. On the defence front, the Indian Navy has 54 ships under construction as of early 2025, all at Indian shipyards[43].

The Maritime India Vision 2030 outlines a transformative growth trajectory for India's shipbuilding sector. It sets forth the ambition for India to become one of the **top 10 shipbuilding nations by 2030,** and to rise to the **top 5 position by 2047**[44]. The policy also targets capturing about **five per cent of the global ship building market by 2030**, up from less than one per cent today[45]. To catalyse this growth, it proposes major interventions including the development of 10 world class shipyards under public private partnership, creation of a dedicated **Maritime Development Fund**, upgradation of existing yards, adoption of automation and green technology, and training of tens of thousands of skilled workers[46].

Maritime Legislation

On the legal front, the year 2025 has been a turning point for India's maritime sector. Parliament passed four major laws that completely update the country's old maritime rules and bring them in line with global standards. This shows India's strong commitment to building a modern and efficient system for managing its maritime related activities.

The **Indian Ports Act, 2025** replaces the more than 100-year-old **Indian Ports Act of 1908.** This legislation creates a modern framework for running and developing ports across the country. The Act established the ***Maritime State Development Council*** **(MSDC)** to improve coordination between the central government and coastal states, helping them work together on port policies and projects. The Act also requires all ports to follow international green standards and strengthen their disaster preparedness, showing India's focus on sustainable and safe maritime operations. In addition, it simplifies port procedures, promotes digital systems, and improves the overall ***Ease of Doing Business*** **(EoDB),** making Indian ports more efficient and globally competitive[47].

The **Merchant Shipping Act, 2025** replaces the outdated **Merchant Shipping Act of 1958**. The new version is shorter and more practical, with 16 parts and 325 clauses instead of the earlier 561 sections. It aligns India's shipping laws with major global conventions such as **SOLAS** (Safety of Life at Sea), **MARPOL** (Marine Pollution), and the **Limitation of Liability for Maritime Claims Convention**. This modern framework makes India's shipping regulations clearer, safer, and more in tune with international maritime practices. It enhances seafarers' welfare, boosts tonnage under the Indian flag, tightens environmental and safety regulations, simplifies registration and compliance processes, and shifts the sector from a heavy regulatory environment towards an enabling one, aimed at making India a globally competitive maritime hub[48].

The Coastal Shipping Bill, 2025 is a landmark reform passed to modernise India's coastal cargo logistics by unlocking the potential of its 11,098 km strategic coastline spread across nine coastal states and four Union Territories. Comprising six chapters and 42 clauses, the Act introduces a simplified licensing system for coastal shipping, sets out a regulatory framework for foreign vessels engaged in coasting trade, and mandates formulation of a *National Coastal and Inland Shipping Strategic Plan*. It also establishes a *National Database for Coastal Shipping*, designed to provide real-time data to investors and stakeholders, thereby enhancing transparency and ease of doing business. The legislation aims to boost India's coastal cargo volume to 230 million metric tonnes by 2030, reduce dependence on foreign flagged vessels, generate employment in coastal regions, and strengthen supply chain resilience by expanding domestic shipping services[49].

The **Carriage of Goods by Sea Bill, 2025** was passed by Parliament to replace the century old Carriage of Goods by Sea Act, 1925, modernising India's maritime cargo law framework and aligning it with international conventions such as the Hague Visby Rules. The legislation, while retaining the core provisions governing the rights, liabilities and immunities of carriers and shippers, simplifies the legal language and structure to promote EoDB. It authorises the central government to issue directions for implementation and to amend the rules through notification, thereby enabling swift alignment with evolving global maritime trade practices.[50]

These comprehensive legislative reforms remove outdated colonial relics, streamline regulation, strengthen security and environmental standards, boost EoDB and open the door to innovative shipbuilding, digitalisation and blue economy growth. With the legal framework freshly updated, India is well positioned to leverage its 11,098 km coastline, its strategic location at the juncture of critical maritime routes, and its long dormant shipbuilding expertise.

India Maritime Week

In 2025, India re-emphasised its maritime resurgence with the India Maritime Week, held from 27 – 31 October in Mumbai, where over 100 countries, more than 100,000 delegates and over 500 exhibitors converged to chart the future of the sea-based economy[51]. This event showcased India's strategic roadmap to become a global maritime hub, with key emphasis on sustainability, innovation, logistics and shipbuilding[52]. During the Week, investment commitments totalling INR 12 lakh crore (approx. USD 145 billion) were announced, of which 20 per cent is earmarked for shipbuilding[53]. Among the many highlights was '*Digi Bandar*', a national framework to make all major ports data-driven, AI-enabled and interconnected, launched as part of the Digital Tech Forum during the Week[54].

Maritime Security

Complementing its maritime economic and civilisational resurgence, India has simultaneously strengthened its maritime security architecture to safeguard national interests across its 11098 km coastline and island territories. A major institutional milestone was the creation of the National Maritime Security Coordinator (NMSC) under the National Security Council Secretariat (NSCS) in February 2022[55], a long pending reform that ensures cohesive inter-agency coordination among the Navy, Coast Guard, and coastal states for maritime domain awareness and response. Parallel efforts under the Coastal Security Scheme (CSS) Phases I and II have equipped coastal police stations with interceptor boats, radar networks, and communication systems, while Phase III, now under implementation, focuses on upgrading surveillance and electronic data sharing between central and state agencies[56]. To enhance vessel tracking, all mechanised fishing boats are being fitted with AIS transponders, and over 20 lakh biometric identity cards have been issued to fishermen to improve security verification and disaster response[57]. The National Command, Control, Communication, and Intelligence (NC3I) network, linking coastal radar chains, Automatic Identification Systems, and the Information Management and Analysis Centre (IMAC) at Gurugram, now provides a real-time, fused maritime picture of the Indian coastline[58]. These reforms together reflect India's seriousness toward a comprehensive maritime security, in which local enforcement agencies, the technological components, and national and level coordination mechanisms, work in a whole of government approach to secure India's maritime interests.

Challenges

Despite considerable progress in areas such as port capacity, legal reforms, and human resource development, India still faces major structural challenges in shipbuilding, fleet ownership, port efficiency, and overall maritime infrastructure. Compared to China, the gap is wide, showing that India still has a long way to go before it can become a true global maritime power. Some of these key challenges are outlined below.

Shipbuilding: India's shipbuilding sector remains inconsequential. While government programmes like *Maritime India Vision 2030* and the *Shipbuilding Financial Assistance Policy* have put the enabling policies in place, the industry still lacks scale, advanced design skills, and well-organised industrial clusters. India's share of global shipbuilding is less than 1 per cent, compared to 50 per cent of the total global output by China controls (in 2024). Chinese shipyards also lead in building green, alternative-fuel vessels, supported by strong state financing and integrated supply chains[59]. For India to compete, it needs to expand shipyard capacity, create specialised industrial clusters, and establish credit and insurance systems similar to those that support the shipbuilding industries in China, Japan and South Korea.

Fleet Size: India's merchant fleet has grown in recent years but is still small compared to the size of India's maritime trade. As of 2025, India's registered fleet includes about 1,549 ships, with a total capacity of 13.5 million GT [60]. In contrast, China's fleet exceeds 280 million GT, making it the largest in the world and giving it huge leverage in global freight markets[61]. Because India's shipping capacity is small relative to its trade volume, it cannot fully benefit from carrying its own imports and exports. Expanding the Indian-flagged fleet through tax breaks, simpler registration rules, and better credit options would help create a stronger ship-owning base and enhance maritime autonomy.

Port Capacity: India has made major strides in developing its ports, but the huge gap with China still remains. For example, in 2024, the port of **Shanghai** alone handled about 50 million containers (TEUs), while all of India's ports together handled only about 13.5 million TEUs. China's ports benefit from large logistics zones, strong inter-port connections, and heavy automation. Although India's ports are growing but this growth is uneven, and the ports are not integrated. To bridge the gap with China, India needs more coordination, new freight corridors, and advanced digital systems to improve efficiency and throughput.

Port Efficiency: The average turnaround time (TRT) for ships at India's major ports has dropped sharply, from 94 hours in 2014 to around 48 hours in 2023–24[62]. However, efficiency still varies widely between ports due to varying levels of automation, inefficient customs procedures, and bottlenecks in hinterland connectivity. In contrast, ports like **Shanghai, Ningbo-Zhoushan,** and **Shenzhen** in China can turnaround container vessels in under 24 hours[63]. To close the operational gap, India needs to standardise procedures, enhance real-time cargo tracking, and implement single-window digital systems across all ports.

Inland Waterways: India's inland waterways growth reflects the success of projects like ***Jal Marg Vikas*** and the development of key river routes such as the Ganga (NW-1) and Brahmaputra (NW-2). Still, infrastructure at terminals, dredging capacity, and integration with rail and road transport are limited. To make waterways a reliable transport option, India needs better infrastructure at multimodal hubs, a larger barge fleet, and digital systems for tracking cargo movement.

Human Capital: India's seafaring workforce is expanding rapidly, making the country one of the top three suppliers of trained seafarers in the world. This rising pool strengthens India's global reputation as a trusted source of seafarers and maritime expertise. However, skill development must move beyond quantity to quality, particularly in areas such as green fuel management, automation, and shipyard engineering. India should expand maritime universities and R&D partnerships to strengthen high end competencies.

Green Transition: India's maritime decarbonisation drive is gathering momentum. Yet, large scale retrofits, alternative fuel vessel production, and financing mechanisms for green projects remain challenging. To narrow the gap, India needs dedicated R&D, pilot projects for hydrogen and ammonia vessels, and fiscal incentives for green technology adoption across ports and shipping.

Financial Aspects: PPP investments in India's ports have increased from INR 16,000 crore in 2014 to INR 40,000 crore in 2025. India Maritime Week 2025 alone generated investment commitments exceeding INR 12 lakh crore (USD 145 billion), with 20 per cent earmarked for shipbuilding[64]. However, obtaining long term ship finance and export credit are still a major challenge for shipowners. To mitigate this, India must establish specialised ship finance windows, export credit insurance for shipowners, and incentives for domestic procurement of Indian built vessels.

Regulatory Modernisation: The year 2025 marked a watershed in India's maritime governance, bringing the country in line with global maritime rules. However, the real challenge lies in implementing the new laws. India needs to quickly frame clear rules, improve coordination between the central and state governments, and build strong digital systems. The focus must now shift to effective enforcement of these enabling legislation.

Connectivity Constraints: Despite India's ambitious plans to improve its maritime connectivity, several practical, political, and infrastructure challenges persist. The strategically important International North–South Transport Corridor (INSTC), struggles with low cargo movement, non-uniform customs rules among partner countries, and logistical problems in the Caspian region, worsened by sanctions and regional instability[65]. The Kaladan Project is almost complete but has faced delays due to rough terrain, cost overruns, and political unrest in Myanmar. The Chennai–Vladivostok Maritime Corridor (CVMC) is still developing and faces gaps in multimodal connections, poor infrastructure at Far Eastern ports, and limited investment in India's Arctic-linked trade readiness in LNG terminal capacities. The India–Middle East–Europe Corridor (IMEC) also hold promise but faces challenges related to financing, route coordination, and political alignment among countries in a volatile West Asian region.

Within India, the problem lies in poor port-to-hinterland connectivity. Last-mile logistics are weak, cargo handling is fragmented, and coordination between shipping, rail, and road systems is limited. Unless these issues are fixed, India's trade corridors will not reach their full potential, limiting both economic competitiveness and its goal of becoming a key maritime hub in the Indo-Pacific.

Maritime Security: Despite the notable recent reforms, India's maritime security system still has serious gaps. Different agencies, the Indian Navy, Coast Guard, state marine police, and other central bodies, often have overlapping responsibilities and jurisdiction. This causes confusion, weakens accountability, and slows down decision-making during emergencies[66].

A major weakness is the absence of a dedicated maritime border-guarding force under the Ministry of Home Affairs (MHA), which is entrusted with the management of India's borders. While India's land borders with every bordering country has a dedicated border-guarding force, such as the Border Security Force, the Assam Rifles, the Indo-Tibetan Border Police, and the Sashastra Seema Bal, no dedicated force is present, under the MHA, for guarding India's maritime borders. This has led to enforcement gaps, particularly in tracking and monitoring small fishing vessels below 20 metres, many of which remain outside the Automatic Identification System (AIS) coverage[67].

In addition, there are no proper performance standards or accountability systems for coastal security operations, making it hard to assess how well current programmes like the Coastal Security Schemes (Phases I and II) are working. While technology and infrastructure have improved maritime surveillance, the lack of unified command, unclear authority, and no dedicated maritime border agency continue to limit India's ability to protect its coastline as effectively as it guards its land borders.

Recommendations for operationalising the Vision of MAHASAGAR

While the articulation of SAGAR and MAHASAGAR has provided India with a visionary maritime outlook, their transformative potential has remained constrained by the absence of an integrated institutional framework. The vision has inspired multiple initiatives such as the *Sagarmala*, the *Indo-Pacific Oceans Initiative*, *Act East Policy*, and various blue economy programmes, but these continue to operate as parallel endeavours, lacking a single coordinating mechanism. The result is a fragmented policy landscape that limits synergy, accountability, and sustained outcomes.

The visionary declarations of SAGAR and MAHASAGAR have provided India's policymakers with a strong and forward-looking maritime guidance. However, the country's full potential in the maritime domain remains to be optimally realised because there is no single, coordinated institutional framework to oversee all maritime related initiatives that may be under the domain of different ministries. Many important programmes such as the *Sagarmala*, the *Indo-Pacific Oceans Initiative*, the *Act East Policy*, Project *Mausam* and other initiatives often operate in isolation, overlap, lack coordination, and fail to achieve their combined impact. This has created a fragmented policy environment that inhibits synergy, accountability, and long-term results.

To turn this vision into action and bring in the desire outcomes, India needs a clear and structured framework for implementing MAHASAGAR. This framework should define the responsibilities of each ministry/institution, provide dedicated funding, and set measurable goals. Because maritime affairs touch multiple areas, such as foreign policy, defence, trade, the environment, and technology, the framework should be coordinated under the Prime Minister's Office (PMO). A PMO-led mechanism would make sure that all ministries work together effectively, maintain accountability, and align maritime goals with national development priorities.

To achieve this, it is proposed to set up a framework that groups all stakeholders into **six functional clusters**, each led by a specific ministry. These clusters would be overseen through a single monitoring body within the PMO. Such a system would ensure proper coordination between ministries and maintain consistency between India's maritime, diplomatic, economic, and security objectives. The six proposed verticals and their coordinating ministries are as follows:

***Sagar Sambandh* External Relations (Ministry of External Affairs)** This pillar would encompass India's diplomatic maritime engagements, including the *Act East Policy, Indo-Pacific Vision, Indo-Pacific Oceans Initiative (IPOI), Indian Ocean Rim Association (IORA), Indian Ocean Naval Symposium (IONS), Project Mausam* and bilateral and multi-lateral maritime dialogues. The MEA would serve as the coordinating ministry, supported by the NSCS and NITI Aayog.

***Sagar Suraksha* Security (Ministry of Defence)** This cluster would oversee India's maritime security architecture, covering **Maritime Domain Awareness (MDA)**, coastal security, maritime border guarding, hydrography, anti-piracy operations, HADR (Humanitarian Assistance and Disaster Relief), and bilateral and multilateral naval exercises. The MoD would coordinate this vertical, ensuring synergy between national defence, regional security, and maritime law enforcement.

***Sagarmala* Connectivity (Ministry of Ports, Shipping & Waterways)** This vertical would focus on strengthening India's connectivity initiatives and maritime logistics and infrastructure, including port led industrialisation, coastal shipping, inland waterways, and digital maritime corridors.

***Sagar Shodh* Scientific Research (Ministry of Earth Sciences)** This pillar would integrate all scientific, technological, and research driven initiatives related to oceanography, polar studies, seabed mapping, blue biotechnology, and marine spatial planning. The Ministry of Earth Sciences (MoES) would coordinate national R&D efforts through partnerships with institutions such as NIOT, NCPOR, NIO, INCOIS, IMD and CSIR, thereby ensuring a seamless integration of all ocean science endeavours in India's maritime domain.

***Sagar Sanskriti* Culture (Ministry of Culture)** This vertical would preserve and promote India's maritime civilisational heritage, including projects such as the *Lothal Maritime Heritage Complex*, *Muziris Heritage Project*, and the *Kaundinya Stitched Ship Project*. It would institutionalise maritime archaeology and promote India's historical engagement with the ocean to further India's interests.

***Sagar Samsadhan* Resources (Ministry of Agriculture, Animal Husbandry & Fisheries)** This cluster would focus on the sustainable development of India's marine resources, including fisheries, deep sea mining, marine energy, and aquaculture. It would also address the blue economy, marine biodiversity, and climate resilience through coordination with the Ministry of Environment, Forest and Climate Change (MoEF& CC) and the MoES.

Each vertical could have a **dedicated action plan and annual budgetary allocation**. A ***National* MAHASAGAR *Coordination Committee* (NMCC)** chaired by the Principal Secretary to the Prime Minister, with representatives from all coordinating ministries, NITI Aayog, and the NSCS, could be established to ensure unified policy implementation and regular monitoring.

This PMO-led institutional framework would have the potential to transform MAHASAGAR from an aspirational vision into a **functional reality**, integrating the diverse maritime clusters under one unified framework. Such a structure would also enable the exercise of a greater strategic coherence and strengthen India's role as a preferred security and maritime partner in the Indian Ocean and beyond.

Conclusion

India's maritime sector has once again emerged as a key component of its comprehensive national power. The country's geographic advantage in the Indian Ocean, along with its proactive engagements and partnerships in the Indian Ocean and the wider Indo-Pacific partnerships, primes it for a leadership role in the region.

For India to turn this geographic advantage into real maritime power, it must bring together its efforts in security, diplomacy, and sustainable development under one coordinated approach. Guided by *Aatmanirbharta* and *Make in India* to build a self-reliant maritime ecosystem, based on indigenous shipbuilding, green technology, and skilled human resources, will be crucial for India to strengthen its position among the top maritime nations in the world.

The six functional areas proposed under the MAHASAGAR framework, monitored by the Prime Minister's Office (PMO), provide a clear roadmap for this. They bring together all aspects of India's maritime domain into one coherent and unified national strategy.[68]

NOTES

1 Sudheer. "Navigation in Ancient India." Sanskriti Magazine. April 28, 2015. https://www.sanskritimagazine.com/navigation-in-ancient-india/

2 Ibid

3 Rao, S. R. "Expedition Magazine." Shipping and Maritime Trade of the Indus People,

30–37. 1964. https://www.penn.museum/sites/expedition/shipping-and-maritime-trade-of-the-indus-people/

4 Tripati, S. "Early Users of Monsoon Winds for Navigation." Historical Notes 113, 1618-1623. 2017. https://drs.nio.res.in/drs/bitstream/handle/2264/7782/Curr_Sci_113_1618a.pdf?sequence=1&isAllowed=y

5 Prasad, Krishna. "Satavahana Trade and Commerce: Ports and Maritime Trade -an Historical Analysis." International Journal of Research and Analytical Reviews, 160-174. 2015. https://www.ijrar.org/papers/IJRAR19D5491.pdf.

6 "The Lost Port of Muziris." Maritime History Society. November 21, 2024. https://mhsindia.org/blogs/the-lost-port-of-muziris/210175/

7 Schoff, Wilfred H. "The Periplus of the Erythraean Sea". New York: Longmans, Green, and Co. 1912. https://dn790003.ca.archive.org/0/items/cu31924030139236/cu31924030139236.pdf

8 Raj, Aarti Kumari. "A Comprehensive Analysis of Cultural Expansion from India to Southeast Asia under the Chola Dynasty." International Journal of History 7, 39–42. 2025. https://doi.org/10.22271/27069109.2025.v7.i4a.392

9 Das, Nandini. "Merchant Guilds of South India." History Notes. March 27, 2021. https://historynotesbook.wordpress.com/2021/03/27/merchant-guilds-of-south-india/.

10 Ray, Himanshu P. "Southeast Asia in the Ancient Indian Ocean World." International Journal of Nautical Archaeology 45, 210–12. 2016. https://doi.org/10.1111/1095-9270.12158.

11 Apte, B. K. "A History of the Maratha Navy and Merchantships". Bombay: State Board for Literature and Culture, Government of Maharashtra. 1973. https://sahitya.marathi.gov.in/ebooks/A%20HISTORY%20OF%20THE%20 MARATHA%20NAVY%20AND%20MERCHANTSHIPS.pdf

12 The famous Maratha war vessel of the seventeenth and eighteenth centuries, known as the *grab*, was described by Robert Orme in his '*History of Hindostan*' as a vessel with two or three masts, broad in proportion to its length, and of about three hundred tons. The term '*ghurab*' in Arabic refers to a crow, a raven, or a type of ship, indicating that the word is evidently of Arabic origin.

13 A Maratha warship having two to three masts. The *pals* were the biggest of the Maratha warship. Original word from Sanskrit '*plu/plav*' to float.

14 The '*galbats*' were larger row boats, built like the '*ghurab*s', but of smaller dimensions. They rarely exceeded seventy tons. They had two masts of which the mizzen was very slight. The mainmast had one large triangular sail. When hoisted, its peak went much higher than the mast itself. The '*galbats*' were usually covered with a spar-deck, made up of split bamboos for lightness. They carried only '*patteraroes*' which were mounted with six or eight pieces of cannon ranging from two to four pounders. They were rowed by forty or fifty stout oars at a speed of four miles per hour.

15 Sahai, B. "Indian Shipping: A Historical Survey". New Delhi: Publications Division, Ministry of Information & Broadcasting, Government of India. 1996. https://dn720401.ca.archive.org/0/items/indianshippinghi00saha/indianshippinghi00saha.pdf

16 "HMS Trincomalee: A Living Prowess of Shipbuilding". Maritime History Society. July 07, 2023. https://mhsindia.org/all/hms-trincomalee-a-living-prowess-of-shipbuilding/210029/

17 Ibid

18 "East India Ships Registry Bill". UK Parliament. June 20, 1815. https://hansard.parliament.uk/lords/1815-06-20/debates/810d5408-669c-46fe-893d-f5e1745f5792/EastIndiaShipsRegistryBill

19 UK Parliament. "Navigation Laws". UK Parliament. https://www.parliament.uk/about/living-heritage/transformingsociety/tradeindustry/importexport/overview/navigationlaws/

20 Op. cit. note no.15.

21 Ibid

22 Ibid

23 "Mutual and Holistic Advancement for Security and Growth Across Regions (MAHASAGAR),"." Ministry of External Affairs, Government of India Press Release. March 12, 2025. https://www.mea.gov.in/newsdetail1.htm?13355/.

24 "Traditionally Built 'Ancient Stitched Ship' Inducted into the Indian Navy as INSV Kaundinya." Press Release, Indian Navy. May 21, 2025. https://indiannavy.gov.in/content/traditionally-built-ancient-stitched-ship-inducted-indian-navy-insv-kaundinya

25 Ibid

26 Durai, S. "India's Maritime Vision: from SAGAR to Indo-Pacific to MAHASAGAR". Embassy of India in Serbia. August 18, 2025. https://eoibelgrade.gov.in/public_files/assets/pdf/SAGAR_to_MAHASAGAR_18_08_2025.pdf

27 "Prime Minister Shri Narendra Modi announced Vision MAHASAGAR for the Global South in Mauritius**".** Ministry of External Affairs, Government of India. March 12, 2025. https://www.mea.gov.in/newsdetail1.htm?13355/

28 "India's Maritime Vision: From SAGAR to Indo-Pacific to MAHASAGAR." Embassy of India in Panama. 2025. https://indianembassypanama.gov.in/eoipa_listview/NjU2

29 "Union Home Minister and Minister of Cooperation Shri Amit Shah inaugurates the India Maritime Week in Mumbai." Press Bureau of India, Government of India. October 27, 2025. https://www.pib.gov.in/PressReleseDetail.aspx?PRID=2182946

30 "Year End Review of Ministry of Ports, Shipping and Waterways 2024." Press Information Bureau, Ministry of Ports, Shipping and Waterways, Government of India. 2024. https://www.pib.gov.in/PressReleasePage.aspx?PRID=2089049.

31 "India and Russia launch Chennai-Vladivostok maritime corridor to boost trade links". TV BRICS. November 21, 2024. https://tvbrics.com/en/news/india-and-russia-launch-chennai-vladivostok-maritime-corridor-to-boost-trade-links/.

32 Seshadri, V. S. "Transforming Connectivity Corridors between India and Myanmar into Development Corridors." New Delhi: Research and Information System for Developing Countries, 1–40. 2014. https://www.ris.org.in/sites/default/files/Publication/Trans.

33 "India-Middle East-Europe Economic Corridor (IMEC) Strategic Choices and Way Forward'. Research and Information System for Developing Countries, 1-40. March, 2025. https://www.ris.org.in/sites/default/files/Publication/IMEC%20Report-Web.pdf

34 Ibid

35 Ibid

36 "Cargo Handling Status for Major Ports During April 2025." Ministry of Ports, Shipping and Waterways, Government of India, 1-7. April, 2025. https://shipmin.gov.in/sites/default/files/Report%20Monthly%20Major%20Port%20April%202252025.pdf.

37 Jagannathan, Shyam. "India's Maritime Opportunity in the Current Context." Vivekananda

International Foundation. September 9, 2025. https://www.vifindia.org/article/2025/september/09/India-s-Maritime-Opportunity-in-the-Current-Context.

38 "Maritime India from Vision 2030 to Amrit Kaal 2047." PIB Headquarters, Government of India. October 26, 2025. https://www.pib.gov.in/PressReleasePage.aspx?PRID=2182563.

39 Op cit. note no. 37.

40 Kumar, M. and Verma, N. "India aims for green shipping on inland waterways in five years". Reuters. March 7, 2024. https://www.reuters.com/world/india/india-aims-green-shipping-inland-waterways-five-years-officials-2024-03-07/

41 "India Maritime Week, 2025 Secures Investment of ₹ 12 Lakh Crores, Set to Bolster Maritime Sector of 'Atmanirbhar Bharat'." Press Information Bureau, Ministry of Ports, Shipping and Waterways. October 30, 2025. https://www.pib.gov.in/PressReleasePage.aspx?PRID=2184349.

42 Op cit. note no. 37.

43 Trivedi, Saurabh. "Indian Navy Scales up Indigenous Shipbuilding with 54 Vessels under Construction." The Hindu. September 22, 2025. https://www.thehindu.com/news/national/indian-navy-scales-up-indigenous-shipbuilding-with-54-vessels-under-construction/article70081584.ece.

44 "India Aims for Global Top 10 in Shipbuilding by 2030." India's World. March 11, 2025. https://indiasworld.in/current-affair/india-aims-for-global-top-10-in-shipbuilding-by-2030/

45 "India Sets 5% Global Shipbuilding Target by 2030; Plans National Container Line, Green Shipping Push." Economic Times. September 15, 2025. https://infra.economictimes.indiatimes.com/news/ports-shipping/india-aims-for-5-share-in-global-shipbuilding-by-2030-with-national-container-line-and-green-initiatives/123899641.

46 Ibid

47 "The Indian Ports Act, 2025—India's Bold Maritime Legislation." Press Information Bureau, Ministry of Ports, Shipping and Waterways, Government of India. September 28, 2025. https://static.pib.gov.in/WriteReadData/specificdocs/documents/2025/sep/doc2025928649401.pdf

48 "Parliament Passes Merchant Shipping Bill, 2025 after Rajya Sabha Adoption." Press Information Bureau, Ministry of Ports, Shipping & Waterways, Government of India. August 11, 2025. https://www.pib.gov.in/PressReleasePage.aspx?PRID=2155271

49 "Parliament Clears Coastal Shipping Bill, 2025 to Boost India's Coastal Economy." Press Information Bureau, Ministry of Ports, Shipping & Waterways, Government of India. August 7, 2025. https://www.pib.gov.in/PressReleasePage.aspx?PRID=2153799

50 "Parliament Passes Carriage of Goods by Sea Bill 2025." News on Air. August 6, 2025. https://www.newsonair.gov.in/parliament-passes-carriage-of-goods-by-sea-bill-2025/.

51 "India Maritime Week 2025." India Maritime Week. October 2025. https://imw.org.in/imw/maritime-week/.

52 Prime Minister's Office. "Prime Minister Shri Narendra Modi Addresses Maritime Leaders Conclave at India Maritime Week 2025 in Mumbai." Press Information Bureau, Government of India. October 29, 2025. https://www.pib.gov.in/PressReleasePage.aspx?PRID=2183881.

53 Op cit. note no. 40.

54 Ibid

55 "National Maritime Security Coordinator Appointed." SP's Naval Forces. 2022. https://www.spsnavalforces.com/story/?id=800&h=National-Maritime-Security-Coordinator-Appointed.

56 "Annual Report 2023-24", 1-376. Ministry of Home Affairs, Government of India. 2024. https://www.mha.gov.in/sites/default/files/AnnualReport_27122024.pdf.

57 "Indigenous Transponders Become Lifeline for Fishermen during Cyclone DANA." Press Information Bureau, Ministry of Fisheries, Animal Husbandry & Dairying, Government of India. October 29, 2024. https://www.pib.gov.in/PressReleasePage.aspx?PRID=2069157.

58 "Coastal Security Network Must Ensure Zero Tolerance to Error: Parrikar." Press Information Bureau, Ministry of Defence, Government of India. November 23, 2014. https://www.pib.gov.in/newsite/printrelease.aspx?relid=111697.

59 Tagoulis, Nikolaos. "India's Market Share in the Global Shipbuilding", Break Wave Advisors. February 19, 2025. https://www.breakwaveadvisors.com/insights/2025/2/19/indias-market-share-in-the-global-shipbuilding.

60 Op. cit. note no. 37.

61 Baskin, Oguzhan. "The New Maritime Superpower: China's Expanding Fleet and Global Influence." More Than Shipping. November 27, 2024. https://www.morethanshipping.com/the-new-maritime-superpower-chinas-expanding-fleet-and-global-influence/.

62 "Average Turnaround Time of Major Ports." Press Information Bureau, Ministry of Ports, Shipping & Waterways, Government of India. December 3, 2024. https://www.pib.gov.in/PressReleaseIframePage.aspx?PRID=2080014.

63 "Chinese Ports' Container Throughput Maintains Expansion in Jan.-Sept." People's Daily. November 5, 2022. https://en.people.cn/n3/2022/1105/c90000-10167689.html.

64 Op. cit. note no. 40.

65 Boltuc, Silvia. "Geopolitics of INSTC: An Interview with Aleksandr Sharov." Special Eurasia. March 17, 2023. https://www.specialeurasia.com/2023/03/17/geopolitics-instc-sharov/.

66 Bisen, Anurag. "India's Maritime Security: Five Concerns." Manohar Parrikar Institute for Defence Studies and Analyses, 1-14. May 18, 2022. https://www.idsa.in/system/files/issuebrief/ib-indias-maritime-security-five-concerns-abisen.pdf.

67 Ibid.

7

Maritime Security Initiatives by IORA, IONS, IPOI and BIMSTEC: Need for Synergy

Vice Admiral A.K. Chawla (Retd)

The Indian Ocean Rim Association (IORA), the Bay of Bengal Initiative for Multi-Sectoral Technical and Economic Cooperation (BIMSTEC), the Indian Ocean Naval Symposium (IONS) and the Indo-Pacific Oceans Initiative (IPOI) represent a multilayered and interconnected maritime security architecture in the Indo-Pacific region. These distinct yet complementary frameworks create a robust network for addressing maritime threats, with significant linkages and opportunities for synergy that enhance regional stability and prosperity.

The Indian Ocean region (IOR) is a critical maritime space, home to nearly a third of the world's population and facilitating approximately 80% of global seaborne oil trade and 75% of global container trade. This strategic importance is accompanied by a complex array of security challenges, which can be broadly categorised under traditional, non-traditional, climate change-related and technological threats. Traditional maritime security threats (apart from inter-state conflicts) include piracy, internal insurgencies/ disturbances that spill over to the maritime domain, and so on. Non-traditional maritime threats include issues such as maritime terrorism, illegal, unreported and unregulated (IUU) fishing, irregular human migration, human trafficking, drugs and contraband smuggling, gun-running, natural disasters, and environmental degradation due to oceanic pollution, among others. Climate change-related threats include issues such as sea level rise, which particularly threatens the stability of coastal states and small island nations, as well as acidification and warming of the oceans resulting in species extinction/ migration, with the attendant impact on food security. Climate change-related natural disasters are another threat, with a disproportionate percentage of such events occurring in the IOR littoral. Finally, advances in technology have resulted in technological threats in the maritime domain, which include cyber warfare/attacks, and the misuse of emerging/future technologies such as AI, unmanned vessels, spoofing, and others.

In response, several regional and sub-regional organisations in the IOR and the wider Indo-Pacific, such as IONS, IORA and BIMSTEC, and initiatives such as the IPOI, have included maritime security as a key focus area within their ambit. Each of the three organisations and one initiative being discussed are different—BIMSTEC and IORA are broad, multi-sectoral intergovernmental bodies, while IONS is a navy-led forum, and the IPOI is an expansive, principle-based diplomatic initiative. However, it is striking that their key focus areas converge on the issue of maritime security—thereby underlining its overarching importance for development and prosperity. This paper examines how these initiatives can be synergised to achieve better results. This is necessary not just because the issues and the region overlap, but also the better use of scarce resources towards achieving the common goal of developing a coherent, inclusive, and rules-based maritime order in the Indo-Pacific. It is also clear that India, through its "Security and Growth for All in the Region" (SAGAR) doctrine and broader Indo-Pacific vision of "Mutual and Holistic Advancement for Security and Growth Across Regions" (MAHASAGAR), needs to play a key role in synergising these initiatives.

Before elaborating on how these disparate initiatives can be synergised, it is necessary to examine how each of them deals with the issue of maritime security.

The Indian Ocean Rim Association

Being the oldest inter-governmental regional multilateral organisation, IORA is the bedrock of comprehensive Indian Ocean cooperation. Established in 1997, IORA brings together 23 member states and 12 dialogue partners across Asia, Africa, and Oceania. Maritime Safety and Security (MSS) is one of IORA's six priority areas. Its approach is broad and policy-oriented, aiming to foster a shared understanding of maritime governance and threats among a diverse membership with varying political and military perspectives. The dialogue within IORA is primarily diplomatic, focusing on establishing a political roadmap for cooperation.

The IORA Action Plan 2022-27 sets out the strategic goals of the MSS Priority Area. IORA has a Working Group on MSS (WGMSS) (currently chaired by Australia), which engages maritime officials and experts across IORA member states to promote regional cooperation. The WGMSS Work Plan focuses on four thematic areas—Search and Rescue, Maritime Partnership, Maritime Crime and Information Sharing. Three other priority areas—Sustainable Fisheries Management, Humanitarian Assistance and Disaster Relief (HADR) and Academic, Science and Technology Cooperation – have direct correlation with maritime security. Sustainable fisheries management focuses on sustainable fisheries management, development and practices in fisheries; cooperation in fisheries management among member states; and protection and conservation of fisheries resources in the Indian Ocean. The HADR priority area is aimed at building a collaborative IORA Disaster Risk Management framework based on the needs and priorities of member states and promoting institutional capability enhancement, capacity building and DRM mainstreaming

Bay of Bengal Multi-sectoral Technical and Economic Cooperation

BIMSTEC (comprising Bangladesh, Bhutan, India, Myanmar, Nepal, Sri Lanka and Thailand), established in 1997, is a smaller sub-regional grouping, which focuses specifically on the Bay of Bengal, a critical sub-region connecting the Indian and Pacific Oceans. The Bay of Bengal's semi-enclosed nature means its littorals share contiguous and overlapping Exclusive Economic Zones (EEZs), making collaborative action essential for managing transnational threats. While initially focused on economic and technical cooperation, BIMSTEC has recognised the exigent need to develop a robust maritime security agenda, which falls under its broader 'Security' pillar. Its focus is largely on non-traditional threats that require collaborative action due to the region's specific geography and shared vulnerabilities.

To coordinate maritime security responses, an 'Expert Group on Maritime Security Cooperation' in the Bay of Bengal, chaired by India, was set up in 2017. Maritime Cooperation in the Bay of Bengal is envisaged in five identified focus areas: Maritime Domain Awareness (MDA), Humanitarian Assistance and Disaster Relief (HADR), Oil Pollution Response and the Blue Economy and Maritime Security. Actions to strengthen maritime security taken thus far include: drafting of guiding principles on 'Conduct by BIMSTEC Maritime Law Enforcement Agencies (MLEAs) during Interaction at Sea with Fishing

Vessels'; drafting guidelines for HADR to provide a framework for HADR operations in the Bay of Bengal region and to develop a common understanding of HADR operations; and drafting an 'Oil Spill Response Mechanism' for BIMSTEC countries.

The Indian Ocean Naval Symposium

The Indian Ocean Naval Symposium, conceived by India in 2008, is a forum for the navies and coast guards of the IOR littoral states. IONS is a functional, operationally focused grouping focused solely on maritime security issues, which aims to enhance maritime cooperation through practical activities and dialogue among naval professionals. It operates through three key working groups: Humanitarian Assistance and Disaster Relief, Maritime Security, and Information Sharing and Interoperability. The working groups have enhanced information-sharing frameworks, thereby advancing Maritime Domain Awareness (MDA), and have harmonised operational guidelines to facilitate coordinated and timely regional responses. Joint exercises like the IONS Maritime Exercise (IMEX) and Milan (a biennial naval exercise) enhance interoperability and participants' understanding of contemporary maritime security challenges.

IONS also provides a platform to harmonise rules-of-engagement, search and rescue procedures, and communication protocols, making combined patrols and crisis responses more effective. Guidelines for HADR for IONS nations have been promulgated, and both table-top and actual exercises have been conducted to simulate disaster response, fostering improved coordination and interoperability for joint HADR operations.

The Indo-Pacific Oceans Initiative

The Indo-Pacific Oceans Initiative (IPOI), proposed by India's Prime Minister Narendra Modi at the 2019 East Asia Summit (EAS), is an expansive, non-treaty-based diplomatic initiative aimed at promoting cooperation for a free, open, inclusive, and rules-based Indo-Pacific. It is structured around seven pillars or spokes, including: Maritime Security; Maritime Ecology; Maritime Resources; Capacity Building and Resource Sharing; Disaster Risk Reduction and Management; Science, Technology, and Academic Cooperation; and Trade, Connectivity, and Maritime Transport.

The IPOI's approach to maritime security is holistic, viewing it as one component within a broader framework for sustainable development and rules-based order, in line with the UN Convention on the Law of the Sea (UNCLOS). The maritime security pillar of the IPOI, led jointly by India and the UK, involves enhanced maritime domain awareness through initiatives such as the Information Fusion Centre – Indian Ocean Region (IFC-IOR) in Gurugram and white shipping agreements with partner nations. The pillar aims to combat piracy, illicit fishing, smuggling, and other maritime crimes, to foster regional cooperation, and to build collective capacity for maritime security across the Indo-Pacific. The IPOI Maritime Security pillar has seen progress through high-level dialogues, the establishment of cooperative frameworks, capacity-building efforts, and joint activities led by India and the United Kingdom.

Current Linkages and Synergies

If we analyse the three organisations and one initiative discussed above, it is evident that each has its unique attributes and advantages. IORA provides the overarching political umbrella for the entire Indian Ocean, while BIMSTEC plays a similar role in a sub-region of the Indian Ocean. The political and policy-making nature of IORA and BIMSTEC is complemented by operational forums like IONS. Finally, the IPOI provides the strategic vision that links regional bodies like IORA, BIMSTEC, and IONS to the wider Indo-Pacific strategy of global partners (e.g., the EU, Quad countries). The primary areas of complementarity of the four organisations lie in addressing non-traditional threats. All four frameworks touch upon MDA, HADR, and capacity building, but at different functional levels (diplomatic, sub-regional, naval, strategic vision).

In recent year, a few initiatives have materialised in synergising maritime security initiatives between the four organisations. The landmark MoU signed between IORA and BIMSTEC in April 2025 formally linked the two organisations, providing a cohesive framework spanning the Bay of Bengal and the wider Indian Ocean Rim. This agreement facilitates coordination on shared priorities like maritime security, connectivity and the blue economy. The most significant step in terms of maritime security cooperation is the initiative to link their respective expert groups and information fusion centres, such as India's Information Fusion Centre - Indian Ocean Region (IFC-IOR,) to create a broader maritime domain awareness network. BIMSTEC is also working to link its Expert Group on Maritime Security with the IFC-IOR in

Gurugram, India, to enhance real-time intelligence sharing and maritime domain awareness among member states.

The second initiative is to have IONS represented at the IORA MSS Working Group. This would ensure that over time, IONS serves as a crucial operational-level implementer for the political and policy discussions held within IORA and BIMSTEC. It is important to note that IONS provides a common link between all the organisations and initiatives, as most members of IORA, BIMSTEC and IPOI are also members of IONS.

Future Possibilities

While nascent steps have been taken to synergise maritime security between IORA, BIMSTEC, IPOI and IONS, there is tremendous scope to expand this synergy in the years ahead. The easiest way to start is in the field of Disaster Risk Management. The region's vulnerability to natural disasters (cyclones, tsunamis) is a key IORA, BIMSTEC, IPOI and IONS focus. Cooperation here involves standardising early warning systems and coordinating humanitarian assistance and disaster relief (HADR) efforts, which directly links to the practical, operational capabilities already operationalised under the IONS framework. As a start point, the cooperation already achieved by IONS under the IONS can be easily replicated *mutatis mutandis* in BIMSTEC, IORA and IPOI. Such cooperation can be operationalised by using the IONS template for HADR cooperation to exercise practical naval cooperation and combined exercises.

There is also substantial scope to use the complex relationship between IORA, BIMSTEC, IONS, and IPOI to further cooperation in maritime domain awareness, particularly to detect dark shipping and IUU fishing, thereby enhancing the security of our maritime commons. Most countries in the IOR and the wider Indo-Pacific do not have the resources and technological capability to do this currently. However, if all our information is pooled, the sum of the MDA will be far greater than its parts.

Combining organisational forces would also help to attract broader international support, funding, and technical assistance from global partners and donors, thereby overcoming the current shortage of funding for various initiatives. Such an approach would also align with India's SAGAR and MAHASAGAR visions, which emphasise a holistic approach to security and growth across regions.

While the possibilities for maritime security cooperation abound, their practical implementation is not easy for a variety of reasons. The diverse memberships of the organisations and differing political perceptions can hinder unified action on sensitive security matters. A way of mitigating this is by using minilateral and bilateral forums to progress issues where multilateral consensus is not feasible/possible in the short term, which could then become more broad-based in the long term. For example, a smaller forum such as BIMSTEC could be used to advance cooperation to a higher level, which could then be replicated on a larger level within IORA. Regional problems are best resolved with regional solutions through regional resources. However, institutional capacity and funding of each organisation can be limited—IORA is a prime example in this regard. Therefore, relying on the voluntary contributions and political will of member states can also lead to implementation delays. This can be overcome by inviting extra-regional assistance through a larger body such as the IPOI. Finally, translating high-level diplomatic consensus into concrete naval operations and SOPs requires effective coordination mechanisms that are not always robust. Here IONS could be the necessary catalyst, with the inherent attributes of maritime forces to advance maritime diplomacy being leveraged towards this end.

Conclusion

The linkages between IORA, BIMSTEC, IONS, and IPOI offer a comprehensive, though still evolving, maritime security architecture for the Indo-Pacific. By leveraging the political legitimacy of IORA, the sub-regional focus of BIMSTEC, the operational capabilities of IONS, and the strategic vision of the IPOI, these frameworks can collectively address the myriad challenges facing the maritime domain. Formalising cooperation through mechanisms like the IORA-BIMSTEC MoU is a positive development, but sustained political will, enhanced capacity building, and effective information-sharing mechanisms will be essential to realising the full potential of these interconnected initiatives and ensure a secure and prosperous Indian Ocean region for all.

8

Integrating Extra Regional Powers in Shaping Indian Ocean Security

Commodore Anil Jai Singh (Retd)

Extra-regional powers have been present in the Indian Ocean for over five centuries. Driven by their self-interest, they first came as colonisers, then as influencers and more recently as partners. In the last two decades or so, with the shift in the global geopolitical and geoeconomic centre of gravity to the Indo-Pacific, their engagement with this region has become a security and economic imperative that has led to many of them articulating their Indo-Pacific strategies. These are centred mainly around the safety of their trade and energy interests in this region. The Indo-Pacific region, which is home to more than 60 per cent of the global population, and generates almost two thirds of the global GDP can neither be ignored nor controlled unlike the past, and figures prominently in the contemporary global strategic discourse. However, within this strategic construct it is the Indian Ocean that is actually shaping the future economic and security contours of this region.

The Indian Ocean, unlike the other two major oceans, the Atlantic and the Pacific, has four unique geographical characteristics which shape the region's political, economic and security dynamics. The first is that the Indian Ocean provides maritime connectivity between the Atlantic and the Pacific Oceans. As a result, more than 1,00,000 ships transit this ocean annually carrying trade and energy across continents. Ensuring the safe passage of this traffic is critical for the smooth functioning of the global economy.

The second significant characteristic of this ocean are the strategic choke points on its east, west and south through which these global arteries of commerce and energy pass, and are therefore both, a strength and a vulnerability.

These choke points are so located that most of the shipping that passes through them converges south of India's southern peninsula, and therefore gives India a pivotal position in the region.

The third defining characteristic is the presence of numerous strategically located island and archipelagic states dotting this ocean whose importance belies their size. These states have large Exclusive Economic Zones (EEZ) and inadequate capacity to secure their own waters. This makes them vulnerable to exploitation by external forces while their strategic location makes them ideal partners for any country seeking to expand its influence in the region.

The fourth characteristic is the geographical conformation of the region. The presence of the huge Eurasian landmass to the north of the Indian Ocean is unlike any of the other oceans and has its own geopolitical dynamics which also impact the maritime domain. Landlocked nations in this landmass also need a linkage to the Indian Ocean through connectivity corridors. The India-led International North-South Transport Corridor (INSTC) connecting the Central Asian Republics to the Arabian Sea is one such[1]. The China-Pakistan Economic Corridor connecting mainland China to the Indian Ocean and linking up with the BRI is another[2].

Each of these four characteristics has a bearing on the individual and collective regional maritime security calculus of the region.

The Maritime Security Challenge

Amongst the many internal and external security challenges in the Indian Ocean, perhaps the most significant ones are the non-traditional threats facing the region, the existential threat of climate change, and the expanding Chinese footprint in this ocean. Each of these has a significant impact on the political and economic dynamics of the region. In the contemporary regional environment, security underpins almost every activity in the maritime domain. Hence, an effective regional maritime security architecture is an imperative that needs immediate and adequate attention.

Since the turn of this century, there has been an exponential increase in the non-traditional threats to maritime security. These include maritime terrorism, piracy, Illegal Unregulated and Unreported (IUU) Fishing, narcotics smuggling, illegal human trafficking, arms smuggling and a host of others. This has forced nations to reconfigure their maritime defence strategies and maritime force structures to address this omnipresent asymmetric challenge.

Since oceans provide connectivity between continents, and with trade and energy dependencies transcending geographies, these non-traditional threats have assumed a transnational dimension. Piracy in the Horn of Africa in the period 2008 to 2013 was one such example. The rise of Somalian piracy which at first seemed innocuous with a bunch of disaffected young men wielding Kalashnikovs in small skiffs boarding vessels passing close to the coast, gradually grew into a threat to the movement of global commerce with ships being hijacked for ransom. It took more than five years and the coordinated actions of more than 20 navies to quell this scourge and restore normalcy. However, high risk areas continued to be notified for many years thereafter with consequential effects on insurance premiums and the cost of shipping. This effort was a good example of a multinational and multidimensional effort by regional and extra regional navies working together to restore the status quo.

Due to various multilateral mechanisms in place to address maritime crime in this region, there has been a reduction in the number of incidents, but non-traditional threats remain a matter of serious concern. The recent Houthi attacks on shipping in the Red Sea in support of Hamas, which led to the rerouting of ships around the Cape of Good Hope, had a major impact on the economies of the Global South and exposed their vulnerability to these asymmetric challenges.

In the last few years, a disturbing trend is the weaponisation of public goods like food, through disruptions in the trade and energy supply chains, and the damage being done to undersea infrastructure including gas pipelines and submarine cables which carry 95 per cent of the global internet and are key to the global communication and global financial systems. All it takes is for an innocuous merchant ship to drag its anchor across a cable laid in shallow water, as has been happening in the recent past[3]. Outer space is also being militarised. Besides the development of space-based weapons, it has implications for cybersecurity and other modern technologies. (e.g. GPS spoofing and jamming to disrupt shipping and aviation). This has further complicated the security challenge.

The visible effects of climate change are now part of our daily lives. The Indian Ocean region in particular is more vulnerable to its effects. The distinct increase in both, the frequency and the intensity of extreme weather events in the region not only wreaks havoc on lives, property and livelihoods, but in regions where good governance is at a premium, also drives local populations to economic despair, making them vulnerable to external and internal pressures, thus further exacerbating the security situation. Unfortunately, despite climate change being an existential threat to humanity and getting a lot of lip service at various summits, COP 30 being the latest[4], the outcomes so far have been dismal to say the least.

Many of the small island states in the Indian Ocean also face an existential threat from the rising sea levels and global warming, with the Maldives, for example, facing the risk of getting fully inundated in a few years from now if urgent measures are not initiated. Low lying areas in major urban centres are also feeling the impact of rising sea levels. Therefore, the Indian Ocean region could soon be facing a major humanitarian and security crisis if the mass evacuation of people becomes necessary, as none of the countries in the region have the capacity to absorb these additional numbers. The disturbance in the ecological balance of the fragile marine biosphere is leading to an environmental catastrophe. The destruction of marine flora and fauna, acidification of the sea and the migration of fish to cooler waters will have a substantial impact on the global economy. Climate change is irreversible and it is beyond the capacity and capability of these countries to arrest, mitigate or reverse this threat. Therefore, the developed world will have to support an effective policy framework, and its speedy implementation with adequate financial commitment and a supportive governance architecture.

The third major challenge facing the region is the rise of China and its relentless ambition to become a global superpower by 2049, euphemistically referred to as the 'Great Rejuvenation of the Chinese nation'. In less than five decades it has developed into a formidable military and non-military maritime power and is steadily expanding its maritime footprint westwards into the Indian Ocean and even beyond. The maritime element of its Belt and Road Initiative connecting its mainland to Europe through a network of connectivity corridors and the development of ports and other important industrial and mobility infrastructure in countries enroute, has given it considerable leverage in most of the important coastal and island states of the Indian Ocean littoral.

The Indian Ocean is China's economic and energy lifeline and justifies the necessity of a military presence for protecting its Sea Lines of Communication (SLOC). However, its maritime expansion is aligned with its long-term grand strategy. Domination of the Indian Ocean is critical for China as it provides the sea space to project its impressive maritime power which its own 'tyranny of geography'[5] does not, and more significantly, the Indian Ocean gives China access to the Atlantic Ocean, which is important for it to realise its global ambitions. The commissioning of its third aircraft carrier, the 80,000 tonne *Fujian* on 7 November 2025 and reports of a fourth aircraft carrier (probably nuclear-powered) under construction is proof, if any was needed, of China's growing maritime ambition to exercise its sea power in its 'far seas'[6]. China has clearly spelt out its intent to reorient the existing rules-based order at sea which it views as a western construct into one with 'Chinese characteristics'. If its behaviour in the South China Sea and the intimidation of its maritime neighbours is any indication, this re-oriented Chinese rules-based order is an ominous sign for all countries with commercial interests in the region. It therefore becomes incumbent on India to ensure that it does not concede its pre-eminent position in the Indian Ocean and develops an effective regional security architecture with other countries in the littoral to shape the outcomes in these waters.

According to a report by the US think tank Council on Foreign Relations, last updated on 26 August 2024, China presently has an active stake in 115 ports worldwide with a majority stake in 17 and a potential for naval base facilities to be created in another 77[7]. This indicates the deep inroads China has made into the maritime domain. The Mumbai based think tank Gateway House in a 2021 paper highlighted that China had an active stake in 17 ports in the Indian Ocean region alone[8]. This is an alarming statistic as its presence at strategic locations in the Indian Ocean could significantly impact the security and freedom of movement of global trade and energy in the Indian Ocean.

Surprisingly however, despite the relatively closed nature of this ocean, its rich maritime heritage of regional trade and its centrality in the movement of global commerce for over three millennia or so, there is little collective convergence on the issues confronting the region. Part of this can be attributed to the disaggregated nature of the region. There are a number of regional multilateral structures like the Gulf Cooperation Council (GCC), the South Asian Association for Regional Cooperation (SAARC), the Bay of Bengal Initiative for Multi-Sectoral Technical and Economic Cooperation (BIMSTEC), the Indian Ocean Commission(IOC), the Djibouti Code of Conduct (DCOC) and its Jeddah amendment, and to some extent, the Association of South-East Asian Nations (ASEAN)—five of whose members have a coastline washed by the waters of the Indian Ocean. Most of these face similar challenges and have overlapping agendas, but attempt to address them through a narrow prism relevant to themselves. Within these constructs, there are also internal fault lines, caused mainly by trust deficits amongst individual members themselves, which render them ineffective. SAARC is a prime example. Many countries in the region are beset by political instability, poor governance, ethnic tensions, disaffected populations and severe economic challenges. Very few of them have their own Indian Ocean Policy, or the capacity to contribute effectively to regional security or even their own maritime interests despite their assurances and commitment to the contrary. Hence, despite the presence of so many multilateral mechanisms or perhaps because of them, and with common members with limited capacities within them, the region falls short in implementing meaningful outcomes to address regional challenges.

Recognising this disparate nature of the Indian Ocean countries, President Nelson Mandela, during his visit to India in 1995 stated that "the natural urge of the facts of history and geography should broaden itself to include the concept of an Indian Ocean Rim for socio-economic cooperation and other peaceful endeavours; recent changes in the international system demand that the countries of the Indian Ocean shall become a single platform."[9]

Indian Ocean Rim Association

This led to the inception of the Indian Ocean Rim Initiative in March 1995, and was followed by the establishment of the Indian Ocean Rim Association (IORA) on 7 March 1997.[10] Over the years, IORA has matured as the premier multilateral mechanism addressing the common concerns of the Indian Ocean Region. IORA presently has 23 members including France which has territories dotted across the Indian Ocean and a large part of its Exclusive Economic Zone (EEZ) in the region. Notable omissions include Pakistan, which despite considering itself a maritime and naval power of some consequence has chosen to distance itself from IORA probably because of its inherent mistrust of India.

IORA also has 12 extra-regional Dialogue Partners, each of which is a stakeholder with considerable maritime interests in the region, thus warranting their presence. Maritime Security and Safety (MSS) is one of IORA's six priority areas and also includes climate change and its impact on the region[11]. IORA's Action Plan 2022-27 lays out the aims in the MSS Priority Area. Effective coordination amongst the member states, the Dialogue Partners and other international organisations is essential for regional capacity building and strengthening regional cooperation to ensure freedom of navigation and combat the non-traditional security challenge.

IORA has established a Working Group for Maritime Safety and Security (WGMSS) which promotes a coordinated approach through regional cooperation amongst all stakeholders in alignment with the objectives of the IORA Action Plan 2022-27[12]. It has four thematic areas and three objectives. The former focuses on Maritime Partnerships, Information Sharing, Maritime Crime and Search and Rescue (SAR) whereas the latter focuses on Maritime Crime and Information Sharing. The objectives include a collaborative IORA MSS framework which has a collective understanding of the region's security requirements and is able to prioritise these based on the requirements of the member states; to encourage collaboration with Dialogue partners, and to develop a standardised approach to enhance effective coordination and identify complementarities with existing mechanisms in the region and beyond. The WGMSS also coordinates its activities with the Working Groups on Disaster Risk Management and Humanitarian Assistance and Disaster Relief (HADR), etc.

Given the nature of the security challenges in the region and the inherent vulnerabilities of many of the Indian Ocean countries, IORA's main priorities would be:

(i) To establish an inclusive, cooperative and collaborative regional capacity building and capability enhancement framework integrating its members and dialogue partners.
(ii) To ensure a robust Maritime Domain Awareness Architecture in the Indian Ocean Region.
(iii) To develop a synergistic approach towards maritime security and coordinate activities both, withing the IORA construct and also with the other multilateral mechanisms in the region.
(iv) To ensure freedom of navigation and overflight and a rules-based order
(v) To provide a transparent forum for interaction amongst all stakeholders on all maritime security issues.
(vi) To encourage Blue Economy Initiatives to ensure sustainable utilisation of marine resources.
(vii) To develop legislation to address maritime crime.

IORA's impressive charter and objectives are challenged primarily by financial constraints, as most of its members are small and developing economies. Despite the presence of developed countries as Dialogue partners, the heavy lifting is done by the smaller states. This limits IORA's capacity to implement effective policies in critical areas particularly related to maritime safety, disaster risk reduction blue economy initiatives, all of which require sustained financial and institutional support.

However, its limitations notwithstanding, it is still the largest and most effective of the numerous multilateral institutions in the Indian Ocean and provides the normative framework for a secure and stable maritime environment in the Indian Ocean. It has to focus on leveraging the strengths of its members and extra-regional dialogue partners to enable a cohesive Indian Ocean multi-dimensional, multi-layered and multi-sectoral architecture in which the other smaller multilateral institutions complement IORA's and each other's objectives. Only then will IORA be able to fulfil its potential as a singular multilateral construct for the entire Indian Ocean region, lay down the normative regional maritime security framework and exercise its influence on the global stage commensurate with the importance of the region it represents.

India has assumed the Presidency of IORA in November 2025 for the next two years[13]. It enjoys considerable regional influence in the Indian Ocean, and has been at the forefront in energising various smaller multilateral constructs within the Indian ocean like IONS, BIMSTEC and the Colombo Security Conclave, etc. As a pivotal Indian Ocean power in various Indo-Pacific constructs, most notably the Quad, it has come to represent the interests of the 'Indo' of the Indo-Pacific. On the global stage, its efforts to include the Global South and the African Union into the framework of the G20 during its Presidency in 2022-23 and its initiatives during its tenure as a non-permanent member of the UN Security Council in 2021-22, where it initiated the first ever debate on maritime security[14], has enhanced its global standing as a champion of multilateralism which has not gone unnoticed in world capitals.

India's Presidency of IORA also coincides with its assumption of the Chairmanship of the Indian Ocean Naval Symposium (IONS)[15], from early 2026, also for two years. IONS was established by the Indian Navy in 2008 'as a voluntary initiative that seeks to increase maritime co-operation among navies of the littoral states of the Indian Ocean Region by providing an open and inclusive forum for discussion of regionally relevant maritime issues. In the process, it endeavours to generate a flow of information between naval professionals that would lead to common understanding and possibly cooperative solutions on the way ahead'[16]. Unlike IORA, Pakistan is a member of IONS and China is part of both fora. IONS has been successful in bringing regional and extra regional navies together on one platform to provide an operational perspective of the maritime security challenges in the region. It has 25 members and nine extra-regional navies as Observers. Many of these are part of both constructs. Hence this provides India a unique opportunity over the next two years to shape the maritime security contours of the region.

India, as the largest maritime power in the Indian Ocean is fully committed to ensuring a rules-based order at sea, and takes this responsibility very seriously. It has established its firm credentials as a preferred security provider and a first responder in the region. However, securing this vast and strategically important sea space, is beyond the capacity of any single nation including India, and requires a collaborative effort from across the region, and perhaps beyond.

In 2015, the Indian Prime Minister, during his visit to Mauritius articulated his vision of SAGAR[17], an acronym for Security and Growth for All in the Region. This vision, which has been the blueprint for India's inclusive and collaborative capacity building in the region with other Indian Ocean states, has since translated into policy and underpins almost every Indian activity in the region. Although, not restricted only to the maritime domain, the acronym SAGAR, which is the Hindi word for 'sea' does highlight its predominantly maritime orientation. Earlier this year, and once again during a visit to Mauritius, the Prime Minister expanded the scope and scale of SAGAR to also include the Global South with MAHASAGAR[18], the Hindi word for 'ocean' and an acronym for "Mutual and Holistic Advancement for Security and Growth Across Regions". However, its centre of gravity remains firmly anchored in the Indian Ocean. Both these policy initiatives are primarily meant to develop an inclusive and cooperative capacity building and capability enhancement approach to the region with all nations doing their bit towards addressing the multitude of security challenges in the Indian Ocean Region.

This would provide India an opportunity to leverage its considerable external influence in charting the future course of IORA as a major stakeholder in the global security and economic calculus, and developing a cohesive way ahead with all its members and dialogue partners into shaping the future security contours of the Indian Ocean Region. With its MAHASAGAR policy as an anchor, it should also endeavour to build convergences amongst the smaller multilateral mechanisms in the Indian Ocean Region (IOR) towards aligning their overlapping agendas with a common and collective approach to the maritime security of the entire region.

There is a perception that the smaller multilateral institutional mechanisms in the Indian Ocean Region like the Indian Ocean Commission (IOC) and the Djibouti Code of Conduct (DCOC) to name just two, have overlapping agendas with IORA regarding the Indian Ocean; this leads to duplication of effort, division of resources and sub-optimal outcomes. Instead, if all these organisations developed complementary agendas addressing specific issues, and a healthy interaction amongst themselves, then perhaps more could be achieved. There is definitely merit in this argument, but one must also be cognisant of the fact that these organisations also address the concerns of nations which are not part of the Indian Ocean littoral but face similar challenges; hence the overlapping of objectives and agendas to some extent is inevitable, but it can perhaps be streamlined better. For example, the IOC's Regional Operations Coordination Centre located in Seychelles which works closely with the Regional Maritime Information Fusion Centre in Madagascar (RMIFC), has a MoU with the Indian Ocean Region Information Fusion Centre (IOR-IFC) located close to New Delhi[19]. An information sharing mechanism between these two Western Indian Ocean Centres, the IFC-IOR in India covering a major portion of the Indian Ocean and the IFC in Singapore covering the eastern flank will be able to provide a comprehensive common operational picture of the entire Indian Ocean which would enable a pro-active approach to combating a developing threat at sea.

Developing the Security Architecture

The two most important pre-requisites for ensuring a safe and secure maritime environment in the Indian Ocean are firstly, building adequate regional capacity and capability to address the threats facing the region that can undermine regional security. To achieve this, it is important to understand the regional maritime environment and either pre-empt or respond decisively to a developing threat. Therefore, the second most important pre-requisite is to establish a robust Maritime Domain Awareness architecture. However, as highlighted earlier, due to their inherent capacity limitations, many of the countries in the IOR littoral, despite their best intentions are unable to contribute meaningfully towards this. Hence, even though a fairly effective MDA capability has been established in the region with effective surveillance assets and information sharing networks, it is still a work in progress. Most of the extra-regional powers in the IORA and IONS constructs with a stake in the security of the Indian Ocean have also supported these efforts through their technical expertise, financial support and deployment of maritime and air assets. However, more coordination between all the agencies will deliver better outcomes.

Extra-Regional Presence

The aftermath of colonialism, the attempt by the newly independent countries to find their feet, and both the Cold War protagonists promoting ideological conflicts to gain influence in the region led to the presence of extra-regional powers being viewed with suspicion by countries comprising the Indian Ocean littoral. From an economic perspective this region remained on the sidelines of a predominantly Euro-Atlantic global order. The Non-Aligned Movement (NAM), most of whose members comprised countries from this region therefore sought to distance themselves from any involvement in the Cold War and the nuclear arms race that defined that era. On 16 December 1971, the UN General Assembly adopted Resolution 2832(XVII) which designated the Indian Ocean as a "zone of peace" for all time. This proposal introduced by Sri Lanka and seconded by Tanzania was very strongly backed and supported by India which understood the vulnerabilities of the region[20].

From the 1990s there has been a paradigm shift in this approach, and over the last three decades, the presence of extra regional powers has become more acceptable as an integral part of the regional maritime security architecture. This has been driven primarily by the geopolitical and geoeconomic shift eastwards to the Indo-Pacific and its importance in the global economic framework. The changing nature of the maritime security challenges in the region with the proliferation of non-traditional and transnational maritime threats in the region have a global impact These, combined with China's rise, its maritime belligerence and naked ambition has led many extra-regional powers to articulate their own Indo-Pacific strategies. These include France, the UK, traditional Euro-centric countries like Germany and the Netherlands, the European Union and even Canada. The European Union has also articulated an Indo-Pacific policy. This signals the increased involvement of extra-regional powers in addressing maritime challenges in the Indian Ocean. Japan and South Korea, although a part of the Indo-Pacific construct but more akin to being extra-regional powers in the Indian Ocean are also engaging more with this region. For most of these countries, their strategy for the region is centred on the safety of their trade, the resilience of global supply chains and periodic naval deployments to this region.

India's foreign policy outreach over the last decade or so, its *Act East* Policy and its multilateral initiatives have sought to integrate its extra regional maritime engagement with its capacity building efforts in the Indian Ocean region, while ensuring a rules-based order as a 'force for good in the region.

Extra-regional maritime security constructs in the region effectively began with the US-UK Combined Maritime Force (CMF) being established in 2001 to address the growing non-traditional threats in the western Indian Ocean and to promote a secure maritime environment[21]. The CMF presently comprises 47 member countries from across the world divided into five task forces with specific mandates; CTF 150 (Gulf of Oman security and counter-terrorism), CTF 151 (counter piracy), CTF 152 (Arabian Gulf security and cooperation), CTF 153 (Red Sea/Gulf of Aden security and cooperation) and CTF 154 (maritime security training). India, which till recently was operating independently in the region joined the CMF as an associate member in 2022 and became a full member in 2024.

The multinational presence in the Horn of Africa gained further momentum when Somalian piracy raised its ugly head from 2008 onwards. It led to the establishment of SHADE (Shared Awareness of Deconfliction Mechanism) led by the US, EU and NATO. Europe also positioned the EU Naval Force (EUNAVFOR) and initiated *Op Atalanta* to combat non-traditional threats, the mandate of which has been extended till 2027. It also provides Humanitarian Assistance and Disaster Relief in the western Indian Ocean Region. Europe has also established a reporting cum information sharing mechanism through its CRIMARIO 1 and 2 initiative, its Maritime Security Centre-Indian Ocean and the development of the Indian Ocean Regional Information Sharing (IORIS) platform in the region to improve situational awareness and coordination with other regional and extra-regional navies operating in the region. The Djibouti Code of Conduct (DCOC), an IMO initiative, was set up in 2009, and the Indian Ocean Commission's Regional Maritime Security Architecture (RMSA) in 2013. Most of these mechanisms were established to combat Somali piracy in the western Indian Ocean and have continued to ensure a secure regional environment.

Countries in the region have also benefited through the transfer of military equipment from extra regional powers including radars for coastal security,

SAR assets and EEZ protection capability. Courses of instruction, training exercises, personnel exchanges and military infrastructure add further value to regional capacity building.

In addition to these activities, extra-regional naval participation from countries invested in this region has increased substantially over the years which have greatly enhanced interoperability, sent a very visible message to potential miscreants and exposed smaller navies to advanced technologies. There has been an incremental increase in the scale and scope of ship visits to the region including Carrier Task Forces. These extend for seven to eight months at a stretch, and include both, port visits and individual and collective exercises with regional navies to get a better understanding of the operational dynamics of the region.

Maritime Domain Awareness (MDA)

Effective MDA is a strategic security imperative. Many extra-regional navies including the CMF Task Forces and the EUNAVFOR operate in various parts of the Indian Ocean. An effective and integrated information sharing and exchange mechanism can greatly enhance the robustness of the regional MDA framework. Hydrographic surveys, foundational agreements and other cooperative arrangements are MDA force multipliers. The region is dotted with strategically located small island states which can be effective strategic outposts covering a wide swath of the Indian Ocean. Commonality of platforms (for example, India, Australia, the US and Japan all operate various versions of the Boeing P8 Maritime Reconnaissance Aircraft with commonalities in their surveillance systems and communication suites, thus facilitating ease of information sharing.

The setting up of the Indo-Pacific MDA mechanism by the four countries comprising the Quad underscores the importance of MDA. In the common understanding, MDA has come to mean a knowledge of security-related developments primarily on the surface of the sea. This is actually an enhanced form of situational awareness. The core of MDA lies beneath the waves, though because of inadequate knowledge of the ocean depths it tends to be considered a sub-set of MDA, and is referred to as UDA or Underwater Domain Awareness. In reality, the converse is true. An understanding of what lies below the surface, either from a security perspective or an economic perspective is critical to developing a comprehensive MDA architecture. The frequent presence of Chinese research ships with their underwater gliders is aimed at gaining a comprehensive maritime domain awareness of the Indian Ocean region for both, its future submarine and anti-submarine operations and to explore the ocean depths from a Blue Economy perspective.

Conclusion

The Indian Ocean is one of the most contested and politically volatile regions in the world. It is also the vital link between the Atlantic and the Pacific Oceans with more than 60 per cent of global trade and energy transiting through its waters. Hence, a secure maritime environment in the region is a critical imperative for the well-being of the global economy. However, many countries in the region are plagued by their own capacity challenges and are hard pressed to contribute significant resources towards a regional security architecture, thus requiring extra regional powers with economic and security interests in the Indo-Pacific to contribute towards regional capacity building and capability enhancement. While these countries have contributed significantly through infrastructure development, naval presence and through other information sharing mechanisms, there has at times been an overlapping of resources and duplication of effort. This is due to the presence of numerous regional initiatives focussed on narrow geographies instead of a single unified institutional mechanism coordinating the regional response. The Indian Ocean Rim Association whose membership covers the entire Indian ocean Region and important Dialogue Partners could become this hub of regional security. It has impressive credentials, an ambitious agenda but is handicapped in implementation by numerous factors, not least being financial constraints. India, which has taken over the reins of IORA for a period of two years from November 2025 onwards has the regional heft, and the credentials to revitalise IORA into the representative mechanism for the entire Indian Ocean Region and even beyond into its contiguous waters. India's own MAHASAGAR policy for capacity building in the Global South can be the catalyst to enable this. It is a happy coincidence that India will soon be at the helm of IONS, also for a period of two years. This will enable India with its sound maritime credentials as the premier maritime power in the region to facilitate maritime security policy and implementation. IORA's extra-regional Dialogue partners who are also part of some of the other smaller regional mechanisms in the region could also rationalise their objectives. This is not to suggest that the other regional mechanisms should become redundant, but should instead integrate their plans and objectives in congruence with those of IORA to ensure an optimal regional maritime security architecture.[22]

NOTES

1 "Question No-1085 International North-South Transport Corridor." Ministry of External Affairs, Government of India. December 8, 2023. https://www.mea.gov.in/lok-sabha.htm?dtl/37388/question+no1085+international+northsouth+transport+corridor.

2 "China-Pakistan Economic Corridor." https://cpecinfo.com/.

3 "Red Sea Undersea Cables Cut: What Damaged Submarine Cables & Impacted Internet? Here Is What Experts Say." The Times of India. September 9, 2025. https://timesofindia.indiatimes.com/business/international-business/red-sea-undersea-cables-cut-what-damaged-submarine-cables-impacted-internet-here-is-what-experts-say/articleshow/123787359.cms.

4 "United Nations Climate Change." https://unfccc.int/cop30.

5 Muhammad, Sahil Yar. "Kaplan's Revenge: Why Geography Still Constrains China at Sea." Geopolitical Monitor. August 1, 2025. https://www.geopoliticalmonitor.com/kaplans-revenge-why-geography-still-constrains-china-at-sea/

6 "Xi Attends Commissioning of China's Fujian Aircraft Carrier." The State Council, Peoples Republic of China. November 7, 2025. https://english.www.gov.cn/news/202511/07/content_WS690d990cc6d00ca5f9a0764d.html.

7 Liu, Zongyuan Zoe. "Tracking China's Control of Overseas Ports." Council on Foreign Relations. August 26, 2024. https://www.cfr.org/tracker/china-overseas-ports.

8 Faridi, Saeeduddin. "China's Ports in the Indian Ocean." Gateway House. August 19, 2021. https://www.gatewayhouse.in/chinas-ports-in-the-indian-ocean-region/.

9 Indian Ocean Rim Association. https://www.iora.int/indian-ocean-rim-association.

10 Ibid

11 Ibid

12 Ibid

13 Bhatt, Pooja. "Charting a Route for IORA under India's Chairship." The Hindu. March 22, 2025. https://www.thehindu.com/opinion/op-ed/charting-a-route-for-iora-under-indias-chairship/article69359008.ece.

14 Chand, Manish. "Modi Chairs UNSC Meet, Unveils 5-Point Maritime Security Framework." India Writes, Blog. August 9, 2021. https://indiawrites.org/india-and-the-world/modi-chairs-unsc-meet-unveils-5-principles-of-maritime-connectivity/.

15 "Indian Ocean Naval Symposium." https://ions.global/.

16 Ibid

17 "Maritime Cooperation with Regional Partners." PIB. March 21, 2025. https://www.pib.gov.in/PressReleasePage.aspx?PRID=1807607.

18 Haldar, Sayantan. "India's MAHASAGAR Vision: Strategic Continuity in the Indian Ocean." Observer Research Foundation. April 23, 2025. https://www.orfonline.org/expert-speak/india-s-mahasagar-vision-strategic-continuity-in-the-indian-ocean.

19 "Maritime Security: Memorandum of Understanding (MoU) between The Information Fusion Centre - Indian Ocean Region (IFC-IOR) and Regional Coordination Operations Centre (RCOC)." Indian Navy. 2025. https://indiannavy.gov.in/node/35588.

20 "Declaration of the Indian Ocean as a Zone of Peace." United Nations Disarmament Yearbook. pp 375-389. December, 1983. https://www.un-ilibrary.org/content/books/9789210579872s005-c003.

21 "Combined Maritime Forces." https://combinedmaritimeforces.com/.

9

Charting India's Maritime Security Path in the Labyrinth of the IOR

Captain Sarabjeet Singh Parmar (Retd)

Introduction

The Indian Ocean Region (IOR), with the existing instability in the Red Sea and South Asia in general, has re-emerged as the maritime theatre most critical to global economic stability, strategic competition, and geopolitical influence. For India, the IOR is not a maritime peripheral frontier but a structural determinant of national security, energy security, trade connectivity, and great-power aspirations. More than 90 per cent of India's trade by volume and 85 per cent of its crude oil imports move by sea, and most of this traffic transits the 11 identified strategic chokepoints that provide entry into and egress from the IOR (Figure 1).[1] With the growing great-power competition, an increase in conflicts that impact the region and related growing instability, the region's maritime environment is not just a passive trade corridor—it is a contested, multi-actor security space marked by threats, risks and challenges (TRCs) emanating from rival naval posturing, territorial contestations, non-state and non-traditional maritime threats, and climate-linked vulnerabilities.

Since 1947, for several reasons, India's national security thinking has been defined by land borders and continental threats. Maritime thinking and strategy occupied a supplementary role until the 1971 war and then accelerated in the post-Cold War era. Decisive guiding points like the 2004 Indian Ocean tsunami, the 2008 Mumbai attacks, and the rise of China as a maritime nation and its growing naval presence in the region gave a major thrust towards the articulation of a coherent maritime doctrine and strategy. The evolution from a coastal-security mindset to the adoption of the term 'Net Security Provider' to the contemporary tags of 'Preferred Security Partner' and 'First Responder' narratives, with a wider focus on the maritime domain is not just institutional, it is a shift in strategic identity.

This paper argues that India has entered a decisive phase in its maritime trajectory and that it has moved beyond rhetoric and begun building an integrated multi-pillar maritime security architecture, but it still faces capability, coordination, and strategic-reach gaps. India's path through the labyrinth of the IOR will depend on its ability to balance power projection, partnerships, diplomacy, blue-economy logic, and developmental legitimacy across multiple maritime sub-regions simultaneously.

Figure 1: The Indian Ocean Region (IOR) Chokepoints

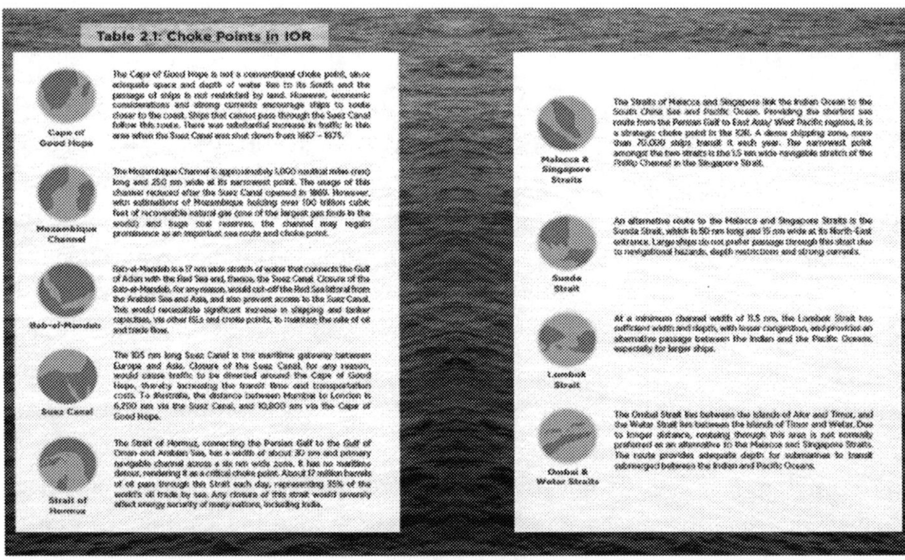

Source: Indian Navy. "Ensuring Secure Seas: India's Maritime Security Strategy," Table 2.1. Integrated Headquarters, Ministry of Defence. 2015.

India in the IOR: Strategic Stakes and Maritime Identity

India's maritime advantages are not accidental—they are geographic, economic, and political. The country sits astride the world's most important sea lines of communication (SLOCs) that connect the region's three continents to the global markets. Further, the geostrategic position of India in the northern Indian Ocean allows a projection of a security umbrella and power in three principal axes, namely, the Strait of Hormuz to the west, the Bab-el-Mandeb to the southwest, and the Strait of Malacca to the east. No other regional state sits at such a crossroads of continental and maritime connectivity.

Reliance on maritime trade defines India's economic strength and weakness. Around 75 per cent of India's overall trade value is seaborne, and the dependency rate of key imports; crude oil, Liquefied Natural Gas (LNG), edible oils, and fertilizers, exceeds 80 per cent.[2] Many nations both in the IOR and beyond face similar dependencies. Hence, if stability and security in the IOR are disrupted, like the Red Sea situation and the tandem rise of piracy, the region's trade and related economic growth are impacted. Therefore, maritime security is closely connected to macro-economic stability. For a rising and growing India there is an increase in geopolitical stakes. As India's foreign policy shifts to multi-alignment, the IOR becomes the primary test of whether India can exercise leadership without formal alliance structures. India's maritime ambitions are not limited to enhancing stability, ensuring security and preserving peace through maritime exercises at the bilateral and multilateral levels and being the *preferred security partner* and *first responder*. These ambitions are also embedded in driving the agendas of regional organisations, multilateral development of capacities and capabilities, port connectivity, and blue-economy ventures.

Chokepoint Vulnerability and SLOC Security

In the maritime domain of the IOR, any instance of instability impacts the security and safety of seaborne trade especially around the chokepoints and along the International Shipping Lanes (ISLs) and SLOCs that crisscross the region (See figure 2).[3] As per a UNCTAD 2023 report, four of the eleven IOR chokepoints; Straits of Hormuz, Malacca, Lombok, and the Bab-el-Mandeb; carry over 60 per cent of the world's maritime oil shipments and nearly half of global container traffic.[4] As per an UNCTAD 2025 report, the Strait of Hormuz carried over 11 per cent of global maritime trade, of which 34 per cent was seaborne oil exports and 30 per cent was LPG exports.[5] It is evident that any disruption due to state/ non-state conflict, piracy, climate disasters, or great-power plays would directly jeopardise the region's and India's food and energy security, and export value chains. While the Indian Navy's mission-based deployments and the conduct of maritime security operations through Op *Sankalp*[6] looks at ensuring the security of shipping in the Gulf of Aden and adjoining areas, the Arabian Sea and off the East Coast of Somalia, there is a need for more cooperative and collaborative efforts with other navies to ensure stability and security over a wider maritime area.

Leveraging Blue Economy

The blue economy is projected to add USD 1 trillion to India's GDP by 2035 if supported by port-led industrialisation, maritime logistics corridors and sustainable marine extraction.[7] India's approach to the blue economy is reflected by the Ministry of Earth Sciences (MoES) as a "potent engine for sustainable growth, unlocking immense potential to propel economic progress while safeguarding our (India's) precious marine ecosystems and empowering coastal communities".[8] Blue economy requires a 'sustainable exploitation' of the ocean resources approach and two aspects stand out indicating India's leadership in this important soft power facet of holistic maritime security[9]:

- During India's Presidency of the G20, world leaders committed to conserving, protecting, restoring and sustainably using the world's ocean and marine ecosystems, thereby mainstreaming the need to build a sustainable and resilient blue economy.
- India's role is further strengthened by global partnerships such as the World Bank's PROBLUE programme and the Asian Development Bank's Blue Bond Guidelines (2022), positioning India as a regional leader in ocean governance.

This approach is part of India's outreach to the region and the broader Indo-Pacific through the lens of SAGAR (Security and Growth for All in the Region) and now MAHASAGAR (Mutual and Holistic Advancement for Security and Growth Across Regions), while reflecting the recognition that maritime resources—shipping, ports, seabed minerals, marine biotechnology—are now strategic assets and will need a stable and secure marine environment to flourish.

Diplomacy

India's maritime diplomacy rests on its ability to provide public goods in a secure environment to the IOR nations, and consists of hydrography, disaster relief, EEZ surveillance, medical aid, and capacity-building, to name a few. The credibility of India being a *preferred security partner* and *first responder* depends on trust built with the nations, which is reflected in its multifield maritime engagements with nations. India's access agreements in Duqm

(Oman), Chabahar (Iran), Assumption Island (Seychelles), and Agaléga (Mauritius) can be placed as successful negotiations under this ambit. India's approach to inclusivity in the region stems from SAGAR and MAHASAGAR.

Announced in 2014, SAGAR is India's first explicit maritime neighbourhood policy, centred on IOR littoral security, humanitarian aid, coastal capacity building, and shared prosperity. The central theme is 'Indian Ocean nations could shape Indian Ocean security'. MAHASAGAR announced in 2025 is an expanded, globalised version of SAGAR, linking IOR security to Africa, Indo-Pacific logistics, green shipping, and digital maritime corridors. The central theme being 'India is no longer just an IOR power—it is an Indo-Oceanic connector of regions.' Table 1 indicates the salient differences between SAGAR and MAHASAGAR.

Figure 2: IOR Chokepoints and ISLs/ SLOCs

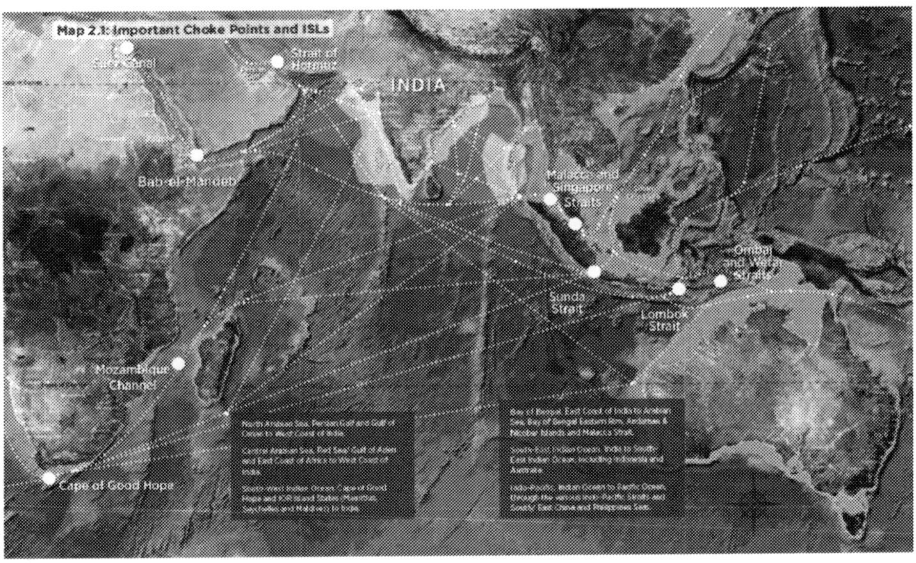

Source: Indian Navy. "Ensuring Secure Seas: India's Maritime Security Strategy," Map 2.1. Integrated Headquarters, Ministry of Defence. 2015.

Africa is an interesting example of India's maritime engagement expansion in the region. Under the Indo-Pacific geographic area outlined by the Indian Prime Minister in 2018 at the Shangri La Dialogue.[10] Africa became the western edge of India's maritime outreach. India has conducted joint patrols with Mozambique and Tanzania, trained over 1,500 African naval officers, supplied coastal radar systems to Mauritius and Seychelles, and executed multiple HADR missions in Madagascar and Mozambique. India's naval deployments to the western IOR tripled between 2017 and 2023—marking the first real operationalisation of the 'net security provider' doctrine.[11] The term *net security provider* has since been replaced by *preferred security partner* and *first responder*.

Table 1: SAGAR vs MAHASAGAR

Aspect	SAGAR (2015)	MAHASAGAR (2024)
Area	IOR	IOR + Africa + Indo-Pacific
Driver	Maritime Security + HADR	Maritime + Trade + Technology + Blue Economy
Mode	India as a Responder	India as a connector and enabler
Partners	Islands + Littorals	Africa + ASEAN + Persian Gulf + Europe
Core Tools(s)	Capacity and Capability Building	Multi-region Connectivity Corridors

Source: Compiled by the Author

Regional Organisations

In the labyrinth of maritime security there are several regional organisations that play central roles in cooperation and collaboration. Primary among them are the Indian Ocean Rim Association (IORA), the Indian Ocean Naval Symposium (IONS), and the Bay of Bengal Initiative for Multi-Sectoral Technical and Economic Cooperation (BIMSTEC). While IORA and BIMSTEC were founded on the basis of economic cooperation, IONS was founded on the basis of increasing maritime co-operation among navies of the IOR. As the scope of cooperation and collaboration in the many facets of the maritime domain increased IORA developed the priority area of maritime safety and security and BIMSTEC the security and energy sector of cooperation. The key strengths and weaknesses of these organisations are outlined in Table 2.

Table 2: Strengths and Weaknesses: IORA, IONS, BIMSTEC

Organisation	Strengths	Weakness
IORA	• Broad pan-IOR legitimacy, linking Africa, Asia, and Australia • Six formalised priority areas	• Limited secretariat capacity, inconsistent funding, and slow project execution • Politically diverse membership hence slow consensus on security initiatives • Largely policy-level, with few operational tools
IONS	• Practitioner-led, enabling trust-building, interoperability, and best-practice exchange among navies • Low political friction and highly flexible engagement mechanisms	• Non-binding outputs hence implementation is dependent on national will • Participation varies widely hence continuity is impacted • Limited ability to integrate coastguards and non-naval agencies
BIMSTEC	• Compact membership enables focused and tangible maritime cooperation in the Bay of Bengal • Structure of sectoral groups supports functional cooperation in security, HADR, and connectivity	• Domestic instability • Institutional delays, resource shortages, and political frictions reduce momentum • Limited mandate and reach beyond the Bay of Bengal.

Source: Compiled by the Author

Actions to Strengthen Regional Maritime Security Resilience

India being a central figure in the IOR and possessing the ability to drive several themes across the region and organisations, can initiate and support actions to strengthen regional maritime security resilience.

Expand Maritime Domain Awareness (MDA) through IFC-IOR and Regional Fusion Centres

This would entail an increase in liaison officers, the integration of IORA and BIMSTEC states, and the provision of connectivity and training, and the conduct of annual multinational MDA table-top exercises anchored around IFC-IOR.

Strengthen IORA's Implementation Capacity

This strengthening would require multi-year financial contributions to professionalise the secretariat and to sponsor flagship maritime projects like HADR coordination, port resilience audits, and fisheries enforcement training to name a few immediate requirements.

Operationalise IORA–BIMSTEC Convergence

The convergence would require the creation of a joint working group on maritime security looking at projects in port security, SAR, and coastal radar networking. India's leadership in the BIMSTEC sector of security and energy and its coordination role in the IORA priority area of maritime safety and security would aid this convergence especially by aligning agendas and avoiding duplication. This a task made easier by the recent signing of the MoU between IORA and BIMTEC on April 03, 2025, aiming to strengthen inter-regional collaboration in key areas of mutual interest.[12]

Use IONS for Interoperability and Standardisation with IORA and BIMSTEC

This would include leading the development of SOPs to counter the various non-traditional threats that impact the IOR, like those developed for HADR. The initial focus could be on piracy and maritime crime response. The conduct of combined workshops with IORA and BIMSTEC with limited-scope sea exercises could lay the foundation for greater integration.

Provide Targeted Capacity-Building Packages

India could expand Mission SAGAR and MAHASAGAR style assistance by expanding the provision of patrol vessels and radar stations, Maritime Law Enforcement (MLE) training with regional characteristics, and EEZ legal advisory support. India is poised to move from a buyer and builder of warships to a builder and seller of affordable, export-ready platforms. These platforms could suit the needs of IOR nations that do not need technology-heavy ships but ships that meet their specific requirements. By building a sustainable export pipeline, from patrol craft to advanced frigates, India can strengthen regional self-reliance, boost its defence industry, and deepen its standing as a preferred security partner.[13] The engagement in areas that require private sector expertise like port development, shipping insurance, and logistics supply chains in IORA/BIMSTEC security dialogue debates could also be encouraged.

The End Game

The IOR is considered a labyrinth as it is multipolar, multi-actor, and multi-domain. India's route through this labyrinth is a hybrid combination of national power and partnership. These will require a credible force posture, reliable logistics, and the consistent provision of maritime public goods that contribute to a rules-based regional order. If India aligns capacity and capability with legitimacy and development with deterrence, it will not merely navigate the Indian Ocean, it will help shape it. This shaping needs a resilient Indian Ocean maritime security architecture that requires political cohesion (IORA), operational interoperability (IONS), and regional focus (BIMSTEC). India is uniquely positioned to knit these strengths together. Targeted investment in MDA, capacity and capability building, institutional strengthening, and maritime legal/regulatory harmonisation will significantly enhance collective security and reinforce India's role as the preferred security partner and first responder in the region. However, to reinforce regional resilience and establish India as a maritime power of consequence the following five internal steps could be considered:

Adopt and Implement a National Maritime Security Policy

This would entail legislation or promulgation of a whole-of-government policy that:

- Defines maritime security with measurable outcomes and clarifies roles across Navy/Coast Guard/line-ministries amalgam.
- Requires the establishment of an integrated maritime operations centre with legal/law-enforcement cells.
- Mandates shared MDA standards and data protocols.

Build Logistics Depth and Forward Access

- Conclude predictable logistics-support and technical-services agreements at key nodes like Duqm, Djibouti/Red Sea ports with partners, Victoria in Seychelles, Agaléga in Mauritius, and the Indonesian archipelago.
- Pre-position humanitarian stores, spares, and deployable radar/communications kits for surge operations in the above places.
- Commission additional fleet support ships, expand the MRO ambit to include other strategic partners and expand fuel and weapons storage at the Andaman and Nicobar Command.

Close the Underwater and Aviation Gaps

- Accelerate Project-75(I) with air-independent propulsion, upgrade P-8I fleet support, and induct ASW helicopters in adequate numbers.
- Expand unmanned underwater and surface vehicle programmes for persistent surveillance of chokepoints and the EEZ.

- Deploy seabed sensors and cable-security protocols to protect undersea infrastructure.

Scale up Economic Diplomacy

- Through MAHASAGAR fuse blue economy projects in the areas of fisheries management, marine biotech, and offshore wind with security outputs like EEZ patrols, search and rescue (SAR), and MDA.
- Offer turnkey packages to IOR nations in areas of coastal radars, specific maritime training, SAR boats, hydrography, and maritime skill scholarships.
- Operationalise green and digital sea corridors linking Indian ports to Africa, ASEAN and Europe and enable time savings and emissions cuts.

Anchor Legitimacy through Public Goods

- Institutionalise an annual Indian Ocean Public Goods Exercise. The exercise could include HADR drills, oil-spill response, IUU interdiction simulations, and cyber-port security exercises with wide IOR participation.
- Expand IFC-IOR's liaison network, open data products to the maritime agencies of IOR nations and publish an annual Indian Ocean MDA Review.

India's position as a maritime nation is no longer aspirational, it now hinges on the operational. The nation has moved from episodic deployments to a structured maritime security model that blends presence, the permanency of that presence, partnerships, and security of public goods. The shift from SAGAR to MAHASAGAR signals an outward-looking India that now connects regions, not just coasts. However, ambition must match the enablers. Naval strength and operational capabilities, domestic resilience in the multifield maritime domain, and industrial capacity will decide whether India can sustain a stabilising maritime presence in the IOR and the broader Indo-Pacific in the coming years.[14]

NOTES

1 Indian Navy. "Ensuring Secure Seas: India's Maritime Security Strategy," Table 2.1. Integrated Headquarters, Ministry of Defence. 2015.

2 UNCTAD. "Review of Maritime Transport," Statistical Annex. 2023.

3 Indian Navy. "Ensuring Secure Seas: India's Maritime Security Strategy," Map 2.1. Integrated Headquarters, Ministry of Defence. 2015.

4 Op. cit. note no. 2

5 UNCTAD. "Maritime Transport Review". 2025.

6 "Indian Navy's Ongoing Maritime Security Operations ('Op Sankalp') 14 Dec 23 To 23 Mar 24," Press Release, Indian Ministry of Defence. March 23, 2024. https://www.pib.gov.in/PressReleaseIframePage.aspx?PRID=2016201

7 "India's Blue Economy Roadmap 2047," NITI Aayog. 2023.

8 "Transforming India's Blue Economy: Investment, Innovation and Sustainable Growth," Ministry of Earth Sciences. May 2025. www.moes.gov.in/sites/default/files/2025-05/White-Paper_Blue_Economy.pdf

9 Ibid

10 "Prime Minister's Keynote Address at Shangri La Dialogue," Press Release, Ministry of External Affairs. June 01, 2018. https://www.mea.gov.in/Speeches-Statements.htm?dtl/29943/Prime+Ministers+Keynote+Address+at+Shangri+La+Dialogue+June+01+2018

11 Mohan, Raja C. "India's Maritime Rise and Africa's Western Littorals," Journal of Indian Ocean Studies. 2023.

12 "Signing of Memorandum of Understanding Between IORA and BIMSTEC," Press Release, IORA. www.iora.int/sites/default/files/2025-04/Press%20Release%20-%20SIGNING%20OF%20MEMORANDUM%20OF%20UNDERSTANDING%20BETWEEN%20IORA %20AND%20BIMSTEC.pdf

13 Parmar, Sarabjeet S. "Indian Shipbuilding: The Case to Become a Warship Sellers Nation", India's World, Volume 1, Issue 6, Nov–Dec 2025.

10

Collaborative Maritime ISR Framework for IORA

Prof. Sudhir Saxena

The Indian Ocean is the third largest water body on the surface of the planet, with 38 littoral states representing more than 2.7 billion people. The ocean connects major economic hubs in Asia, Africa, Europe, and the Americas, making it a vital global trade corridor. It provides global access to essential resources like food, energy, and precious minerals, handling more than half of the global maritime trade including around four-fifths of global oil shipments and more than one-third of bulk cargo annually. More than 90,000 vessels operate in the region annually carrying more than 12 billion tonnes of bulk cargo. The Indian Ocean Region (IOR) accounts for around 15 per cent of the world's total fish catch.

The IOR seabed provides vast deposits of polymetallic nodules and other valuable minerals. The region is also home to a vast, complex and high value network of Sub- Sea cables network that carry more than 99 per cent of the global Internet traffic. IOR houses more than 17 major subsea cables carrying more than 400tbps of data for the regional and extra-regional economies, linking European and West Asia with South, South-East and East Asian tele-cyberspace.

As a sea faring nation India has around 11,000 km of coast line and a large strategic interest in the security cooperation with the maritime neighbours and like-minded nations linked to the IOR. Amongst other stakes in the region's security and development, due to its peninsular geography, India has a unique location in the subsea cable topology.

As is applicable for any other multi-stakes region the progress of IORA objectives is dependent on the success of its maritime security framework. This in turn is linked to the collective Intelligence, Surveillance, and Reconnaissance (ISR) capabilities of the member states. This paper attempts to analyse the ISR options for the IORA member states keeping in view the common maritime security objectives.

Security Challenges

Given the enormity of global resources and assets invested in the region, security challenges are a logical precipitate for both regional and extra regional stakeholders. The geography and geo-politics of IOR have led to evolution of three major chokepoints, two of which are located near the conflict ridden West Asian and North African regions.

(a) The Strait of Hormuz as one of the vital oil chokepoints, has had a historical impact on the crucial supply channels from the oil producing sources. It connects the Persian Gulf to the rest of the region handling around 40 per cent of all seaborne oil trade connecting some of the biggest oil consumers in the world like India and China.

(b) The Bab el-Mandeb Strait connects the Red Sea to the Indian Ocean (via the Gulf of Aden) and is the gateway to the Suez Canal. It is a critical link for trade between Asia and Europe.

(c) The Strait of Malacca. As a primary sea connection between the Indian Ocean, Pacific Ocean and the other East Asian seas, it is vital for Asian economies, including China, which conducts around 80 per cent of its energy imports through this route.

As is the case with other multi-stake issues, IOR also experiences global and regional power contention along with a sinusoid of geopolitical stresses. After the end of Cold War, especially during the last two decades the US-China rivalry has dominated large parts of the IOR, with other emerging global and regional powers like India and Japan adding to the complexity of the security matrix even further.

In addition to the big power play, the region is also challenged by other commercial and sub-military contentions by State, State supported non-State and non-state actors. These include terrorists, pirates, smugglers, human traffickers, environment criminals and activities of sanctioned entities. Many of these actors have armed capabilities which are employed to defend and pursue their respective objectives. The case of pirates operating from the East/

North-East Africa and Yemen based terrorist groups are representative examples of the influence exercised by the non-State actors.

The IOR is also known for its rich fishing resources, which have attracted both industry-scale and illegal fishing operations. Over time the fishing commerce has become another domain of economic contention amongst fishing powers. The large scale and illegal fishing combine has also resulted in irreversible damage to the IOR bio-ecosystem. The sea-bed mining largely mirrors the challenges in the fishing domain, with some additional strategic aspects. In the domain of non-traditional security, the adverse environmental impact due to exploitative practices by bigger regional and extra regional economies have further added to challenges faced by some of the poorer member nations.

The region is home to military bases of ten littoral and extra-regional powers. Some of these are not members of the IORA forum. While US maintains a large military presence in Diego Garcia and other African/West Asian locations, China has been ramping up its military presence in strategically important coasts in the Horn of Africa, Djibouti, Pakistan, Sri Lanka, and elsewhere, both as part of BRI initiative and through bilateral arrangements.

Notwithstanding the geopolitical competition, the IORA forum has anchored its objectives in peaceful and sustainable development, a goal which does not collide with any global power play. However, even non-contentious objectives cannot be completely delinked from the common maritime security objectives of the forum, even if limited in scope. The IORA forum has evolved for itself a modest Maritime Security mechanism including Maritime Security Dialogues, Cooperative Capacity Building, Information Sharing and Cooperation Agreements. In addition, various technological initiatives in partnership with other international organizations like the International Maritime Organization (IMO) have been put in place to further strengthen the maritime security framework. These have resulted in certain constructive outcomes like the interactions for human resource development, agreements for enhancing navigation safety, addressing marine pollution etc. The counter piracy cooperation in sync with other regional anti-piracy initiatives can be considered as one of the relative successes for the forum. However, given its long period of existence, a macro assessment will reveal that the forum has fallen short of its overall desired goals. While there are other factors which have impacted the progress, maritime security is one of the important aspects where efficacy of the forum has been lagging behind.

IORA-ISR Framework

Most maritime security issues eventually get anchored on the contributed ISR capabilities of the member nations, information sharing and willingness to cooperatively develop capabilities to achieve the common maritime ISR and security objectives.

Unlike land mass, oceans have a peculiar ISR requirement due to absence of sustained physical human presence over time and space. Further, the reaction times to mitigate an ISR triggered crisis are far longer as compared to those over land mass, where a sustained human presence can be exercised. And yet, the maritime ISR requirements demand persistence in time and space, similar to the land mass. The challenge gets more complex when the IOR security issues interweave with extra-regional and global security issues, especially due to the stakes of extra-regional powers which are also part of the IORA framework. The physical maritime security frameworks are further stretched when linked to cybersecurity issues associated with strategic and economic dependencies on structures like the subsea cables network.

In addition to addressing the regional maritime security challenges, the member nations are also required to meet the security requirements towards their role in other bi-lateral and multi-lateral forums, with equally pressing demands. The less enabled member states are challenged by resource constraints and find it difficult to viably contribute to the maritime security objectives of the forum.

It is logical to conclude that the complex IOR maritime security matrix and related ISR requirements can only be addressed by technology driven solutions which can provide a persistent coverage over large spatial and temporal swaths. While the world is witnessing a golden age of technology, the ISR technologies have created their own universe of capabilities, dependencies, contention and conflict. A large part of surface, above surface and sub-surface maritime ISR requirements are being addressed by space based and floating/sub-surface mechanisms coupled with limited airborne coverage. It needs no highlighting that these are high end assets, both in terms of technological complexity and cost, which many member states cannot afford or do not possess. This capability differential invariably leads to a maze of dependencies driven by bigger players who have the technological and financial capabilities to sustain such ISR activities.

Given the differentials in the maritime security requirements of IORA member states and ISR capabilities, there is a need to evolve inclusive, common, minimum, maritime ISR objectives. These will need to be realistic enough to address the IORA Maritime Domain Awareness and security objectives while enabling the less capable member states. While the richer and technologically enabled member states can take on the deployment of costlier assets, the less enabled members can contribute manpower-intensive local ISR coverages.

The above ISR collective will need to be fructified through an information sharing mechanism which can benefit all member states, particularly the less enabled nations. This in turn would require creation of a dedicated IORA Information Sharing infrastructure which can be accessed and jointly manned by the member states. Given its legacy of maritime security cooperation, technological capabilities and its location in the IOR, India is one of the most suitable candidates to house such a capability.

The IORA-ISR forum could also provide an additional nucleus for a collaborative capacity development, training and joint R&D possibilities which can plug-in to other dimensions of IORA cooperative framework. It needs no emphasis that the bulk of technological and financial load would have to be borne by more capable nations initially with the less capable members enabled to increase their contribution gradually. A practical sharing of Space borne and Surface maritime ISR capabilities by the more capable members could be a realistic measure to further the common security objective.

The IORA maritime security is an important element of the forum's overall development objectives. A progressive IORA maritime ISR structure will go a long way toward strengthening the forum's overall capability to pursue its objectives.

11

India and Indian Ocean: Importance and Vulnerabilities of Undersea Cables

Dr. Neha Kumar

Introduction

In contemporary times, undersea cables have gained immense importance due to their linkage to global communications and the rise of the digital economy.[1] Recent disruptions to undersea communication cables in regions such as the Red Sea[2] and the Baltic[3] have highlighted the strategic significance and growing vulnerability of seabed infrastructure. Nearly 95 per cent of global digital communications including financial transactions, government communications, and data exchange supporting strategic and military decision-making travel through these cables.[4]

While such incidents are often categorised as *grey-zone operations*[5] i.e., actions conducted below the threshold of conventional conflict, they can nonetheless have direct implications for economy and broader digitalisation. As India has established itself as an emerging digital economy,[6] its dependence on undersea cables has correspondingly increased. Prime Minister Narendra Modi emphasised this significance when he stated, *"The optical fibre project connecting Andaman and Nicobar to the rest of the country and to the world is a symbol of our commitment towards Ease of Living."*[7]

This chapter explores India's economic and digital vulnerabilities linked to undersea cables, particularly in the context of China. The undersea cables located in the Indian Ocean form the central focus of this discussion. It argues that these cables are not only critical economic assets but also strategic infrastructures whose security and resilience have far-reaching implications for India's communication networks and digital economy. The chapter explore China's capability to target undersea cables and India's vulnerabilities in Indian Ocean.

India, the Indian Ocean, and Undersea Cables

The Indian Ocean has emerged as the *digital artery* of the global economy,[8] consisting of a network of undersea cables that carry over 95 per cent of the world's international data traffic. Given India's geographical proximity to the Indian Ocean, these cables have become digital lifelines and economic multipliers for the nation.

India's expanding digital economy is characterised by rapid growth in information technology, financial services, e-commerce, and telecommunications. Any disruption to these cables would have a profound impact on this "digital economy," bringing business operations to a standstill. Moreover, dependence on undersea cables is no longer confined to urban or corporate sectors. Agriculture (both land-based and fisheries), transport (road, air, and sea), healthcare, and rural development have all become increasingly reliant on timely digital information, thereby deepening India's dependence on these cables.[9]

Currently, the undersea cables at Mumbai, Chennai, Kochi, Tuticorin, and Visakhapatnam serve as gateways linking Southeast Asia, the Middle East, Africa, and Europe.[10] In 2023–24, India's services exports were valued at USD 341.11 billion, the vast majority of which relied on undersea cables for delivery. This figure is expected to rise to approximately USD 618 billion by 2030, surpassing merchandise exports.[11]

The extent of India's dependence on undersea cables was demonstrated by the severance of multiple cables off the coasts of Egypt and Dubai, which resulted in a loss of more than 80 per cent of international service capacity. During this period, India lost 60 million users in two weeks, and its business processing industry experienced a 60.23 per cent drop in connectivity—causing serious economic repercussions.[12]

To enhance security, it is essential to understand the points of vulnerability in the submarine cable system. The submarine communication network comprises both the **wet plant** (the optical fibre cable undersea) and the **dry plant** (cable landing stations and beach manholes). Beach manholes are structures located at the shoreline where subsea cables connect to terrestrial fibre-optic lines that extend to landing stations. Therefore, vulnerabilities exist both **offshore** and **onshore**.[13]

In addition to these physical vulnerabilities, **cyberattacks** against cable systems pose significant risks. Common forms of cyberattacks are outlined in **Table 1** below.

Table 1: Types of Cyberattacks on Undersea Cables

Type of Attack	Method	Impact	India-Specific Context
Network Layer Manipulation (BGP/DNS Attack)	Hijacking or leaking routes; DNS poisoning to divert and intercept traffic	Traffic interception, misrouting, and service outage	Indian ISPs and government networks are increasingly exposed due to high traffic via Mumbai and Chennai gateways
Intrusion of Landing Stations	Cyberattacks on control systems or servers	Loss of operational control and data breaches	India's cable landing points in Mumbai, Chennai, and Kochi are high-value nodes requiring stringent access control
Malware Targeting Operators	Compromise of operators' IT systems and infrastructure	Denial of access, ransom payments, and operational paralysis	Reliance Jio, Tata Communications, and BSNL undersea operations require coordinated CERT-IN oversight
Insider Threats	Coercion, bribery, or phishing of personnel at landing stations	Unauthorised access, sabotage, and data leakage	Private cable operators employ contractors; insider threat mitigation remains weak

Source: Compiled by the Author

Beyond direct cyberattacks, cable disruptions may also facilitate **disinformation campaigns** within the political domain. An adversary could exploit temporary communication blackouts to depict the government as ineffective in protecting national infrastructure, thereby eroding public confidence. By targeting specific cables, hostile actors could create "information vacuums" that enable the spread of false narratives and intensify information warfare.

Such hybrid threats, combining physical sabotage, cyber intrusion, and psychological operations, underscore the complex nature of contemporary security challenges.[14] In India's case, where digital and economic interdependence is rapidly expanding, the manipulation of information flows could have profound political, economic, and strategic consequences.

Strategic Vulnerabilities in the Indian Ocean

From the Indian Ocean perspective, cables such as the **Bay of Bengal Gateway (BBG), SEACOM,** and **SAFE** connect India to regional and global information networks.[15] These systems sustain digital connectivity, commerce, intelligence-sharing, and military coordination. Their geographic concentration at hubs such as Mumbai and Chennai enhances efficiency but simultaneously increases vulnerability.[16] An adversary targeting a limited number of chokepoints could disrupt a substantial portion of India's external communications.

In the evolving landscape of hybrid warfare, civilian infrastructure assumes unprecedented strategic importance. The consequences of such disruption ranging from economic paralysis to loss of trust in digital governance, demonstrate how infrastructure vulnerability can translate into strategic instability.

Moreover, India's growing reliance on digital and maritime infrastructures places it at the intersection of global power competition in the Indian Ocean. The Indian Ocean, once viewed primarily as a trade corridor, has become a **data corridor**, where cables, satellites, and digital networks collectively shape geopolitical influence. The intersection of economic interdependence and strategic rivalry renders India's maritime domain an increasingly contested digital frontier.

Therefore, securing undersea cables is not only a matter of economic necessity but a **core national security imperative.** Protection of these critical infrastructures requires coordination among maritime, cyber, and intelligence agencies to ensure resilience against both physical and virtual disruptions.

China's Expanding Maritime and Digital Footprint

China's strategic presence in the Indian Ocean is multifaceted. While often framed in economic terms, particularly its dependence on energy imports [17] transiting through the region, China has also invested heavily in maritime access, naval deployments, and digital infrastructure development. Chinese-financed ports at **Gwadar, Hambantota, Kyaukpyu,** and **Djibouti** provide logistical depth and dual-use potential for military operations.[18] These ports, while commercially justified, serve the parallel purpose of expanding Beijing's strategic reach across vital maritime and communication chokepoints.

Simultaneously, technological advancements have expanded China's operational reach. Chinese research institutions have developed deep-sea submersibles and cable-interference technologies capable of cutting or tapping fibre-optic lines at significant depths. Although such capabilities are often presented as civilian tools for maintenance or resource exploration, they possess clear dual-use characteristics. The integration of these technologies with Beijing's broader maritime and digital strategies underscores its capacity to influence the security of global information networks. This is explained ahead in the chapter.

Dual-Use Capabilities

China's strategy of ***civil–military fusion***[19] enables the seamless transfer of commercial and military technologies. A fleet of ostensibly civilian oceanographic and research vessels is frequently deployed for data collection relevant to national defence.

For instance, the ***Song Hang*** vessel was detected loitering in the Sulu Sea, engaging in activities beyond conventional fishing.[20] As one maritime analyst noted, *"The Song Hang exhibited deliberate loitering patterns directly over critical infrastructure, movements typically associated with mapping or surveillance rather than fishing."*[21] Similarly, the ***Xiang Yang Hong*** and ***Haiyang Dizhi*** classes routinely conduct hydrographic and geophysical surveys across the Indian Ocean Region.[22] While these operations are described as peaceful, they provide the People's Liberation Army Navy (PLAN) with valuable undersea mapping data.

Such dual-use activities raise legitimate concerns that these vessels could map or even target submarine cable routes and landing approaches, enabling potential disruption or intelligence collection during crises. The dual nature of China's maritime scientific missions thus blurs the line between research and reconnaissance.

Unmanned Underwater Vehicles and Remotely Operated Vehicles

Technological evolution has significantly expanded the sophistication of underwater systems. **Unmanned Underwater Vehicles (UUVs)** operate autonomously, without direct human supervision, while **Remotely Operated Vehicles (ROVs)** are guided by operators but possess advanced manoeuvrability.

These systems serve multiple functions, such as monitoring adversarial movements, detecting and neutralising naval mines, tracking submarines, and mapping the ocean floor.[23] Their development has enhanced China's capability to conduct persistent, covert undersea operations, including the surveillance or potential interference of submarine cables. As UUV and ROV technology matures, China's capacity to operate undetected in sensitive undersea environments will continue to grow, intensifying risks for India's maritime domain awareness.

Naval and Logistical Reach

Since 2008, China has routinely deployed naval forces under the guise of anti-piracy operations in Indian Ocean.[24] In parallel, Beijing has consolidated access to strategic regional ports such as **Gwadar** and **Hambantota**. These deployments, coupled with port facilities and replenishment capabilities, enable China to sustain long-term missions in the Indian Ocean.

Such infrastructure facilitates not only enhance naval endurance but also have the potential for **undersea cable surveillance** and **data-gathering operations** near Indian maritime zones under the cover of benign commercial or research activities. The blurred boundary between economic expansion and military projection creates a persistent ambiguity in China's regional behaviour—one that complicates India's ability to distinguish between legitimate scientific activity and covert strategic operations.

China and Cyber Warfare

China's **People's Liberation Army (PLA)** and the **Ministry of State Security (MSS)** have frequently been linked to global cyber intrusions targeting telecommunications and critical infrastructure networks.[25] Through these state-sponsored groups, China could infiltrate **landing station networks, network operation centres (NOCs)**, or **supplier ecosystems**, thereby enabling data interception, manipulation of systems, or preparatory operations for physical interference.

This integration of cyber and physical capabilities highlights the **hybrid nature** of the threat India faces in protecting its undersea cable systems. China's strategy does not rely solely on physical presence but also on leveraging cyber infiltration, technological dependency, and industrial partnerships to shape the global information environment.

India's Challenges with Undersea Cables

India faces significant operational and strategic challenges in the repair and security of undersea communication cables, primarily because the existing repair capacity relies on foreign-based maintenance vessels.[26] The mobilisation of these vessels often entails delays ranging from several weeks to months, arising from procedural requirements such as customs clearances, naval permissions, and crew approvals. Moreover, these ships require additional time to mobilise from their home ports and transit to Indian waters and the wider Indian Ocean Region (IOR).

To address these challenges, the National Security Secretariat has been collaborating with the Department of Telecommunications (DoT) to establish indigenous repair vessels dedicated to undersea fibre-optic maintenance.[27] However, progress toward the development of such indigenous capability has been limited. The delay in repair operations continues to be compounded by complex administrative and regulatory procedures involving multiple agencies.

Another critical concern pertains to the geographical concentration of cable landing stations in India. At present, these facilities are located in only five cities—Mumbai, Chennai, Kochi, Tuticorin, and Thiruvananthapuram.[28] Cable landing stations play a vital role by supplying power to undersea cables and connecting them to terrestrial communication networks. The clustering of cables around a limited number of landing sites heightens the risk of sabotage or espionage, as a coordinated attack could simultaneously disrupt multiple cables. Such an incident would have severe repercussions for global internet connectivity and communication channels, potentially undermining India's national security and military coordination capabilities.

The protection of these critical assets presents additional challenges. While India has designated undersea cables and their landing stations as critical infrastructure and placed them under the security of the Central Industrial Security Force (CISF), their geographic concentration increases vulnerability. The broader protection of submarine cable infrastructure is managed through a three-tier coastal security framework involving the State Marine Police, the Indian Coast Guard, and the Indian Navy. However, specialised training programs for seabed infrastructure protection and undersea cable maintenance have yet to be instituted, limiting the effectiveness of existing security mechanisms.

Way Forward

To address the aforementioned challenges, this chapter proposes the following measures:

1. **Develop indigenous cable maintenance and rapid-repair capability:** Establishing domestically operated maintenance vessels and technical facilities would reduce India's dependence on foreign entities and ensure timely restoration of damaged cables.
2. **Diversify cable landing locations to reduce clustering risk:** Expanding the number of landing sites across India's coastline would minimise vulnerabilities arising from geographical concentration and enhance redundancy in network connectivity.
3. **Expand maritime surveillance of seabed infrastructure:** Strengthening the monitoring capacity of the Indian Navy and the Coast Guard to include undersea infrastructure would help detect and deter potential threats to submarine cables.
4. **Enhance regional cooperation for seabed security in the Indian Ocean:** Building collaborative frameworks with littoral states and regional partners would improve information-sharing, joint response mechanisms, and resilience against transnational maritime threats.
5. **Integrate undersea infrastructure protection into India's broader maritime and nuclear deterrence strategy:** Embedding cable security within strategic doctrines would align technological, military, and policy measures to safeguard national communication networks critical to command-and-control systems.

Finally, **policy alignment** must integrate cable protection within the broader frameworks of national cyber strategy, blue economy planning, and maritime security policy. Ensuring that undersea cables are recognised as critical infrastructure will help channel resources and political attention toward their protection. A coherent national doctrine connecting data sovereignty, digital resilience, and maritime strategy will not only secure India's economic future but also reinforce its strategic credibility as a responsible power in the region.[29]

NOTES

1 Matis, Michael. "The Protection of Undersea Cables: A Global Security Threat." United States Army War College, Strategic Research Project, 2012, p.1-32. 2012. https://apps.dtic.mil/sti/pdfs/ADA561426.pdf

2 "Undersea cables cut in Red Sea: Internet disturbed across Asia, Middle East, India and

Pakistan among affected". Times of India. 2025. https://timesofindia.indiatimes.com/business/international-business/undersea-cables-cut-in-red-sea-internet-disrupted-across-asia-middle-east-india-pakistan-among-affected/articleshow/123744508.cms

3 Kotasova, Ivana; Stockwell, Billy and Murphy, P. Paul. "Two undersea cables in Baltic Sea disrupted, sparking warning of hybrid warfare." CNN. 2024. https://edition.cnn.com/2024/11/18/europe/undersea-cable-disrupted-germany-finland-intl

4 Mital, Neeraj. "International Advisory Body formed to strengthen the resilience of submarine telecom cables." Ministry of Communications, Government of India. 2024. https://www.pib.gov.in/PressReleasePage.aspx?PRID=2081003,

5 "Underwater Fiber Optic Cable Security and Gray Zone Operations." Defstrat. https://www.defstrat.com/magazine_articles/underwater-fiber-optic-cable-security-and-gray-zone-operations/

6 Kumar, Santosh, Meena, Sarla and Rane, Kritika. "Future Ready: India's Digital Economy to Contribute One-Fifth of National Income by 2029-30." Press Information Bureau, Government of India. 2025. https://www.pib.gov.in/FactsheetDetails.aspx?Id=149096.

7 "Prime Minister Shri Narendra Modi Launches Submarine Cable Connectivity to Andaman & Nicobar Islands (CANI)." Press Information Bureau, Government of India. August 10, 2020. https://www.pib.gov.in/PressReleasePage.aspx?PRID=1644712.

8 Arha, Kaush. "India at the Centre of the Indian Ocean Submarine Cable Network: Trusted Connectivity in Practice." Observer Research Foundation. 2024. https://www.orfonline.org/research/india-at-the-centre-of-the-indian-ocean-submarine-cable-network-trusted-connectivity-in-practice.

9 Agarwal, Soham and Lahiri, Debesh. "Disaster-Resilience of India's Undersea Communications Cable Systems." National Maritime Foundation. 2024 https://maritimeindia.org/disaster-resilience-of-undersea-communication-cable-systems-in-india/

10 "India Poised to Become Global Hub for Submarine Telecom Cable Network." The Economic Times Business Verticals. 2025. https://government.economictimes.indiatimes.com/news/technology/india-poised-to-become-global-hub-for-submarine-telecom-cable-network/118873661

11 Khanna, Monty. "A Roadmap for Securing India's Undersea Cables." Observer Research Foundation. 2025. https://www.orfonline.org/research/a-roadmap-for-securing-india-s-undersea-cables

12 Op. cit. note no.10.

13 Chesnoy, José and Jean-Christophe Antona (ed.). "Undersea Fiber Communication Systems," Academic Press, p 3–21. 2025. https://www.sciencedirect.com/science/chapter/edited-volume/abs/pii/B9780443298868000013

14 Voo, Julia and Singh, Virpratap Vikram. "Competition in Cyberspace: A Distorted Representation." International Institute for Strategic Studies. 2025. https://www.iiss.org/online-analysis/charting-cyberspace/2025/04/competition-in-cyberspace-a-normalised-misrepresentation/.

15 Op. cit. note no. 8.

16 Op. cit. note no. 10.

17 Kumar, Atul. "Indian Ocean Chokepoints: Is China Still Vulnerable?" Observer Research Foundation. 2025. https://www.orfonline.org/expert-speak/indian-ocean-chokepoints-is-china-still-vulnerable.

18 "China Strategic Ports Worldwide under Chinese Control." Indian Military Review, IMR Media Pvt Ltd. 2025. https://imrmedia.in/china-strategic-ports-worldwide-under-chinese-control/.

19 Stone, Alex and Wood, Peter. "China's Military-Civil Fusion Strategy: A View from Chinese Strategists." China's Aerospace Studies Institute. 2020. https://www.airuniversity.af.edu/Portals/10/CASI/documents/Research/Other-Topics/2020-06-15%20CASI_China_Military_Civil_Fusion_Strategy.pdf.

20 Reklai, Leilani. "Palau Reports Unauthorized Entry of Chinese Research Vessel for Fourth Consecutive Year." Island Times. 2024. https://islandtimes.org/palau-reports-unauthorized-entry-of-chinese-research-vessel-for-fourth-consecutive-year/

21 McCartney, Micah. "China Research Ship 'Loitering' near Undersea Cables: Report." Newsweek. 2025, https://www.newsweek.com/china-research-vessel-undersea-cable-threat-2074705.

22 "Chinese Research Vessels Operating in the Indian Ocean." Reuters. February 22, 2024. https://www.reuters.com/world/asia-pacific/chinese-research-vessels-operating-indian-ocean-2024-02-22/.

23 Semenyuk, Vladislav et al. "Advances in UAV Detection: Integrating Multi-Sensor Systems and AI for Enhanced Accuracy and Efficiency." International Journal of Critical Infrastructure Protection, Volume 49, 1–14. July 2025. https://doi.org/10.1016/j.ijcip.2025.100744

24 "India's Response to China's Naval Expansion in the Indian Ocean." Only IAS. 2025. https://pwonlyias.com/editorial-analysis/indian-ocean-dominance/

25 "Countering Chinese State-Sponsored Actors Compromise of Networks Worldwide to Feed Global Espionage System." Cybersecurity and Infrastructure Security Agency, U.S. Department of Homeland Security. 2025. https://www.cisa.gov/news-events/cybersecurity-advisories/aa25-239a.

26 Agarwal, Soham and Chauhan, Pradeep. "Underwater Communication Cables: Vulnerabilities and Protective Measures Relevant to Indian Part 1." National Maritime Foundation, p 1–9. 2021. https://www.maritimeindia.org/wp-content/uploads/2021/04/Soham-Agarwal-Pradeep-Chauhan-Underwater-Communication-Cables-Part-1.pdf.

27 Deka, Bidisha. "Securing the Bay: Undersea cable security in India's Bay of Bengal strategy Introduction." CENJOWS. July 28, 2025. https://cenjows.in/securing-the-bay-underseas-cable-security-in-indias-bay-of-bengal-strategy-introduction/#:~:text=Famously%20referred%20to%20as%20%E2%80%98submarine%20cables%E2%80%99%2C%20these%20fibre-optic,national%20security%2C%20making%20their%20protection%20and%20reliability%20crucial.3

28 Op. cit. note no.10.

12

Translating India's Maritime Trade Strategy for the Indian Ocean Region: Addressing Vulnerabilities and Building Resilience

Dr. Richa Srimal and Dr. Shishir Shrotriya

> "*Ocean health is a moral imperative, a business imperative and a matter of global and national security. It should be recognized as a vital building block of peace and prosperity.*"[1]
>
> —H.M. Queen Noor of the Hashemite Kingdom of Jordan

The Indian Ocean region has been significant trade entity for centuries. Covering about 74 million square kilometres—roughly 20 per cent of the world's ocean area—the Indian Ocean ranks as the third-largest ocean, after the Pacific and the Atlantic Ocean. Bounded by Asia to the north, Africa to the west, Indochina to the east, and Antarctica to the south[2], the region is home to thirty-three nations and 2.9 billion people[3], representing 36 per cent of the global population. The Indian Ocean Rim Association (IORA) GDP has grown from USD 9.21 trillion in 2015 to USD 13.18 trillion in 2022, registering a CAGR of 5.26 per cent. Thus, it is a significant area for global trade and economic activity.[4] The region contains three key Sea Lanes of Communication (SLOCs) essential for trade and energy security connecting countries across West to East.[5]

India, the United States, France, Australia, the United Kingdom, and Japan form the traditional players of the region as they have a long history of diplomatic, economic, development, and military engagement throughout the Indian Ocean. Whereas, China, the UAE, Saudi Arabia, Türkiye, and Russia are the key emerging players in the region owing to their growing investments and evolving partnerships with the traditional states in the region.[6] [Figure 1]

Figure 1: The Indian Ocean Region-Countries and the Choke Points

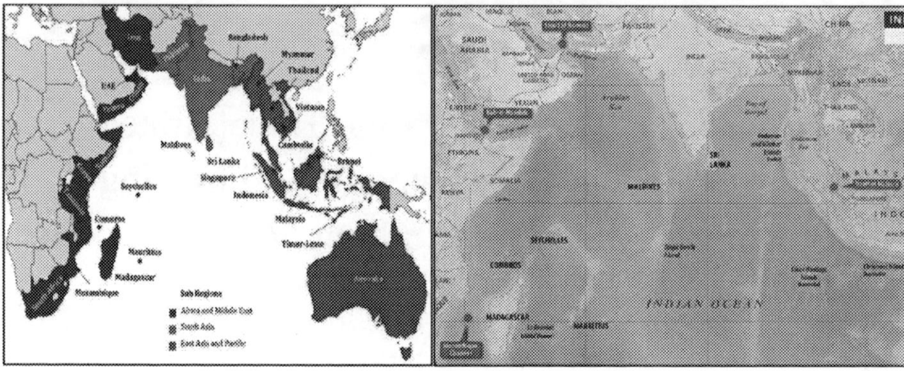

Source: "India and Indian Ocean Region." Lotus Arise. January 26, 2023. https://lotusarise.com/india-and-indian-ocean-region-upsc/

This region has emerged as the fulcrum of global trade, international powerplay and energy transfer. It has attracted a lot of global attention owing to presence of a vast, densely populated littoral with some of the fastest growing economies of the world including India, Australia, Singapore, Iran and South Africa. The Indian Ocean is rich in natural resources, including seabed deposits of nickel, cobalt, iron, manganese, copper, zinc, silver, and gold. Its coastal sediments also contain titanium, zirconium, tin, and other valuable minerals, along with rare earth elements.[7] It accounts for almost 15 per cent of the world's total fishing and transports 75 per cent of the world's maritime trade and 50 per cent of daily global oil consumption.[8] This region also estimates to have three-quarters of global oil reserves, iron, and tin. Around 80 per cent of the world's maritime oil and 9.84 billion tonnes of cargo pass through the Indian Ocean region annually. The region produces a combined total of USD 1 trillion in goods and services and intra-IORA trade is billed around USD 800 billion.[9]

Also, referred to as 'sea of stability', Indian Ocean serves as a vital link between the Middle East, Africa, and East Asia with Europe and the Americas, and is the world's busiest maritime trade corridor with four key maritime chokepoints—the Suez Canal, Bab-el-Mandeb, Strait of Hormuz, and Strait of Malacca.[10] Every day, these choke points provide transit to over 36 million barrels of oil, about 40 per cent of global oil production.[11] Almost 90,000 vessels, carrying 9.84 billion tonnes of cargo, travel every year through the Indian Ocean and move through its choke points for destinations in Africa, Asia, and Europe.[12] Unlike the Atlantic and Pacific regions, intra-regional trade within the Indian Ocean accounts for only about 20 per cent of total commerce, while nearly 80 per cent is extra-regional, such as crude oil exports to Europe, the United States, and Japan.[13]

Mineral products are the number-one export and number-two import commodity in the region. The mineral products category includes all mineral fuels, lubricants, and related materials that are derived from coal, such as coal briquettes, petroleum, and petroleum products. [Figure 2] This region is critical for movement of liquid energy as almost 65 per cent of the world's oil reserves belong to ten of the Indian Ocean's littoral states. For instance, approximately 80 per cent of China's and India's oil imports move through this region from the Arabian Gulf.[14]

Passage of these primary and intermediate goods across the Indian Ocean is crucial to maintain the industrial and technological value chains. As Asia's industrial base continues to expand, demand for these resources is expected to remain strong, further enhancing the strategic relevance of the region's trade routes and chokepoints.[15] Any disruption in maritime trade within the Indian Ocean Region can create critical bottlenecks, effectively choke global supply chains and impact international commerce.

Figure 2: Major Commodities Traded through IOR (2020)

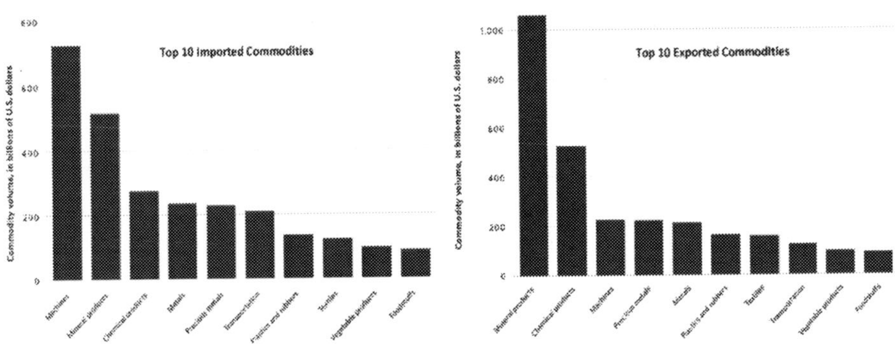

Source: Baruah, Darshana M., Nitya Labh, and Jessica Greely. "Mapping the Indian Ocean Region." Carnegie Endowment for International Peace. 2023. https://carnegieendowment.org/research/2023/06/mapping-the-indian-ocean-region?lang=en.

The New-Age Supply Chain Challenges in IOR

The Indian Ocean Region (IOR) is today exposed to diverse maritime threats, including smuggling, terrorism, sea robberies, human and drug trafficking, illegal fishing, arms and wildlife trade, and climate-related risks. Extremists use regional sea routes for illicit trade and illegal businesses. Piracy, particularly around the Malacca Strait and the Horn of Africa, continues to endanger maritime security. A spectrum of new-age threats have evolved in the present digital and politically vulnerable times, creating a big concern for the member countries as these create

- **Sea Route disruptions**: The unrest mushrooming across various countries, like, Israel-Iran, Russia-Ukraine, India and its neighbouring states have highly affected the maritime trade rhythm. Major sea routes like Red Sea route, Suez Canal and the Bab-el-Mandeb Strait, have been disrupted leading to heavy losses to the trading community. Notably, 12 per cent of global trade, valued at over USD 01 trillion, encompassing 30 per cent of global container traffic, traversed through the Red Sea annually.[16]

  The Red Sea route facilitated 8 per cent of the global grain trade and also handled 40 per cent of the Asia-Europe trade, encompassing various goods such as food products, palm oil, grains, oil, diesel, and containerised items. The Suez Canal alone witnessed the passage of 17,000 ships, contributing to 10 per cent of global trade, and more than 1 million barrels of crude oil daily. Major ports along the Red Sea including Egypt, Saudi Arabia, and Yemen, served as crucial hubs for loading and unloading cargo, warranting a smooth international trade flow. Thus, security and stability of this region have been a paramount concern for nations.[17] Major shipping companies started avoiding the route. The lengthening of supplier delivery times and rerouting of ships around Africa's Cape of Good Hope leading to a 30 per cent increase in transit times, and this implied an approximately 9 per cent reduction in effective global container shipping capacity.[18] The economic ramifications have been threatening for the global supply chain.[19] Delivery schedules got affected by re-routing, generally showing delays in the shipments.[20]

  For India and other Indian Ocean littoral states like Indonesia, Kenya and Bangladesh, the fallout includes rising freight costs, delayed imports and inflationary pressure on essentials. Island nations such as Seychelles and Mauritius face severe supply insecurities threatening economic and social stability.[21] India is heavily reliant on the Red Sea route through the Suez Canal for its trade with Europe, North America, North Africa and the Middle East. According to CRISIL Ratings, these regions made up about 50 per cent of India's INR 18 trillion (USD 217 billion) exports and 30 per cent of its INR 17 trillion (USD 205 billion) imports in FY 2023. Shipment delays of 21–28 days caused due to disruption impacted the export earnings by around 6.8 per cent.[22]

- **Trade corridor plans:** IOR members planned- US-backed trade route initiative IMEC (The India–Middle East–Europe Corridor) for addressing supply chain resilience. The corridor was expected to increase efficiencies, reduce costs, enhance economic unity, generate jobs, and lower greenhouse gas emissions—resulting in a transformative integration of Asia, Europe and the Middle East. But following Israel-Iran-Gaza conflict the, the corridor now faces insurmountable political and infrastructural obstacles. The UAE, Saudi Arabia, and Jordan – all formal stakeholders in IMEC –are facing mounting public pressure against any cooperation with the occupation state.[23]
- **Piracy and Maritime Terrorism**: One of the persistent maritime security challenges in the Indian Ocean Region is piracy, particularly near Somalia in the Horn of Africa. Somali pirates have long targeted merchant vessels, seizing ships and crews for ransom, disrupting maritime trade. According to the Information Fusion Centre–Indian Ocean Region (IFC-IOR), piracy and armed robbery cases rose to 194 in 2023, up 20 per cent from 161 in 2022, with monthly incidents increasing from 13 to 16. This escalation has raised safety concerns and disrupted freight movement. After the October 2023 Israel–Hamas conflict, Houthi rebels also began attacking merchant ships in the southern Red Sea, endangering vessels passing through key routes like the Suez Canal and Bab-el-Mandeb Strait.[24]
- **Environmental concerns:** Illegal, unreported, and unregulated (IUU) fishing poses a growing threat to trade and sustainability in the Indian Ocean. Foreign trawlers intruding into India's Exclusive Economic

Figure 3: Maritime Incidents in Western Indian Ocean

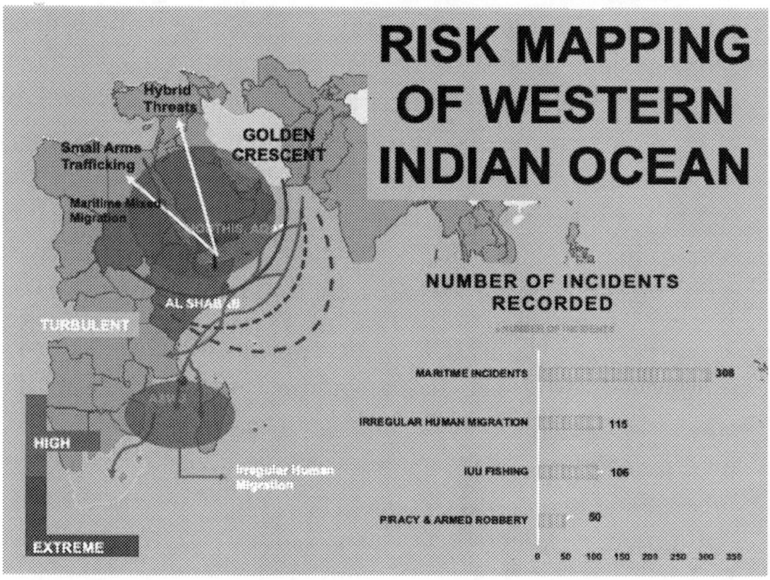

Source: Khan, Anum. "Data As A Facilitator In Maritime Risk Profiling Of The Western Indian Ocean (WIO)". National Maritime Foundation. April 21, 2024. https://maritimeindia.org/data-as-a-facilitator-in-maritime-risk-profiling-of-the-western-indian-ocean-wio/

Zone cause overfishing, biodiversity loss, and economic hardship for coastal communities. Rising sea levels and frequent cyclones disrupt trade routes and displace populations, especially in vulnerable nations like the Maldives and Bangladesh. These challenges underscore the urgent need for ethical, green, and sustainable maritime practices to protect regional trade and livelihoods.[25]

- **Increasing influence of China:** China has expanded its presence in the IOR to secure energy and trade routes, heightening competition over vital Sea Lines of Communication (SLOCs) and chokepoints. Through its "String of Pearls" strategy, China has established footholds in Pakistan, Sri Lanka, Myanmar, Bangladesh, and several island nations.[26] China's Maritime Silk Road, a part of the Belt and Road Initiative (BRI), is enhancing its naval presence in the Indian Ocean, leading to a security dilemma for India. Growing US–China rivalry in the Indian Ocean has fuelled political divisions within coastal states, disrupting regional cooperation and trade flows. Chinese-funded projects like Sri Lanka's Hambantota Port and infrastructure deals in the Maldives have stirred domestic controversy, while alliances such as the QUAD, may further deepen polarization if progressed primarily towards Defence cooperation. These tensions have complicated shipping logistics, raised insurance costs, and weakened maritime supply-chain stability.[27]

- **Weak Regional Mechanisms**: The Indian Ocean Region includes various groupings and forums like IORA, Indian Ocean Naval Symposium (IONS), Bay of Bengal Initiative for Multi-Sectoral Technical and Economic Cooperation (BIMSTEC), and South Asian Association for Regional Cooperation (SAARC), which aim to enhance regional cooperation, economic development, maritime security, and environmental sustainability. IORA struggles with funding and institutional gaps, limiting its impact, while BIMSTEC faces setbacks due to India-Bangladesh Teesta water disputes and Myanmar's political crisis.[28]

The evolving new-age threats across IOR signal a turning point demanding a deeper re-evaluation of regional resilience, cooperative strategies and the evolving meaning of maritime security today.

India and IOR

India has a historic relevance in the Indian Ocean region. The Indian Ocean, commonly referred to as the "*Hind Mahasagar*," takes its name from the historical and cultural influence that India has long exerted over the nations in the region.[29] Covering 11098 kilometres of coastline and a strategic location, India has a crucial role in shaping the geopolitical and economic landscape of the Indian Ocean Region. India has an Exclusive Economic Zone (EEZ) of over 2.37 million square kilometre making India a strategic nation in the region.

The Indian Ocean serves as a critical conduit for India's trade and energy supply chains. India's 95 per cent of trade by volume and 74 per cent by value, travels via Indian Ocean. It also supports key maritime sectors such as shipping, fisheries, and aquaculture, which are critical for livelihoods and exports. The Indian Ocean is vital to India's trade and energy security, as much of the country's commerce and oil imports transit through its waters. A large share of India's energy supply depends on maritime routes, around 93 per cent of offshore oil production and petroleum exports are seaborne. Moreover, India ranks as the world's fourth-largest importer of liquefied natural gas (LNG), with about 45 per cent of these imports arriving by sea.[30]

Being the founding member of the IORA and as the largest import and export economy in the IOR, followed by Singapore, Malaysia, Australia, and Thailand, India's maritime presence is indispensable to the region's economic vitality.[31] [Figure 4]

To take advantage of its strategic position, long coastline, increasing maritime traffic and the escalating sea-power, India created a detailed policy framework to build its presence strong in IOR. A number of initiatives to enhance the military, economic and security backup in the region were introduced by Government from time to time. The basic premise of these policies was to enhance trade, security and co-operation among the members of the region.

Figure 4: Trade Volumes of Countries in IOR (2020)

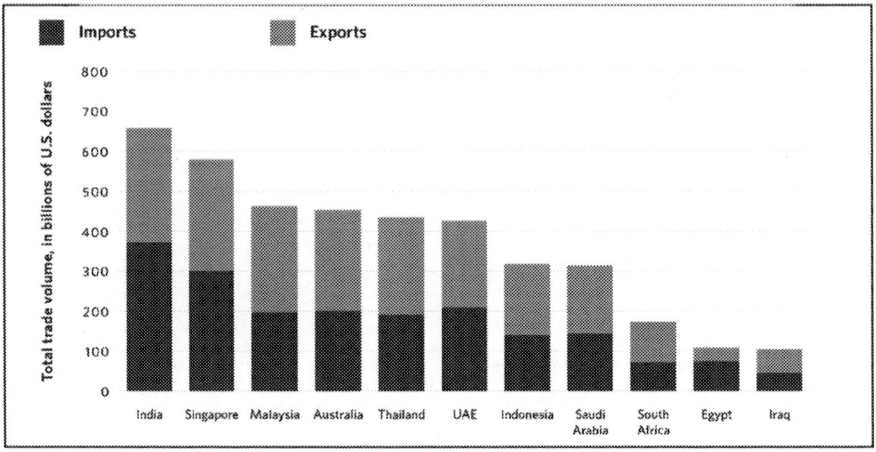

Source: Baruah, Darshana M., Nitya Labh, and Jessica Greely. "Mapping the Indian Ocean Region." Carnegie Endowment for International Peace. 2023. https://carnegieendowment.org/research/2023/06/mapping-the-indian-ocean-region?lang=en.

In 2015, India unveiled her strategic vision for the Indian Ocean i.e. Security and Growth for All in the Region (SAGAR). It was an increasing recognition of the importance of maritime security, maritime commons and cooperation. Through SAGAR, India sought to deepen economic and security cooperation with its maritime neighbours and assist in building their maritime security capabilities along with promoting blue economy. For this, India focused on cooperating on the exchange of information, coastal surveillance, building of infrastructure and strengthening their capabilities. Furthermore, through the doctrine, India also sought to safeguard her national interests and ensure that the IOR remains inclusive, collaborative and in consonance with the international laws.

Despite all the strengths India possesses in the region, its capacities are still limited. With series of new security, geo-political, environmental and piracy challenges evolving in the region, there is a pressing need for the nation to become more forward-leaning in order to create supply chain resilience.

India's Strategies to Build Value Chain Resilience

- **India's Maritime Vision 2030**

  India's Maritime India Vision 2030 (MIV 2030) outlines a long-term strategy to enhance the nation's maritime trade and logistics network. The plan includes over 150 developmental projects with an estimated investment of INR 3–3.5 lakh crore, complemented by a INR 69,725 crore initiative to boost shipbuilding. Its objectives include modernising ports, increasing cargo-handling capacity, and improving inland waterway transport. Over the past decade, port capacity and cargo volumes have nearly doubled, while vessel turnaround times have significantly improved. In FY 2024-25, major ports handled about 855 million tonnes of cargo, marking a steady rise from 819 million tonnes the previous year. Growth in Indian-flagged vessels, coastal shipping, and the seafarer workforce further illustrates India's strengthening role in global maritime trade and supply chains. The SAGARMALA Programme, central to MIV 2030, targets 840 projects worth Rs 5.8 lakh crore by 2035 to cut logistics costs and generate jobs. The government has also outlined a long-term Maritime Amrit Kaal Vision 2047, with nearly Rs 80 lakh crore earmarked for ports, shipbuilding, green shipping, and inland waterways.[32]

- **Making India a Shipping Hub**

  The Government of India aims to position the country as a major shipping and shipbuilding hub in the Indian Ocean Region, attracting global investment and enhancing maritime dominance. In September 2025, new reform schemes worth INR 69,725 crore were launched to strengthen the sector. Key measures include a Shipbuilding Financial Assistance Scheme (INR 24,736 crore), the National Shipbuilding Mission and Maritime Development Fund (INR 25,000 crore), and a Shipbuilding Development Scheme (INR 19,989 crore) offering capital and risk support. Granting infrastructure status to large vessels further encourages domestic production. Collectively, these reforms aim to modernize infrastructure, expand capacity, and enhance India's competitiveness in global maritime trade.[33] Vizhinjam Port, a transshipment port developed in Kerala, is an impressive initiative towards creating India a shipping hub of the IOR.[34]

- **Geopolitical and Strategic Co-operation**

  India seeks to balance China's expanding naval footprint and infrastructure influence in the Indian Ocean Region by reinforcing regional stability and cooperation. Through its SAGAR vision and the Indo-Pacific Oceans Initiative, India promotes inclusive maritime growth and security. Active engagement in QUAD, IORA, BIMSTEC, and ASEAN underscores its commitment to collaborative regional governance. Strengthening strategic and economic partnerships with nations such as Oman, the Maldives, and the Seychelles further deepens India's maritime presence, enhances connectivity, and consolidates its leadership role in ensuring a stable and secure Indian Ocean. [Figure 5] India prioritizes its regional neighbours in its foreign policy and aims to maintain stability and security in the region, despite the influence of China. This approach is guided by the "Neighbourhood First" policy, which includes two of its maritime neighbours—Sri Lanka and Maldives—in the South Asia-Indian Ocean Region.[35]

Figure 5: India in the IOR

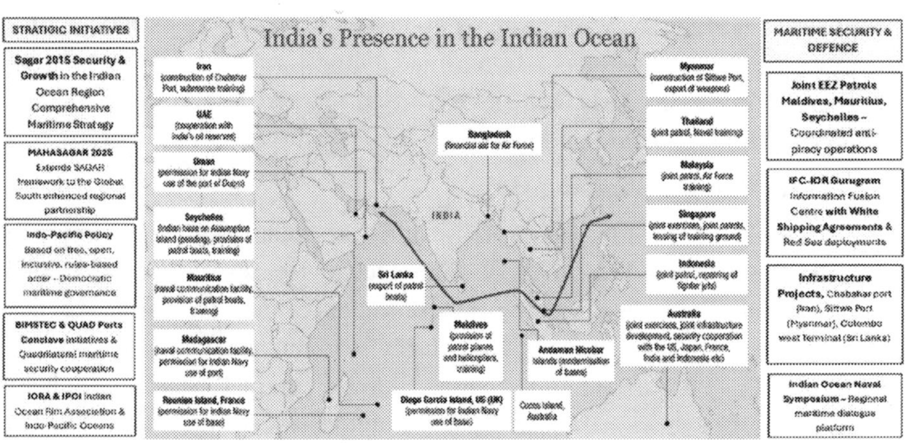

Source: Adapted by Author from "India's Maritime Security Strategy - Drishti IAS", https://www.drishtiias.com/current-affairs-news-analysis-editorials/news-editorials/2020-07-10

- **From SAGAR to MAHASAGAR**

  In March 2025, Prime Minister Narendra Modi expanded India's maritime vision from SAGAR to MAHASAGAR (Mutual and Holistic Advancement of Security and Growth for All in the Region), highlighting the Global South's role in the Indian Ocean. The first MAHASAGAR session, hosted by the Indian Navy, gathered leaders from ten IOR nations to promote collective maritime security. Through the Africa-India Key Maritime Engagement (AIKEYME) and participation of INS Chennai and INS Kesari, India strengthened cooperation with African and South Asian partners, advancing a unified, resilient, and inclusive maritime framework for regional trade and security.[36]

- **Enabling Legislative Reforms**

  The Indian Ports Bill, 2025, replaces the century-old Indian Ports Act, 1908 with a modern legal framework designed to align India's port governance with international standards. It mandates streamlined procedures, digitalisation of operations and transparent tariffs to improve the ease of doing business. The Act also introduces a consultative central-state structure through the Maritime State Development Council and empowers State Maritime Boards, thereby aiming to position India as a globally competitive maritime hub by optimising coastline utilisation, waste management, sustainable operations and trade-related logistics.[37]

  India's new maritime legislation, especially the Bills of Lading Bill, 2025 and the Carriage of Goods by Sea Bill, 2025, modernises decades-old shipping laws to bring them into line with international norms. These reforms simplify documentation like bills of lading, clarify carrier and consignee liabilities, and permit digitalisation of shipping records. By replacing colonial-era statutes and enabling clearer, more efficient processes, the laws are designed to reduce delays, lower legal risk and transaction costs, and make India's maritime trade and supply-chains more competitive and streamlined.[38]

- **Investments in International Ports**

  India is enhancing its economic and strategic presence in the Indian Ocean by investing heavily in infrastructure and connectivity projects. Key initiatives such as the Chabahar Port in Iran and the Sittwe Port in Myanmar aim to boost regional trade and strengthen supply-chain links.

Collaborations with Japan and ASEAN on island development and smart port projects further reinforce maritime logistics and sustainability.[39]

- **Digitalisation**

  India's digitalisation initiatives such as MAITRI (Master Application for International Trade and Regulatory Interface) are being designed to integrate trade portals to create a seamless, paperless Virtual Trade Corridors (VTC). Such could streamline export-import (EXIM) and trade harmonization processes by enabling real-time data exchange, improving logistics, and reducing processing times through the use of advanced digital technologies.

Systems Approach to Mutual Growth and Prosperity

India is marching forward to be the power centre and trade magnet of the Indian Ocean region. But focusing on creating a resilient supply chain involves much more than only policy initiatives. It involves a collective approach where all the stake holders including the Government, Business entities, Ports and Shipping industry and the researchers need to work together to make the supply chains sustainable and robust.

- To enhance supply chain resilience and maritime security in the IOR, India should adopt a multi-dimensional strategy. At first, we must continue to diversify maritime routes by enabling logistical efficiencies, beyond traditional passages such as the Red Sea and the Cape of Good Hope to sustain uninterrupted shipping operations amid geopolitical or environmental disruptions. Concurrently, India should operationalize new multi-modal trade corridors, including initiatives similar to the India–Middle East–Europe Corridor (IMEC) and International North South Transport Corridor (INSTC), to strengthen transregional connectivity.
- Strategic investments in international ports and logistics infrastructure are a must, particularly across the eastern seaboard, to balance China's growing maritime influence. Similarly, expanding bilateral and multilateral trade agreements, including Free Trade Agreements (FTAs) within the IOR, would promote deeper intra-regional integration. Advancing digital transformation of the maritime sector, through initiatives such as MAITRI, Electronic Bills of Lading and Blockchain-

enabled logistics systems, will enhance transparency and operational efficiency.

- The success of Indian start-ups can strengthen her role as an enabler in the IOR for economic growth, port-led industrialisation, and technological innovation. India needs to focus on smaller nations in the IOR with frugal grassroot-level innovations by Indian industry and start-ups with their technology-led economic cooperation and contributions for regional prosperity and the sustainable Blue-economy.
- Sustainability is not just a priority; it is embedded at the core of India's maritime strategy. India's ocean resources offer immense opportunities in fisheries, tourism, marine biotechnology, renewable energy, and logistics. Our technology-led Blue Economy initiatives can unlock the full potential of smaller island states in the IOR, while maintaining ecological integrity.
- India's maritime doctrines have positioned the country as a net security provider. India's leadership fosters trust and cooperation, reducing the risk of conflicts and enhancing collective prosperity. India's Global South advocacy, and the transition to MAHASAGAR highlight India's ambition to lead the Global South, addressing shared challenges like climate change and economic disparity.
- India has actively contributed to building the institutional, financial, legal and infrastructural frameworks for developing countries. India's role in Capacity building for the Global South in the IOR, in the coming decades can be a big enabler for the region's growth.
- Finally, India should intensify her efforts towards larger participation of the countries in the IOR into the global economy value chain, with increased manufacturing and integration of high-tech and finished products. India's will have to further accelerate regional integration and act as a cooperative force multiplier, through regional mechanisms such as IORA, BIMSTEC, IONS and IPOI, emphasizing logistics harmonization, maritime security, and joint disaster-response frameworks to ensure sustainable and resilient supply chains across the region.

As the famous maritime strategist, Admiral Alfred Thayer Mahan aptly has observed, "Whoever controls the Indian Ocean will dominate Asia; the destiny of the world will be decided on its waters."[40] The IOR indeed represents the strategic and economic centre of gravity in contemporary geopolitics. For India, maintaining a robust maritime presence is essential not only for securing trade routes but also for reinforcing its position as a regional logistics and supply-chain hub. By combining infrastructure development, technological innovation, and strategic diplomacy, India can transform the IOR into a space of stability, sustainable growth, and resilient global connectivity—cementing its role as a pivotal maritime power in the twenty-first century.

India's initiatives in the IOR, guided by the SAGAR doctrine have been instrumental in establishing India as a key maritime power in the Indian Ocean region, promoting security, economic growth, and regional cooperation. Its integration with India's Indo-Pacific strategy has strengthened partnerships, enhanced trade networks, and addressed critical challenges like piracy, climate change, and disaster preparedness. The recent evolution into MAHASAGAR in 2025 reflects India's commitment to adapting its maritime vision to encompass the Global South, ensuring continued relevance in a changing geopolitical landscape. Through SAGAR and MAHASAGAR, India not only advances her strategic interests but also contributes to the collective well-being of nations connected through the seas, fostering a systems approach for a stable, sustainable and prosperous maritime ecosystem.

NOTES

1 "Quotes on the Future of Our Ocean from Queen Noor of Jordan, Marc Benioff and More." World Economic Forum. June 2, 2020. https://www.weforum.org/stories/2020/06/quotes-ocean-future-environment-climate-change/.

2 Chaturvedi, S. "Indian Ocean." International Encyclopaedia of Human Geography. July 8, 2009. https://doi.org/10.1016/B978-008044910-4.00287-X.

3 Baruah, Darshana M., Nitya Labh, and Jessica Greely. "Mapping the Indian Ocean Region." Carnegie Endowment for International Peace. 2023. https://carnegieendowment.org/research/2023/06/mapping-the-indian-ocean-region?lang=en.

4 "World Development Index," World Bank. https://data.worldbank.org/

5 "India and Indian Ocean Region." LotusArise. January 26, 2023. https://lotusarise.com/india-and-indian-ocean-region-upsc/.

6 Ibid.

7 Jaishankar, Dhruva. "Indian Ocean Region: A Pivot for India's Growth." Brookings Institution–India Center. September 12, 2016. https://www.brookings.edu/articles/indian-ocean-region-a-pivot-for-indias-growth/.

8 Op. cit. note no. 5.

9 Op. cit. note no. 4.

10 Op. cit. note no. 2.

11 Albert, Eleanor. "Competition in the Indian Ocean." Council on Foreign Relations. May 19, 2016, https://www.cfr.org/backgrounder/competition-indian-ocean; and Ashraf, Sajjad.

"America Seeks Partner to Contain China in the Indian Ocean." China–US Focus. July 22, 2021, https://www.chinausfocus.com/peace-security/america-seeks-partner-to-contain-china-in-the-indian-ocean.

12 "China's Maritime Silk Road Initiative: Economic Drivers and Challenges." Asia Maritime Transparency Initiative, Center for Strategic and International Studies. April 4, 2018. https://www.csis.org/analysis/chinas-maritime-silk-road-initiative-economic-drivers-and-challenges-0.

13 Op. cit. note no. 2.

14 Op. cit. note no. 3.

15 Ibid.

16 Ludwikowski, Mark R., Williams, Kevin R., and Alghazali Sally. "The Red Sea Shipping Crisis: Lessons for Importers." Reuters. February 22, 2024. https://www.reuters.com/legal/legalindustry/red-sea-shipping-crisis-lessons-importers-2024-02-21/.

17 Mukherjee, Ishasree. "The Red Sea Crisis in Global Trade." Intueri Global. February 6, 2024. https://intueriglobal.com/the-red-sea-crisis-in-global-trade/.

18 Op. cit. note no. 16.

19 Hussain, Afaq and Malik, Akhtar. "Can the IMEC Address the Red Sea Crisis? Explained." The Hindu. February 26, 2024. https://www.thehindu.com/news/international/can-the-imec-address-the-red-sea-crisis-explained/article67885961.ece.

20 "Mapping the Red Sea Attacks: How Houthi Attacks on One of the World's Main Maritime Trade Routes Have Impacted International Trade." Al Jazeera. February 22, 2024.

21 Guhathakurta, Rahul. "Quantifying the Threat to Indian Ocean Supply Chains in 2025." Indrastra. 2025. https://www.ssoar.info/ssoar/bitstream/handle/document/101765/ssoar-indrastraglobal2025-3-guhathakurta-Risk_and_Resilience_Quantifying_the.pdf?sequence=1&isAllowed=y.

22 Pradhan, Bibhudatta. "How Escalating Red Sea Crisis Poses Billions of Dollars of Risk for India." Al Jazeera. January 31, 2024. https://www.aljazeera.com/economy/2024/1/31/how-escalating-red-sea-crisis-poses-billions-of-dollars-of-risk-for-india.

23 Karan, Suleyman. "IMEC's Imperial Illusion: Why the US-Backed Trade Corridor Will Fail." The Cradle. August 5, 2025. https://thecradle.co/articles/imecs-imperial-illusion-why-the-us-backed-corridor-will-fail.

24 Raafi , Mohamed M., and Pathak, Shreesh K. "Navigating the Waters: Maritime Security Challenges and Countermeasures in the Indian Ocean Region." International Journal of Humanities Social Science and Management (IJHSSM). May 6, 2024. https://ijhssm.org/issue_dcp/Navigating per cent20the per cent20Waters per cent20 per cent20Maritime per cent20Security per cent20Challenges per cent20and per cent20Countermeasures per cent20in per cent20the per cent20Indian per cent20Ocean per cent20Region.pdf.

25 Ibid.

26 Ghosh, Prabol. "Indian Ocean Dynamics: An Indian Perspective." East Asia Forum. April 5, 2011. https://eastasiaforum.org/2011/04/05/indian-ocean-dynamics-an-indian-perspective/.

27 White, Joshua T. "China's Indian Ocean Ambitions: Investment, Influence, and Military Advantage." Brookings Institution. June 2020. https://www.brookings.edu/wp-content/uploads/2020/06/FP_20200615_chinas_indian_ocean_ambitions_white-1.pdf.

28 "Indian Ocean Region & India's Path to Maritime Leadership." PMF IAS. 2025. https://

www.pmfias.com/indian-ocean-region/.

29 Ram, Madhav. "What India Needs to Do in the Indian Ocean." The Indian Express. February 15, 2025. https://indianexpress.com/article/opinion/columns/what-india-needs-to-do-in-the-indian-ocean-9836874/.

30 Chauhan, Anu. "India's Strategic Position in the Indian Ocean: Geopolitical Significance, Challenges, and Opportunities." Nickeled & Dimed. April 14, 2024. https://nickledanddimed.com/2024/04/14/indias-strategic-position-in-the-indian-ocean-geopolitical-significance-challenges-and-opportunities/.

31 Op. cit. note no. 3.

32 "Maritime Sector Drives India's Economic Surge as 95 per cent of Trade Moves Through Sea Routes." *The Economic Times*. October 26, 2025. https://economictimes.indiatimes.com/news/economy/indicators/maritime-sector-drives-indias-economic-surge-as-95-of-trade-moves-through-sea-routes/articleshow/124825829.cms.

33 "Setting Sail: India's Shipbuilding Revival." Press Information Bureau. October 14, 2025. https://www.pib.gov.in/PressNoteDetails.aspx?id=155540&NoteId=155540&ModuleId=3#:~:text=Conclusion:.

34 Maritime Hub: On the Vizhinjam Port." The Hindu. May 6, 2025. https://www.thehindu.com/opinion/editorial/maritime-hub-on-the-vizhinjam-port/article69537588.ece.

35 Op. cit. note no. 30.

36 "Prime Minister Shri Narendra Modi Announced Vision MAHASAGAR – 'Mutual and Holistic Advancement for Security and Growth Across Regions' for the Global South in Mauritius." Ministry of External Affairs. March 12, 2025. https://www.mea.gov.in/newsdetail1.htm?13355/.

37 Rathore, Anamika and Sharma, Gaurav. "Indian Ports Act 2025 – Transforming India's Maritime Landscape." Lawrbit. August 26, 2025. https://www.lawrbit.com/article/indian-ports-act-2025/.

38 Parashar, Vaishnavi. "Lok Sabha Passes Bills of Lading Bill 2025, Revamps 169-Year-Old Shipping Law." *India Today*. March 13, 2025. https://www.indiatoday.in/amp/information/story/lok-sabha-passes-bills-of-lading-bill-2025-revamps-169-year-old-shipping-law-2693025-2025-03-13.

39 "Building a Secure and Prosperous Indian Ocean Region." Drishti IAS. February 17, 2025. https://www-drishtiias-com.translate.goog/hindi/daily-updates/daily-news-editorials/building-a-secure-and-prosperous-indian-ocean-region?_x_tr_sl=hi&_x_tr_tl=en&_x_tr_hl=en&_x_tr_pto=sc.

40 Op. cit. note no. 26.

13

Global Models Addressing IUU Fishing and Their Applicability in the Indian Ocean Region for Sustainable Fishing

Dr. Pooja Bhatt

Introduction

Several governance models addressing Illegal, Unreported, and Unregulated (IUU) fishing have emerged, highlighting the importance of the issue at national, regional, and global levels. The multifaceted impact of IUU fishing manifests itself in national security, such as food and economic security, as well as biodiversity. Since the 1950s, sustainable fisheries governance has evolved to address the overexploitation of fish stocks, with international legal frameworks such as United Nations Convention on the Law of the Sea (UNCLOS) 1982 and the FAO's Port State Measures Agreement (PSMA) supporting cooperative efforts.[1]

Despite these advances, IUU fishing continues to account for up to 20 per cent of global seafood catches, causing billions in economic losses and threatening the livelihoods of coastal communities.[2] The Indian Ocean Region (IOR), characterised by diverse coastal states and extensive high seas, faces unique challenges due to limited enforcement capacity and complex jurisdictional issues.[3]

IUU fishing exacerbates the challenges of humanity. Globally, IUU fishing undermines sustainable fishing practices, leading to overfishing, depletion of fish stocks, and disruption of the marine ecological balance. It significantly impacts the environment and has a cascading impact on coastal communities, challenging their food and economic security. Moreover, IUU fishing boats are increasingly linked to human rights abuses, drug and human trafficking, and other illicit activities, thereby challenging the security of states. Underdeveloped and developing economies are acutely impacted, as fisheries provide vital employment and protein sources for millions of people.

The growth in IUU fishing in recent years can be attributed to various reasons. First, an increasing population has driven the need for more food sources, and fisheries provide a readily available source of protein to millions. Second, technological innovation has enabled fishermen to venture farther into the seas, using larger vessels and more advanced technologies to catch a greater variety of species. This has led to fisheries becoming an unorganised industry. Fishing fleets from various coastal states, such as China, Vietnam, and Indonesia, are operating as industries on the high seas.[4] Since the high seas are open to all under UNCLOS, fishing communities often exploit weak and often non-existent legal frameworks and enforcement mechanisms. Lastly, the emerging issues of maritime crimes and complex laws around vessel registrations and operations add to the complex nature of IUU fishing. The rising geopolitical tensions and insufficient international cooperation have further propelled rampant illegal fishing activities globally.

The complexity and scale of these illegal activities are exacerbated by inadequate enforcement, vast maritime zones, and transnational criminal links, which make IUU fishing a formidable challenge that transcends national boundaries. Without decisive, coordinated action, the social, economic, and environmental consequences of unchecked IUU fishing will further endanger regional prosperity and the long-term viability of marine resources in the Indian Ocean. The following section further discusses the existing debates on various models addressing IUU fishing.

Institutions and Scope

The persistence of IUU fishing highlights the significant problem of the inadequacy of current global and regional governance mechanisms in effectively deterring and managing these activities independently.[5] On the one hand, international instruments such as Regional Fisheries Management Organisation (RFMOs) and the PSMA provide frameworks for cooperation; on the other, some gaps remain in enforcement, information sharing, and technological integration.[6] Moreover, existing studies indicate that the securitisation of the maritime commons and geopolitical tensions in regions such as the Indian Ocean, exacerbate reluctance among states to cooperate fully, undermining collective action.[7] Various scholars also provide contrasting perspectives on whether enhanced legal frameworks or technological innovations offer more promise in addressing the illegal fishing problem; yet, both approaches face limitations due to a lack of robust regional collaboration.[8] Apart from food and economic security, newer dimensions of security threats from IUU fishing boats, including espionage, trafficking, etc., have added to the perils of illegal fishing.[9] Needless to say, a failure to address these gaps risks the continued depletion of fish stocks and the destabilisation of regional maritime security.[10]

This study provides a conceptual overview of existing sustainable fisheries governance, international legal cooperation, and technological monitoring systems to analyse global models for combating IUU fishing. Sustainable governance is largely defined as the coordinated legal, social, and economic arrangements that ensure the long-term viability of fishery resources.[11] It also surveys multilateral agreements and RFMOs, which facilitate compliance and enforcement for their role and scope.[12] Studies highlight that technological monitoring, such as vessel tracking and electronic reporting systems, enhances transparency and detection.[13] This framework guides the assessment of model applicability within the Indian Ocean context.

By synthesising legal, institutional, and technological approaches, this study aims to identify effective strategies and highlight regional challenges, thereby contributing to improved governance and sustainable fisheries management in the IOR. This review fills a critical gap by aligning global best practices with regional realities, supporting policy development and cooperative enforcement.

Existing Governance Models

Presently, the issue of IUU fishing has been addressed by various methods, ranging from legal conventions and institutional frameworks to monitoring and surveillance architectures, at domestic, regional, and global levels. These methods can be broadly classified as governance models based on their operational features. Many of the models also share overlapping characteristics, such as the Port States Measures Act, a binding treaty that addresses IUU fishing through inspections at ports, which is a unique strength of the model and makes it more suitable for adoption both at the domestic and regional levels. Since most models are implemented under existing international laws and conventions, such as UNCLOS, it would be easier and more effective for states to adopt them and harmonise their processes and operations. This will also avoid duplication of efforts and resources, which remain a crucial concern for several underdeveloped and developing states in the IOR.

The table below classifies and provides the various governance models based on their key features:

Model Type	Key Feature	Examples
Legal, Institutional	Treaties/ Conventions, RFMOs National Laws	UNCLOS, PSMA, EU, Indonesia
Port or Market Access-Based	Uses Traceability Through Port Inspections, Bans And Sanctions	PSMA, EU, US
MCS and Technology-Based	Focus On Detection Using MDA, VMS, AIS Etc	RPOA-IUU
Cooperative	Regional, Sub-Regional	ASEAN, Honduras-Guatemala, Belize, BOB-IGO
Criminalisation	Treated as Crime by Individual Nations or Group of Nations	Indonesia, Norway, EU
Community Engagement-Based	Voluntary Participation at Domestic Levels	
Geographical/ Area-Based	Area Based Management	Marine Protected Areas

Source: Compiled by the Author

Legal and Institutional Frameworks

At the global and regional levels, international legal instruments such as the PSMA, the International Plan of Action to Prevent, Deter and Eliminate Illegal, Unreported and Unregulated Fishing (IPOA-IUU)[14], and RFMO[15] mandates have established comprehensive frameworks to combat IUU fishing.[16] While these frameworks are a helpful start, several studies highlight enforcement capacity gaps, especially in developing countries and disputed maritime areas, underscoring the need for harmonised laws and stronger flag state responsibilities.[17] Another emerging issue within the illegal fishing domain is the integration of labour protection and environmental justice into fisheries governance, which relates to the socio-ecological impacts of IUU fishing.[18] Scholars have critiqued the fragmentary and discretionary nature of legal frameworks, calling for more binding and coordinated international cooperation.[19] In this regard, regional legal cooperation, particularly in the Indian Ocean and Asia/Indo-Pacific, has been identified as essential but often hindered by political and capacity challenges.[20]

Market and Port Measures

Another approach to addressing illegal fishing has been through port inspections and discouraging market access where fishing landings are likely to occur. For this reason, the PSMA is widely recognised as a cornerstone legal instrument for port state controls, with studies documenting its deterrent effect on IUU fishing through inspections and port denials.[21] The PSMA is designed to prevent IUU-caught fish from entering markets by standardising inspections and denying port access to vessels flagged for IUU fishing.

Similarly, market-based measures, including import regulations and certifications, are increasingly recognised as crucial complements to legal and enforcement efforts, as they restrict access to markets for IUU products.[22] Challenges include inconsistent implementation, reflagging to avoid port measures, and limited capacity in developing countries.[23] Studies highlight the need to integrate catch reporting, documentation, and traceability systems through technology to enhance market transparency and enforcement.[24]

Needless to say, it requires strong enforcement mechanisms to be effective. Challenges, such as reflagging and the inclusion of domestic fleets, require strengthening both foreign and domestic port controls, as well as the harmonisation of legal frameworks. This provides an opportunity to integrate the PSMA with the local maritime law enforcement agencies for more robust and effective operation.

Monitoring, Control, and Surveillance (MCS) and Technology-Based

An increasing number of studies indicate that the greater use of advanced technologies such as AI, satellite tracking, vessel monitoring systems, and electronic monitoring can enhance the detection and enforcement of IUU fishing.[25] Integration of multiple monitoring systems into intelligent platforms is proposed to overcome institutional and technical limitations. [26] Predictive models and spatial analysis technologies are now increasingly used to identify high-risk zones and to optimise surveillance efforts.[27] Capacity constraints and resource limitations in developing regions hinder the full deployment of these technologies, necessitating capacity-building initiatives.[28] Emerging technologies are also linked to improving traceability and transparency in seafood supply chains, supporting market-based controls.[29]

Criminalisation

Treating IUU fishing not merely as a regulatory violation but as a criminal offense allows for stronger legal instruments, investigative tools, and international cooperation to suppress these activities. Numerous international conventions and agreements (such as the PSMA) promote criminal sanctions and enforcement measures to deter and penalise offenders.

Some countries, like Norway and Indonesia, have been at the forefront of criminalising IUU fishing within their maritime jurisdictions. Norway has combined a stringent legal framework with active enforcement in its territorial waters and the Barents Sea, cooperating closely with neighbouring states to share intelligence and conduct joint operations. Indonesia has also toughened its legal stance, including prosecuting and even sinking vessels involved in illegal fishing in the past few years, signalling a strong commitment to addressing the IUU fishing challenge through deterrence. By establishing IUU fishing as a crime, states and regional bodies can leverage criminal justice tools such as asset seizures, criminal investigations, and international law enforcement collaboration.

Area-Based Protection Zones

This study proposes that the establishment of ecological zones, such as Marine Protected Areas (MPAs), in the IOR can address the challenge of the lack of adequate RFMOs and their scope in the region. These regionally agreed-upon MPAs will empower the protection of transboundary marine resources and help prevent the destruction of ecological resources through regional cooperation. These MPAs can complement the efforts of the Biodiversity Beyond National Jurisdiction (BBNJ) or the High Seas Treaty at the regional level. Existing regional organisations can facilitate consultation among members to establish the necessary zones based on their importance. Under this framework, national-level fisheries ministries, enforcement agencies and other related research institutions can collaborate within these MPAs for effective coordination. At the national level, these institutions can support and engage in the development of community-based cooperative approaches from a coastal development perspective, as detailed below.

Cooperative Models

Effective IUU fishing mitigation relies on strengthening regional cooperation mechanisms and capacity building, particularly in developing countries with limited resources. Interagency collaboration among UN bodies, RFMOs, and national agencies, along with multi-stakeholder involvement, is identified as a consistent enabler of effective fisheries management. Case studies from the Indian Ocean and Asia-Pacific regions emphasise the need for coordinated governance, communication platforms, and shared enforcement responsibilities to overcome fragmented efforts.

The role of regional cooperation in addressing the IUU fishing challenges cannot be understated. Studies emphasise the importance of frameworks, such as RFMOs and regional organisations like IORA, for effective IUU fishing governance in the Indian Ocean and adjacent regions.[30] However, cooperation is often challenged by geopolitical tensions, sovereignty disputes amongst neighbouring coastal states, and uneven capacities of countries.[31] Successful examples include coordinated enforcement, data sharing, and joint capacity-building projects, which improve compliance and surveillance.[32] Some studies call for new or reformed regional governance arrangements tailored to the Indian Ocean's unique ecological and political context. [33] Community participation and whole-of-society approaches are recognized as complementary to formal regional cooperation.[34]

The IUU Fishing in the Indian Ocean Context: Challenges and Opportunities

The Indian Ocean is marked by vast EEZs, overlapping claims, and diverse governance. Addressing the IUU fishing challenges is multifaceted and therefore demands a joint approach. Regional cooperation (ASEAN, RPOA-IUU, RFMOs) is vital for harmonising enforcement and sharing intelligence, while advanced MCS technologies (VMS, satellite, AI) are essential for monitoring vast and remote areas

The Indian Ocean faces unique governance complexities due to maritime disputes, geopolitical tensions, and security concerns that undermine fisheries regulation. The securitisation of fisheries issues often leads to confrontation rather than cooperation, thereby exacerbating IUU fishing risks. Studies recommend various strategies focused on improved legal frameworks and inclusive domestic governance that can enhance regional collaboration and sustainable fisheries management.[35]

The growing overlap between maritime security threats and IUU fishing necessitates an integrated policy response. IUU fishing also poses a significant transnational maritime threat impacting economic stability and regional security, especially in the Indian Ocean. The transnational impact of crimes such as drug and human trafficking and other illicit activities calls for stronger legal enforcement and inter-state collaboration.[36]

The emerging issue of human rights and labour abuse in the IUU fishing industry is also surfacing, which needs urgent attention as well. Tracing global labour abuse risks highlights the need to integrate social justice and inclusive participation into fisheries governance as well. While measures are provided by port states and RFMOs, the issue of labour exploitation needs to be addressed simultaneously, along with the need to tackle both illegal fishing.[37]

While IUU fishing has emerged as a maritime security challenge in the Indo-Pacific region in recent times, the responses to tackling it have not been sufficient. One of the reasons for the inadequate tackling of this emerging maritime challenge is the confounding semantics, the unclear role of maritime law enforcement agencies, and the lack of regulatory infrastructure both domestically and regionally.

One of the efforts to create awareness about IUU fishing has been made by the IFC-IOR in Gurugram. Its regular reports and publications mention IUU Fishing amongst other maritime crimes and incidents. It categorises the incidents of IUU fishing separately from those of poaching. In its working definitions, it uses the term 'poaching' which is an ad-hoc term. It has been understood that operationally, it is very difficult to catch/ classify Unregulated and Unreported components of IUU fishing. Only the Illegal component is caught, if at all. It notes that some vessels of a foreign country poaching in another country's waters, or that foreign-flagged vessels of the same country flout rules and regulations.

The FAO defines IUU fishing largely as illegal fishing within and outside the EEZ of the coastal state. However, operationally, the issues related to IUU fishing are multifaceted and often interlinked with other maritime crimes. This makes targeting IUU fishing difficult. On the other hand, UNODC takes a wider view of the illegal fishing from the vantage point of crimes taking place in the maritime domain, such as drugs and narcotics smuggling, human trafficking, piracy, gun running and so on.

Most of the solutions in the existing literature for addressing IUU fishing focus on strengthening the flag state's responsibility, Port State measures, and the regulatory measures of the RFMOs. It has been adequately understood that the subsidies provided by the Flag states to fishermen for their welfare are often misused for overexploiting fisheries resources within and outside the EEZ. Although the State is responsible for taking action against the culprits, which it does, it is often bound by domestic and regional constraints. Operationally, RFMOs request that the flag state take action against the culprit vessel and may place it on the black list. More often than not, the flag state releases the fishing vessel, and the owner changes the registration details to resume operations.

Similarly, to address the issue of illegal fishing, port states are required to be signatories to a US-led legal instrument that provides them with the necessary tools, such as information sharing and other technical assistance, to block the entry of illegally caught fish. While these instruments are sound, it has been observed that countries are finding it increasingly difficult to participate in such regional and international mechanisms, as there is no universally accepted definition of IUU fishing.

IUU fishing, therefore, remains a broad and abstract concept. This is especially true in the unreported and unregulated domains, which are operationally more challenging. Indeed, due to the increasing maritime domain awareness initiatives of several countries, there exists immense data to support the claims; however, there is precious little for executioners to implement on the ground, or in this case, on the seas. How to stop Unregulated and Unreported fishing? It's doable in theory, but more challenging to address on reality.

There are also perceived dual standards regarding IUU fishing by developed countries. These nations are largely concerned with IUU fishing by certain countries like China and Vietnam, or the subsidies that countries like India give to their fishermen (which are considered among the primary causes of IUU fishing). However, data provided by various agencies, including the IFC-IOR (Gurugram), IUU Fishing Index,[38] and the US National Oceanic and Atmospheric Administration (NOAA),[39] also indicates that some European countries, such as Italy and Spain, as well as Asian and Latin American nations, are known to be engaged in IUU fishing. Notably, the EU has the most stringent rules against the import of illegally caught fish.

Lastly, maritime enforcement agencies struggle to address the issues of IUU fishing and other maritime crimes beyond apprehending the perpetrators.

Needless to mention, navies largely operate within the EEZ and on the high seas, where such crimes often take place. However, by training, these forces are trained to deter the next war. Their assets, training, and so on are all aligned in that direction. While Navies and coastguards are increasingly drawn into non-traditional maritime security roles, the forces have yet to be structured accordingly.

Additionally, addressing the IUU fishing becomes even more difficult as it's a Herculean task to connect the security threat to this activity. It is more of an economic and environmental issue, rather than a maritime security issue. Fishermen, in the form of maritime militias, operating in the far seas, presents another security dimension.

Lack of definitional clarity, as well as the universal acceptance of the IUU fishing concept, are among the reasons why existing frameworks face challenges. This study suggests that raising the possibility of separating IUU fishing from poaching semantically can serve as a helpful foundational block in addressing the issues of IUU fishing. In this regard, the established practice of IFC-IOR's periodic reports and database provides a helpful starting point for developing a vessel classification framework to address the IUU fishing challenge. Once IUU fishing and poaching are established on their own merits, nations might find it easier to develop their domestic legislation and law enforcement infrastructure. However, the issue of poaching involving foreign vessels can be addressed through diplomatic and political cooperation.

Role of IOR Regional Organisations for Governance

As governance structures, the Indian Ocean Rim Association (IORA), the Bay of Bengal Initiative for Multi-Sectoral Technical and Economic Cooperation (BIMSTEC)[40] and the Bay of Bengal Inter-Governmental Organisation (BOB-IGO)[41] are organisations that play a crucial role in providing frameworks of cooperation to their member states. These bodies provide formal platforms for member states to collaborate on common challenges, including combating Illegal, Unreported, and Unregulated (IUU) fishing, which transcends national jurisdictions and requires a coordinated response.

IORA, with its broad membership spanning the Indian Ocean, has prioritised fisheries management as a key thematic area within its Blue Economy framework. The organisation facilitates dialogue, capacity building, and the sharing of best practices among member countries to enhance enforcement capabilities and sustainable resource use. These institutions promote the ratification and enforcement of international treaties, such as the FAO's PSMA, which prevents IUU vessels from landing their catch or entering ports. They assist member states in developing national legislation aligned with these frameworks.

Similarly, BIMSTEC has emerged as a regional organisation that fosters multi-sectoral cooperation among countries around the Bay of Bengal, emphasising not only economic integration but also environmental and fisheries sustainability. Through its collaboration with IORA, BIMSTEC supports joint initiatives in ocean governance and fisheries, aiming to build a cohesive regional governance architecture.

Adding to the governance models provided by the regional institutions and mechanisms requires effective enforcement mechanisms. The Indian Ocean Naval Symposium (IONS)[42] is an existing naval forum that complements these efforts by enhancing maritime security cooperation among littoral states. By promoting interoperability, information sharing, and coordinated patrols, IONS contributes to the enforcement of fisheries regulations and the deterrence of IUU fishing activities. IONS, along with regional Maritime Coordination Centres such as IFC-IOR, works toward harmonising policies, sharing intelligence, and adopting common standards for vessel monitoring, catch documentation, and sanctions, which collectively strengthen regional and sub-regional enforcement.

Conclusion

This study is a foundational step toward effective regional governance by providing a set of models addressing IUU fishing that the region can use to develop its unique approach through its existing regional organisations. A hybrid, multi-layered model combining regional cooperation, advanced monitoring, legal harmonisation, and community-based management can offer the best prospects for addressing IUU fishing in the IOR. This approach can ensure the optimal use of resources, ensure accountability for efficient results, and avoid duplication of efforts at the regional level through enhanced capacity building and capability enhancement. The study suggests standardising IUU fishing terminology and definitions across all regional organisations. Standardising terminology will enable clearer communication, harmonised policies, and unified action plans, thereby strengthening the institutional capacity of these regional bodies to comprehensively address IUU fishing.[43]

NOTES

1 Geest, van der C. "Redesigning Indian Ocean Fisheries Governance for 21st Century Sustainability". Global Policy, 8 no. 2, 227–236. 2017. https://doi.org/10.1111/1758-5899.12447; Palma-Robles, Mary Ann. "Combating IUU Fishing: International Legal Developments." Navigating Pacific Fisheries: Legal and Policy Trends in the Implementation of International Fisheries Instruments in the Western and Central Pacific Region. Wollongong, NSW, Australia: University of Wollongong, 71-103. 2009. https://ro.uow.edu.au/articles/chapter/Combating_IUU_fishing_international_legal_developments/27690975?file=50428515

2 Saccareau, T., S. Magon de la Giclais, M. Lalire, M. Atché, and A. Conchon. "Mapping Risks of IUU Fishing Using Vessel Trajectories and Species Distribution Models." One Ocean Science Congress 2025, Nice, France, June 3–6. 2025. https://doi.org/10.5194/oos2025-1167; Selig, Elizabeth R., Shinnosuke Nakayama, Colette C. C. Wabnitz, Henrik Österblom, Jessica Spijkers, Nathan A. Miller, Jan Bebbington, and Jessica L. Decker Sparks. "Revealing Global Risks of Labor Abuse and Illegal, Unreported, and Unregulated Fishing." Nature Communications, 13 no.1, 1-15. 2022. https://doi.org/10.1038/s41467-022-28916-2.

3 Pandey, S. K. "IUU Fishing and Maritime Threat: A Rise in Transnational Maritime Non-Traditional Threat to Security with Particular Reference to the Indian Ocean." International Journal of Science and Research, 12 no. 4, 1574-1578. 2023. https://doi.org/10.21275/sr23425183314; Zeleneva, I. V. "Interaction of the Indian ocean rim association members in ensuring marine security". Social'no-Politiceskie Nauki, 13 no. 6, 77–83. 2023. https://doi.org/10.33693/2223-0092-2023-13-6-77-83

4 US Congressional Reports. "China's Role in the Exploitation of Global Fisheries: Issues for Congress." Congress. 2022. https://www.congress.gov/crs-product/R47065.

5 Lim, S.S., and B.K. Jung. "Study on Improving International Cooperation Frameworks for Combating Illegal, Unreported, and Unregulated Fishing to Achieve Sustainable Use of Fishery Resources." Water, 17 no. 17, 1-16. 2025. https://www.mdpi.com/2073-4441/17/17/2518; Lobach, T. "Combating IUU Fishing: Interaction of Global and Regional Initiatives." In D. Vidas (Ed.), Law, Technology and Science for Oceans in Globalisation. Brill Academic Publishers,109–129. 2010. https://doi.org/10.1163/ej.9789004180406.i-610.35

6 Seling et al. "Revealing Global Risks of Labor Abuse and Illegal, Unreported, and Unregulated Fishing" ; Hutniczak, B., Delpeuch, C., & Leroy, A. "Intensifying the Fight Against IUU Fishing at the Regional Level". OECD Food, Agriculture and Fisheries Papers, 121, 1–54. 2019. https://doi.org/10.1787/b7b9f17d-en

7 Luo, G., & Chi, Z. "Conflicts and Challenges of Sustainable Fisheries Governance Cooperation under the Securitization of the Maritime Commons". Fishes, 8 no. 1. 2022. https://doi.org/10.3390/fishes8010001; Chen, Xidi, Qi Xu, and Lun Li. "Illegal, Unreported, and Unregulated Fishing Governance in Disputed Maritime Areas: Reflections on the International Legal Obligations of States." Fishes 8 no. 1, 36, 1-19. 2023. https://doi.org/10.3390/fishes8010036

8 Lim, S.S., and B.K. Jung. "Study on Improving International Cooperation Frameworks for Combating Illegal, Unreported, and Unregulated Fishing to Achieve Sustainable Use

of Fishery Resources." Water, 17 no. 17, 1-16. 2025. https://www.mdpi.com/2073-4441/17/17/2518

9 Bhatt, Pooja. "IUU Fishing as a National Security Threat: Revisiting India's Domestic Framework and Compliance with International Regimes." International Law Studies, U.S. Naval War College 96, 445-463. 2020. https://digital-commons.usnwc.edu/cgi/viewcontent.cgi?article=2928&context=ils;
Bisen, Anurag. "China and IUU fishing in IOR: Need for India to lead mitigation efforts". VIF. 2024. https://www.vifindia.org/article/2024/april/11/China-and-IUU-Fishing-in-IOR-Need-for-India-to-Lead-Mitigation-Efforts

10 Pandey, S. K. "IUU Fishing and Maritime Threat: A Rise in Transnational Maritime Non-Traditional Threat to Security with Particular Reference to the Indian Ocean."

11 Geest, Van der C. "Redesigning Indian Ocean Fisheries Governance for 21st Century Sustainability"; Oral, F. "Examination of the literature on SDG 14-IUU-trade and maritime security". Marine Development. 2024.

12 Lobach, T. "Combating IUU Fishing: Interaction Of Global And Regional Initiatives."

13 Lim, S.S., and B.K. Jung. "Study on Improving International Cooperation Frameworks for Combating Illegal, Unreported, and Unregulated Fishing to Achieve Sustainable Use of Fishery Resources." Water, 17 no. 17, 1-16. 2025. https://www.mdpi.com/2073-4441/17/17/2518
Faiyaz, T., and Al Arif, A. "Towards a Blue Revolution in the Bay of Bengal: Tackling Illegal, Unreported and Unregulated Fishing Through Effective Regional Cooperation". The Journal of World Investment and Trade, 23(1), 9–38. 2022. https://brill.com/view/journals/jwit/23/1/article-p9_2.xml?language=en&srsltid=AfmBOopuOu7CGHwE48rBOK0mjMy664pSz1lObo1yL0hNabpOdIL7FR0J

14 The IPOA-IUU provides as comprehensive toolbox, i.e. it is a full range of tools that are available for use in a number of different situations to combat IUU fishing. It covers flag, port, coastal and market State responsibilities, envisages broad participation and coordination among States, as well as representatives from industry, fishing communities and non-governmental organisations (NGOs) and the use of a comprehensive and integrated approach, so as to address all impacts of IUU fishing. See: https://www.fao.org/iuu-fishing/international-framework/ipoa-iuu/en/

15 RFMOs are international organisations set up to establish binding measures such as agreements or treaties for conservation and sustainable management of specific fish species, particularly those that migrate across regions or straddle multiple jurisdictions. They consist of countries with fishing interests in a given area and are open to coastal states, as well as nations with historical or potential future fishing activities in these areas. Presently, there are 17 RFMOs operating globally.

16 Lim, S.S., and B.K. Jung. "Study on Improving International Cooperation Frameworks for Combating Illegal, Unreported, and Unregulated Fishing to Achieve Sustainable Use of Fishery Resources." Water, 17 no. 17, 1-16. 2025. https://www.mdpi.com/2073-4441/17/17/2518 Lobach, T. "Combating IUU Fishing: Interaction Of Global And Regional Initiatives."

17 Chen, Xidi, Qi Xu, and Lun Li. "Illegal, Unreported, and Unregulated Fishing Governance in Disputed Maritime Areas: Reflections on the International Legal Obligations of States." ;
Pandey, S. K. "IUU Fishing and Maritime Threat: A Rise in Transnational Maritime Non-

Traditional Threat to Security with Particular Reference to the Indian Ocean."; Wei Yuan and Yen-Chiang Chang. "Curbing IUU Fishing by Enforcing the Port State Measures Agreement." 2025. https://www.preprints.org/frontend/manuscript/57213b0e6d4d91bcbc465406834e782b/download_pub

18 Wang, K. "From Fishery Resources Conservation to Labor Protection: RFMOs and the Development of Combating IUU: An Essay in Honor of Ted L. McDorman". *Ocean Development & International Law*, 55, 579–594. 2024. https://doi.org/10.1080/00908320.2024.2413610; Yuru He, Yan Li, Yanan Li and Jiangfeng Zhu. "Integration of spatial justice into navigating the combat on illegal unreported and unregulated fishing in ocean and coastal areas". Frontiers in Marine Science. 2024.

19 Luo, G., and Chi, Z. "Conflicts and Challenges of Sustainable Fisheries Governance Cooperation under the Securitization of the Maritime Commons".

20 Auld, Kathleen, Raphael Baumler, Deukhoon Peter Han, and Francis Neat. "The Collective Effort of the United Nations Specialised Agencies to Tackle the Global Problem of Illegal, Unreported and Unregulated (IUU) Fishing." Ocean & Coastal Management 243, 1-12. 2023. https://doi.org/10.1016/j.ocecoaman.2023.106720; Mallik, A. "IUU Fishing as an Evolving Threat to Southeast Asia's Maritime Security. Asia Maritime Transparency Initiative" Center for Strategic and International Studies. 2022. https://amti.csis.org/iuu-fishing-as-an-evolving-threat-to-southeast-asias-maritime-security/

21 Yuan, W., & Chang, Y. Curbing IUU Fishing by Enforcing the Port State Measures Agreement. 2025; Lobach, T. "Combating IUU Fishing: Interaction of Global and Regional Initiatives."

22 Long, T., Widjaja, S., Wirajuda, H., & Juwana, S. Approaches to Combatting Illegal, Unreported and Unregulated Fishing. 1(7), 389–391. 2020.

23 Selig et al, "Revealing Global Risks of Labor Abuse and Illegal, Unreported, and Unregulated Fishing."; Salahuddin, G., Bellefontaine, N., & Qamar, N. Polaris Journal of Maritime Research. Polaris - Journal of Maritime Research. 2023.

24 Roberson, Leslie, Gilles Hosch, Chris Wilcox, Rosa Mar Domiguez-Martinez, Glenn Sant, and Carissa Klein. "A New Seafood Import Policy for Nations to Combat Illegal Fishing." Conservation Letters 18 no. 11-8. 2025. https://doi.org/10.1111/conl.13091.

25 Saccareau, et al. "Mapping Risks of IUU Fishing Using Vessel Trajectories and Species Distribution Models."; Lim, S.S., and B.K. Jung. "Study on Improving International Cooperation Frameworks for Combating Illegal, Unreported, and Unregulated Fishing to Achieve Sustainable Use of Fishery Resources." Water, 17 no. 17, 1-16. 2025. https://www.mdpi.com/2073-4441/17/17/2518

26 Lim, S.S., and B.K. Jung. "Study on Improving International Cooperation Frameworks for Combating Illegal, Unreported, and Unregulated Fishing to Achieve Sustainable Use of Fishery Resources." Water, 17 no. 17, 1-16. 2025. https://www.mdpi.com/2073-4441/17/17/2518; Chuaysi, B., and S. Kiattisin. "Fishing Vessels Behavior Identification for Combating IUU Fishing: Enable Traceability at Sea." Wireless Personal Communications 115, 2971–2993. 2020. https://link.springer.com/article/10.1007/s11277-020-07200-w.

27 Saccareau, et al. "Mapping Risks of IUU Fishing Using Vessel Trajectories and Species Distribution Models."; Park, J., Van Osdel, J., Turner, J., Farthing, C. M., Miller, N. A., Linder, H. L., Ortuño Crespo, G., Carmine, G., & Kroodsma, D. "Tracking elusive and shifting identities of the global fishing fleet. Science Advances". 2023.

28 Neat, F., Auld, K., and Baumler, R. "Regional cooperation and capacity development are key to effective implementation of international instruments to tackle IUU fishing in developing countries." 2025.

29 Chuaysi, B., and S. Kiattisin. "Fishing Vessels Behavior Identification for Combating IUU Fishing: Enable Traceability at Sea."; Roberson, et al., "A New Seafood Import Policy for Nations to Combat Illegal Fishing."

30 Li, S. "Combating IUU fishing: an examination of interaction between China and regional fisheries management organizations". Frontiers in Marine Science. 2025.

31 Pandey, S. K. "IUU Fishing and Maritime Threat: A Rise in Transnational Maritime Non-Traditional Threat to Security with Particular Reference to the Indian Ocean."; Chen, Xidi, Qi Xu, and Lun Li. "Illegal, Unreported, and Unregulated Fishing Governance in Disputed Maritime Areas: Reflections on the International Legal Obligations of States.""; Gou, Yiping, and Cuibai Yang. "Dilemmas and Paths of International Cooperation in China's Fight against IUU Fishing Analysis." Marine Policy 155, 1-9. 2023. https://doi.org/10.1016/j.marpol.2023.105789.

32 Hutniczak, B., Delpeuch, C., and Leroy, A. "Intensifying the Fight Against IUU Fishing at the Regional Level"; Österblom, H., and Ö. Bodin. "Global Cooperation among Diverse Organizations to Reduce Illegal Fishing in the Southern Ocean." Conservation Biology 26 no. 4, 638–648. 2012. https://conbio.onlinelibrary.wiley.com/doi/abs/10.1111/j.1523-1739.2012.01850.x; Österblom, H., & Bodin, Ö. "Global cooperation among diverse organizations to reduce illegal fishing in the Southern Ocean". Conservation Biology, 26(4), 638–648. 2012.

33 Geest, Van der C. "Redesigning Indian Ocean Fisheries Governance for 21st Century Sustainability".

34 Hübschle, A., and J. Lindley. "Blue Crimes and Ocean Harmscapes: Strategies for Tackling Transnational Maritime Environmental Crimes in the Global South." Frontiers in Conservation Science, 5. 2024. https://doi.org/10.3389/fcosc.2024.1448316; Kumar, A., and K. P. Parameswaran. "Sustainable Fishery: Combating IUU Fishing through People's Participation to Ensure Environmental Justice." Maritime Affairs: Journal of the National Maritime Foundation of India, 18 no. 2, 37–57. 2022. https://doi.org/10.1080/09733159.2022.2131248.

35 Chen, Xidi, Qi Xu, and Lun Li. "Illegal, Unreported, and Unregulated Fishing Governance in Disputed Maritime Areas: Reflections on the International Legal Obligations of States."; Luo, G., and Chi, Z. "Conflicts and Challenges of Sustainable Fisheries Governance Cooperation under the Securitization of the Maritime Commons"; Hasan, Y. A. "The Urgency of Handling Illegal, Unreported and Unregulated Fishing in the Indonesian Border Region Perspective: Marine Security in the Makassar Strait". Journal of International Law, 8(1). 2024.

36 Hübschle, A., and J. Lindley. "Blue Crimes and Ocean Harmscapes: Strategies for Tackling Transnational Maritime Environmental Crimes in the Global South."

37 Selig et al, "Revealing Global Risks of Labor Abuse and Illegal, Unreported, and Unregulated Fishing."

38 Co- Developed by a Geneva based NGO, the Index provides a measure of the risk of IUU fishing in and by different countries based on diverse indicators. The Index provides an IUU fishing risk score for all coastal states of between 1 and 5 (1 being the best, and 5

the worst). The Index allows countries to be benchmarked and ranked, and assessed for their vulnerability, prevalence and response to IUU fishing. For more details, see: https://www.iuufishingindex.net/about

39 The US government organization, NOAA's using its assets including research programs, vessels, satellites, science centers, laboratories and a vast pool of distinguished scientists and experts, provide data backed information on daily weather forecasts, severe storm warnings, and climate monitoring to fisheries management, coastal restoration and supporting marine commerce. See; https://www.noaa.gov

40 "Fisheries & Livestock - Home-the Bay of Bengal Initiative for Multi-Sectoral Technical and Economic." BIMSTEC. https://bimstec.org/fisheries-livestock

41 BOBP is a Regional Fisheries Advisory Body (RFAB) of the countries bordering the Bay of Bengal region. It serves as the think tank on transboundary and contemporary national issues of the member countries concerning fisheries management. See: https://www.bobpigo.org

42 For more details, see: https://ions.global

14

India's Humanitarian and Disaster Relief Cooperation: Focus on Africa in the Indian Ocean Region

Ruchita Beri

In recent years, India has emerged as a trusted friend and prominent responder to the multiple natural disasters and calamities that have struck African countries in the Indian Ocean Region (IOR). Whether it is cyclones in Mozambique, Madagascar and Zimbabwe, floods in Kenya, famine and drought in Somalia and Djibouti, the oil spill in Mauritius or the COVID-19 pandemic, India has been at the forefront in providing Humanitarian and Disaster Relief (HADR) to African states in the IOR. According to India's Defence Minister Rajnath Singh, India's leadership in disaster relief across the Indian Ocean has been possible due to "India's unique position in the IOR, and capabilities of our armed forces."[1]

There is no doubt that India's armed forces have garnered considerable experience in dealing with natural disasters both within the country and its neighbourhood. India's policy of humanitarian and disaster relief is guided by India's age-old tradition of *Dana* (charity), the philosophy of *Vasudhaiva Kutumbakam* (World is one family), the vision of Security and Growth for All in the Region (SAGAR) and the recently updated Mutual and Holistic Advancement for Security and Growth Across Regions (MAHASAGAR) vision of regional and global cooperation. This paper examines India's approach to humanitarian assistance and disaster relief and the evolving HADR cooperation with African states in the IOR.

India's Approach towards Humanitarian and Disaster Relief

India has been providing humanitarian assistance and disaster relief to countries in the immediate and extended neighbourhood for a long time. How does India define HADR? Is it any different from the global norms? The Organisation for Economic Cooperation and Development (OECD) defines humanitarian assistance as efforts "designed to save lives, alleviate suffering and maintain and protect human dignity during and in the aftermath of emergencies."[2] In the case of India, there is no clear definition available, however, there are some principles that guide its global contribution towards HADR.

First, it is guided by India's age-old cultural and spiritual values that foster a tradition of charity towards people in need. In India, the concept of *Dana* is considered as a way of life.[3] The Hindu scripture, *Bhagvad Gita*,[4] preaches that charity should not be guided by any selfish interest, rather it should be given "without consideration of anything in return." Thus, India's humanitarian assistance is guided by the idea of selfless support to friendly countries.

Second, India's humanitarian assistance is also guided by the ancient Indian philosophy of *Vasudhaiva Kutumbakam*. This philosophy emphasises the common goals and shared vision of prosperity, peace and stability across the world. It calls for greater cooperation amongst humans in all aspects of life.

Third, India's HADR policy is guided by the SAGAR and MAHASAGAR visions.[5] The SAGAR maritime vision emphasises a safe, secure and stable IOR. It also calls for deepening development and maritime security cooperation with the countries in the Indian Ocean, including those in Africa. This vision was announced by Prime Minister Narendra Modi during his visit to Mauritius, an Indian Ocean Island state, in 2015. On the 10th anniversary of SAGAR, Prime Minister Modi announced the MAHASAGAR vision during his visit to Mauritius in March 2025. The MAHASAGAR expands India's maritime vision from the regional to the global level. It encompasses all countries in the world, particularly those in the global South.

Fourth, India's humanitarian assistance is demand driven. It is guided by the requirements of countries affected by a disaster, calamity or any crisis. This is clearly mentioned in the ten guiding principles of India's engagement with African countries, announced by Prime Minister Modi during his address to the Ugandan Parliament in 2018.[6] In the past, Indian officials have explicitly stated that humanitarian assistance should be provided only after obtaining the affected states consent and receiving their request or appeal. India has also stressed respect for the sovereignty of the affected country. Unlike India, the Western countries have invoked the use of Responsibility to Protect (R2P) in dealing with major disasters.

On the issue of organisation and implementation of HADR, India's Ministry of External Affairs (MEA)—through the Development Partnership Administration, in particular the Rapid Response Cell (RRC)—is the nodal point. The MEA coordinates with the Indian Armed Forces and other organisations for speedy dispatch of relief to the affected countries. One of the most important developments is the release of guidelines on international humanitarian assistance and disaster relief by India's National Disaster Management Authority (NDMA) in October 2024.[7] These guidelines provide details about:

1. The scope of India's disaster management, the category of support to be provided (personnel, equipment, transportation, financial assistance);
2. The operational framework for implementation of HADR operations;
3. Standard Operating Procedures (SOPs) on receiving a request from an affected foreign country, along with an explanation of the roles and responsibilities of each organisation/stakeholder like the MEA, particularly the Rapid Response Cell, India's Diplomatic Mission abroad, Ministry of Home Affairs, NDMA, Ministry of Defence, Indian Armed Fores (Army, Air Force, Navy, Coast Guard), Ministry of Health, and other concerned Ministries.

While India has not developed a formal HADR policy it has been active in supporting the disaster relief efforts domestically, and in its immediate and extended neighbourhood. These efforts were undertaken either to deal with disasters, pandemics, or the evacuation of Indian diaspora from conflict zones. India has responded actively in disaster relief efforts and evacuations, some of these instances include its response to Indian Ocean Tsunami (2004), evacuating the Indian diaspora from war torn Lebanon (2006), providing post conflict relief in Afghanistan (2008) and Libya (2011), and initiated Operation Maitri to provide support to Nepal (2015) after a massive earth quake. During COVID 19 pandemic, India launched the SAGAR and SAGAR II missions to deliver medical relief. India also launched Operation *Dost* to provide relief to the victims who suffered in the massive earthquake in Turkey, and in Syria (February 2023), initiated Operation *Karuna* to provide support to Bangladesh

(May 2023) after a devastating cyclone and launched Operation *Brahma* after an earthquake in Myanmar (2025). India has been equally swift in evacuating the Indian diaspora and citizens of neighbouring countries during the COVID 19 pandemic, and from the conflict-ridden regions like; onset of conflict / instability in Afghanistan (Operation *Devi Shakti*), Ukraine (Operation *Ganga*), South Sudan (Operation *Sankat Mochan*), Sudan (Operation *Kaveri*) and Israel (Operation *Ajay*). India was in the forefront to deliver relief to African countries in the IOR.

India's HADR Cooperation with Africa in the Indian Ocean Region (IOR)

The Indian Ocean islands and littoral countries in Africa are greatly vulnerable to various types of natural disasters. Tropical cyclones and recurring floods are common phenomenon, along with droughts and famines in some parts of the region. These natural disasters have caused tremendous loss of life and property in the affected countries, and climate change has only added to the problems. The latest Intergovernmental Panel on Climate Change's (IPCC) report released in 2023 states that due to human activity the global temperatures have risen to 1.1 degree centigrade (°C) above the pre-industrial levels. This increases the intensity of extreme weather events globally, including in Africa and the IOR.[8] However, there is a growing recognition that Africa carries a disproportionate climate burden. Africa's contribution to greenhouse gas emissions is miniscule compared to other countries in the world. The African continent as a whole, contributes just 4 percent of global carbon emissions at 1.45 billion tonnes.[9] In comparison, China contributes 11.47 billion tonnes and the United States, 5 billion tonnes.[10] Nevertheless, the African region, has borne the brunt of climate related disasters, like; floods, droughts and other extreme events have become more intense and regular in recent years. The COVID 19 pandemic and recent conflicts in countries such as Sudan and South Sudan have added to the grave humanitarian situation in the larger African region. In the face of these natural disasters and national emergencies, the African countries have often looked for support from external partners like India.

In recent years, India has provided humanitarian and disaster relief to various African littoral and island countries in the IOR including Comoros, Djibouti, Eritrea, Kenya, Madagascar, Mauritius, Mozambique, Madagascar, Seychelles and Somalia. The HADR primarily comprised food and medical assistance to deal with natural disasters faced by these countries (Refer to

Table-1). The aid includes food supplies, essential medicines, medical equipment, temporary shelter items and energy resources (for example – solar lanterns).[11] The Indian Navy and Air Force were deployed to deliver this assistance.

During the COVID 19 pandemic, India continued its engagement with the African continent. The engagement flourished and stood in contrast to several major powers that closed their borders and significantly restricted external assistance.. India took the lead and supplied medical assistance to 32 countries and vaccines under the "Vaccine Maitri," an initiative extended towards 42 countries in Africa including the Indian Ocean Island and littoral states.[12] This was in line with Prime Minister Modi's "One Earth, One Health" initiative. Seychelles, the first African country to receive Indian made vaccines appreciated India's gesture. The Foreign Minister of the country noted that this cooperation "cements the ties of solidarity, friendship and cooperation which exist between our two countries."[13] These views were echoed by other countries that received India's vaccines and medical support during the pandemic.

In March 2019, Cyclone Idai caused widespread destruction in Mozambique, Zimbabwe and Malawi. In response to a request from Mozambique, India immediately launched Operation *Sahayata* and diverted three Indian naval ships INS *Sujata*, INS *Shardul* and ICGS *Sarathi* to provide HADR. The Indian crew assisted the Mozambique government in rescuing and evacuating hundreds of locals and also provided food, medicines and water supplies.[14]

In January 2020, when Madagascar was hit by Cyclone *Diane*, the Indian Navy launched Operation *Vanilla* in a bid to support the people of the island nation. The Indian Navy Ship *Airavat* was dispatched to provide clothing, emergency food, medical assistance and support for transportation and evacuation of people in the country.[15]

As the COVID 19 pandemic spread across the world, India launched Mission *Sagar* in response to requests for assistance from Indian Ocean Island countries. Indian government dispatched Indian Naval Ship *Kesari* to Mauritius, Madagascar, Comoros and Seychelles, with medical teams, and COVID 19 related essential medicines and food items. The medical teams were deployed in Mauritius and Comoros. This mission was unique, as during these tough times, when many developed countries were denying access to medicines and vaccines to developing countries, India, extended a helping hand to its maritime neighbours and fellow countries from the Global South. This emphasised India's commitment towards humanitarian assistance in the IOR.[16]

As part of Mission *Sagar*, in June 2020, Indian Naval Ship Kesari delivered essential medicines to Seychelles, to deal with the COVID 19 pandemic. This mission highlights the importance accorded by India to relations with the countries in the IOR.[17]

In August 2020, in response to a request from Mauritius for assistance in dealing with the environmental crisis due to an oil spill on its coastal areas, India promptly dispatched over 30 tonnes of technical equipment, material and a technical team to Mauritius.[18]

In November 2020, in response to floods and resultant food insecurity faced by some of the Indian Ocean littoral countries in the Horn of Africa like Eritrea and Djibouti, India dispatched INS *Airawat* to provide relief. India donated food aid of around 50 metric tonnes to Eritrea consisting of 30 MT of white wheat flour, 10 MT of rice and 10 MT of sugar.[19] Around the same time, India also delivered 50 metric tonnes of food aid to Djibouti.[20] This aid was delivered as part of the Indian Navy's Sagar II mission.

In May 2024, in the wake of devastation caused by the floods in Kenya, India dispatched Indian Naval Ship *Sumedha* for immediate disaster support. Later, additional 22 tonnes of relief material was sent through an Indian Air Force plane. This included food and medical supplies such as lifesaving drugs, surgical equipment, diagnostic test kits, tents, blankets and power generators.[21]

Table 1: India's HADR to African States in Indian Ocean Region (2020-25)

S. No.	Country	Year	HADR supplies
1.	Comoros	2020	14-member Indian Medical Team along with medical supplies sent to mitigate Dengue and COVID 19
		2021	1000 MT of rice
		2022	Anti-TB Drugs
2.	Kenya	2020	Essential medicines worth USD 1.54 million
		2024	Flood relief by INS *Sumedha* & 22 tonnes of food, medicines and equipment
3.	Madagascar	2020	600 tonnes of rice in wake of floods; 1 lakh HCQ tablets & 43.95 thousand Azithromycin tablets
		2021	1000 MT Rice and 1000 MT HCQ as drought relief
		2022	5000 MT of rice

S. No.	Country	Year	HADR supplies
4.	Mauritius	2020	30 tonnes of technical equipment,10-member Technical Response Team to mitigate Wakashio oil-spill crisis
			13 tonnes of medicines, 10 tonnes of Ayurvedic medicines
			14 – member Indian Rapid Response Medical Team to help combat COVID
		2021	1 lakh doses of free Covishield vaccines, 1 lakh doses of Covishield and 2 lakh doses of COVAXIN, on commercial basis
5.	Mozambique	2020	Essential medicines
		2021	500 MT of rice
		2022	PPE Kits & Face Mask worth INR 54.58 lakh
6.	Somalia	2020	65 lakh units of Paracetamol tablets
7.	Seychelles	2020	Essential goods, medicines and relief material, two 'air evacuation pods', indigenously designed by the Indian Navy to support urgent medical evacuation
		2021	Deployment of Indian medical team
		2022	Anti-TB Medicines
8.	Tanzania	2020	Essential medicines (nearly USD 1 million)

Sources: Various Reports by the Ministry of External Affairs[22]

Through the foregoing discussion of India's HADR cooperation with African countries in the IOR, there have emerged several implications, and some prominent trends.

First, the Indian armed forces, primarily the Indian Navy, responded swiftly to various humanitarian crises and disasters in the region. It was often first to reach the affected country, sometimes even within a day. There is no doubt that India has earned a lot of respect as a first responder and key partner in the region. India has astutely used its HADR efforts as a soft power tool for enhancing cooperation with African countries in the IOR. It has catapulted India to a dominant maritime power in the IOR.

Second, India's humanitarian aid and disaster relief to partner countries is focused on providing timely assistance to save lives and alleviate suffering in the affected country. This humanitarian assistance is specific to each disaster and is driven by the requirements and requests of the host country. There is no overt strategic interest that guides this policy, rather it is driven by the deep empathy to alleviate human suffering, a philosophy of *Vishvamitra* (Global Friend).

Third, the Indian armed forces play a crucial role in the implementation of HADR in the region. Over the years, the India armed forces have gained expertise and ability to deliver a swift response to the multiple crisis in the region. The Indian Air Force has expanded its capacities, with platforms to deal with long range airlift, such as, the C-130 Super Hercules and C-17 Globemaster military transport aircraft. Similarly, Indian navy has developed a robust infrastructure to deliver disaster relief within the country and beyond. While India has emerged as a dominant maritime power in the IOR, India's Chief of Defence Staff General Anil Chauhan, has cautioned that this brings an "added responsibility of always being the first responder in the region".[23] As India expands its role in delivering HADR in the IOR it is equally important that the Indian Navy enhances its capacity to deliver and transport large quantities of relief materials, upgrade its medical services and its capacity to deliver medical aid.

Fourth, India has showcased its emerging food security status as a provider of global food solutions through its HADR cooperation in the IOR. In the past, India's food security was a matter of global concern. Today, India is a food surplus country with the capacity to deliver food aid. It is the largest producer of milk, spices and pulses and the second largest producer of food grains, fruits, vegetables, tea and sugar.[24] India's proactive approach to support regional and global agricultural demand calls for a deeper focus on agricultural development and greater access to adequate and nutritious food in the country. Similarly, India's medical aid reflects India's emerging capability as a global pharma hub in the world. This was quite clear during India's supply of medicines and vaccines through the *Vaccine Maitri* initiative during COVID 19 pandemic. Nevertheless, there is a dire need to enhance domestic skills, capabilities and governance norms to maintain the status of "pharmacy of the world".

Finally, India's HADR cooperation with Indian Ocean states in Africa emphasises India's image as a key partner of the countries in the Global South. While India has a deep and historical connect with countries in the Global South, in recent years India has taken extra steps to articulate the common concerns and priorities of the developing countries at the global stage. It has also developed strategic partnerships for sustainable development based on common priorities to achieve common objectives. Nonetheless, there is a need to enhance cooperation at all levels to help the African countries in the IOR and the larger Global South to navigate future challenges and opportunities.[25]

NOTES

1 "India first responder in Indian Ocean Region: Rajnath Singh." The Hindu. November 25, 2021. https://www.thehindu.com/news/national/disaster-relief-india-has-proved-itself-to-be-first-responder-in-indian-ocean-region-says-rajnath/article37667077.ece.

2 Chakradeo, Saneet. "Neighbourhood First Responder: India's growing Humanitarian assistance and disaster relief." Policy Brief. Brookings India. August, 2020. https://www.brookings.edu/articles/neighbourhood-first-responder-indias-humanitarian-assistance-and-disaster-relief/.

3 Meier, Claudia and CSR Murthy. "India's growing involvement in humanitarian assistance." GPPi Research Paper No. 13. Global Public Policy Institute, Berlin. January, 2011. https://www.jnu.ac.in/sites/default/files/India's%20Growing%20Involvement%20in%20Humanitarian%20Assistance.pdf.

4 Bhagavad Gita: Chapter 17, Verse 20. https://www.holy-bhagavad-gita.org/chapter/17/verse/20/.

5 "India's Maritime Vision: From SAGAR to Indo-Pacific to MAHASAGAR by Amb Suchitra Durai". Ministry of External Affairs, Government of India. August 13, 2025. https://www.indembassydili.gov.in/section/articles-commissioned-by-xpd-division/india-s-maritime-vision-from-sagar-to-indo-pacific-to-mahasagar-by-amb-suchitra-durai/.

6 "Prime Minister's address at Parliament of Uganda during his State Visit to Uganda." Ministry of External Affairs, Government of India. July 25, 2018. https://www.mea.gov.in/Speeches-Statements.htm?dtl/30152/Prime+Ministers+address+at+Parliament+of+Uganda+during+his+State+Visit+to+Uganda

7 "Guidelines on International Humanitarian Assistance and Disaster Relief." National Disaster Management Authority, Government of India. October, 2024. https://ndma.gov.in/sites/default/files/PDF/Guidelines/HADR_Guideline_Oct_2024.pdf.

8 Boem, Sophie and Clea Schumer. "10 Big Findings from the 2023 IPCC Report on Climate Change." World Resources Institute. March 20, 2023. https://www.wri.org/insights/2023-ipcc-ar6-synthesis-report-climate-change-findings.

9 AJ Labs. "How much does Africa contribute to global carbon emissions?" Al Jazeera. September 4, 2023. https://www.aljazeera.com/news/2023/9/4/how-much-does-africa-contribute-to-global-carbon-emissions.

10 Ibid

11 "Question No-4683 Emergency Medical Assistance," Ministry of External Affairs, Government of India. March 2025. https://www.mea.gov.in/lok-sabha.htm?dtl/39288/QUESTION+NO4683+EMERGENCY+MEDICAL+ASSISTANCE.

12 "India supplied 'Made in India' COVID vaccines to 42 African countries: EAM." Economic Times. June 15, 2023. https://health.economictimes.indiatimes.com/news/policy/india-supplied-made-in-india-COVID-vaccines-to-42-african-countries-eam/101009408.

13 Beri, Ruchita. "India's Vaccine Maitri with Africa." Institute for Defence Studies and Analyses (IDSA). March 11, 2021. https://www.idsa.in/publisher/comments/indias-vaccine-maitri-with-africa.

14 "Humanitarian Assistance and Disaster Relief to Mozambique-Operation Sahayata 2019." Ministry of External Affairs, Government of India. March 23, 2019. https://www.mea.gov.in/press-releases.htm?dtl/31174/Humanitarian+Assistance+and+ Disaster +

Relief+to+MozambiqueOperation+Sahayata+2019.

15 Singh, Mayank. "Operation Vanilla: India sends INS Airavat to provide aid to disaster-hit Madagascar." The New Indian Express. January 29, 2020. https://www.newindianexpress.com/nation/2020/Jan/28/operation-vanilla-india-sends-naval-ship-to-provide-aid-to-disaster-hit-madagascar-ins-airavat-2095815.html.

16 "Mission Sagar: India's helping hand across the Indian Ocean." Ministry of External Affairs, Government of India, PIB. May 10, 2020. https://www.mea.gov.in/press-releases.htm?dtl/32678/Mission_Sagar_Indias_helping_hand_across_the_Indian_Ocean

17 "Mission Sagar - INS Kesari at Port Victoria, Seychelles." PIB, Ministry of Defence, Government of India. https://www.pib.gov.in/PressReleasePage.aspx?PRID=1630101.

18 "Indian assistance to Mauritius to deal with the environmental crisis due to oil spill." Ministry of External Affairs, Government of India. Press Releases. August 16, 2020. https://www.mea.gov.in/press-releases.htm?dtl/32896/Indian_assistance_to_Mauritius_to_deal_with_the_environmental_crisis_due_to_oil_spill.

19 "India-Eritrea – Bilateral Relations." Embassy of India, Asmara (Eritrea). Ministry of External Affairs, Government of India. September 25, 2025. https://www.mea.gov.in/Portal/ForeignRelation/India-Eritrea-Bilatera-May-2025.pdf.

20 "India gifts food Items to Djibouti." Press Release. Embassy of India, Djibouti. November 11, 2020. https://www.mea.gov.in/Portal/CountryNews/13364_Press_Release_Gift_of_Food_items_website.pdf.

21 "India sends US$ 1 million flood relief assistance to Kenya." Press Releases. Ministry of External Affairs, Government of India. May 14, 2024. https://www.mea.gov.in/press-releases.htm?dtl/37809/India_sends_US_1_million_flood_relief_assistance_to_Kenya.

22 "Relief and Medical Assistance to other Nations." Unstarred Question No 2324. Details of humanitarian assistance provided by India over the last 5 years. Annexure-I. Rajya Sabha. March 20, 2025. https://www.mea.gov.in/rajya-sabha.htm?dtl/39214/QUESTION+NO2324+RELIEF+AND+MEDICAL+ASSISTANCE+TO+OTHER+NATIONS.
"India-Mauritius Bilateral Relations." High Commission of India Port Louis, Mauritius. August, 2025. https://hcimauritius.gov.in/pages?id=9avme&subid=yb8md&nextid=RdG7d.
"India-Tanzania Bilateral Relations." High Commission of India Dar es Salaam, Tanzania. July, 2025. https://www.hcindiatz.gov.in/india-tanzania-bilateral-relation.php.

23 "Indian Ocean region's 'first responder' India both continental, maritime power: Chief of Defence Staff." The Week. November 9, 2025. https://www.theweek.in/news/defence/2025/11/09/indian-ocean-region-s-first-responder-india-both-continental-maritime-power-chief-of-defence-staff.html.

24 "India is a food surplus country; we are working on solutions for global food security: PM Modi." Economic Times. August 3, 2024. https://economictimes.indiatimes.com/news/economy/agriculture/india-is-a-food-surplus-country-we-are-working-on-solutions-for-global-food-security-pm-modi/articleshow/112239114.cms?utm_source=con tentofin terest&utm_medium=text&utm_campaign=cppst.

15

Cyber-Physical Threats at Sea: Rethinking UNCLOS and Maritime Accountability

Dr. Sanjeet Ruhal

Introduction: A Legal Regime Confronting a New Threat Paradigm

The 2017 'NotPetya' malware attack, which resulted in a catastrophic operational failure for the global shipping giant Maersk, revealed the maritime industry's profound digital vulnerability.[1] While initially viewed as an information technology (IT) incident, its true significance lay in demonstrating a pathway to the more perilous cyber-physical attack: a scenario where a digital breach is leveraged to produce direct, kinetic consequences at sea.

The modern "smart ship" paradigm, driven by demands for efficiency and environmental compliance, has systematically erased the traditional operational separation between administrative data networks (IT) and the critical systems controlling navigation, propulsion, and cargo (Operational Technology, or OT).[2] This IT/OT convergence, facilitated by network integration, remote diagnostics, and the use of commercial off-the-shelf (COTS) components, creates a direct vector for malicious intrusions.[3] Such intrusions are no longer theoretical and could result in kinetic scenarios, including navigational manipulation through Global Navigation Satellite System (GNSS) or Electronic Chart Display and Information System (ECDIS) spoofing to induce a collision or grounding[4], loss-of-control via the remote disabling of propulsion or steering, effectively weaponising a ship in a critical chokepoint like the Suez Canal or the Strait of Malacca;[5] and environmental attacks involving the deliberate manipulation of cargo or ballast systems to trigger an intentional pollution event, thereby implicating international liability regimes.[6]

These are direct, kinetic threats to the core objectives of the international maritime legal order—safety of life at sea, maritime security, and protection of the marine environment.

The international legal framework, with the 1982 United Nations Convention on the Law of the Sea (UNCLOS) at its core, was conceived in a pre-digital era to govern physical acts and tangible threats.[7] Its provisions face structural limitations in effectively addressing a threat paradigm characterised by remote actors, the use of intangible code as a weapon, and the instantaneous, multi-jurisdictional effects of incidents. These limitations, particularly the jurisdictional ambiguities, raise legal questions that challenge the foundational balances of jurisdiction.

The International Maritime Organization (IMO)[8] adopted Resolution MSC.428(98) on Maritime Cyber Risk Management in Safety Management Systems (SMS), determining that an approved SMS should integrate cyber risk management in accordance with International Safety Management (ISM) Code objectives.[9] The Resolution encouraged Administrations to ensure that cyber risks were adequately addressed within the SMS by the first annual verification of the company's Document of Compliance (DOC) after 1 January 2021.[10] However, this approach is procedural rather than jurisdictional and does not fully address the broader conflicts arising under public international law. This article examines the implications of technological change and the limitations of the existing legal framework, identifying three key governance gaps. It proposes a comprehensive legal approach to interpret and complement UNCLOS, thereby enhancing its effectiveness in the digital era. Additionally, under India's chairmanship of the Indian Ocean Rim Association (IORA),[11] the article considers how regional initiatives—particularly those related to Maritime Safety and Security—can be leveraged to address these gaps. Drawing on the capacity-building focus of the SAGAR doctrine,[12] it explores opportunities to promote harmonised standards, strengthen jurisdictional clarity, and advance liability reforms, thereby supporting a more resilient model of maritime governance.

The Jurisdictional Quagmire: UNCLOS and the IMO's Proceduralism

UNCLOS was drafted for a physical, state-bounded maritime world and does not speak directly to intangible, instantaneous cyber operations that cross borders without moving a ship. That mismatch produces persistent legal uncertainty about which State may act when a ship-borne or ship-originated cyber operation harms a coastal State.

On the high seas, the rule of exclusive flag-State jurisdiction remains central: a ship generally falls under the jurisdiction of the State whose flag it flies, save for a few treaty-defined exceptions.[13] This principle significantly limits coastal States confronting hostile cyber activity originating from foreign ships outside their national jurisdiction. Absent an established legal exception or the consent of the flag State, the ability of the coastal State to undertake interdiction, prescriptive regulation, or direct enforcement against the ship is legally constrained.

IMO safety and security instruments have sought a practical fix by including cyber into existing risk regimes. The ISM Code requires companies to assess identified risks and establish safeguards, and the Maritime Safety Committee's Resolution MSC.428(98) made clear that cyber risks fall within that duty; the ISPS/SOLAS regime likewise requires routine security risk assessment and mitigation.[14] Those measures have made cyber-risk management an auditable, compliance-based obligation for owners and operators, but they do not create new coastal-State enforcement powers under UNCLOS.[15]

The regime of the territorial sea represents a dynamic balance between coastal State sovereignty and the right of innocent passage. UNCLOS allows the coastal State to prevent passage that is "not innocent" and to take "necessary steps" to protect its interests,[16] but the text prescribes specific prejudicial acts (e.g. collecting information prejudicial to security) and limits coastal legislation: laws may not regulate the "design, construction, manning or equipment" of foreign ships except to give effect to generally accepted international rules and standards (GAIRS).[17] That limitation means a coastal State cannot simply impose bespoke cyber-equipment standards on foreign-flagged ships unless backed by accepted international rules.[18]

In the Exclusive Economic Zone (EEZ), the dilemma reappears in environmental terms. Coastal States enjoy sovereign rights to protect the marine environment and may claim that poor cyber hygiene on transiting ships (if it foreseeably risks catastrophic pollution) conflicts with the duty of other States to act with "due regard." But prescribing mandatory technical cyber standards for all foreign ships in an EEZ would challenge the flag-State primacy and requires careful legal and political justification—most plausibly by linking cyber requirements to recognised international standards (e.g. MARPOL-related obligations) or by an IMO elevation of guidance into binding norms.[19]

Criminal law instruments provide a complementary route. The 1988 SUA Convention (Convention for the Suppression of Unlawful Acts against the Safety of Maritime Navigation) criminalises placing "devices" on ships and obliges States to extradite or prosecute offenders;[20] a good-faith, contextual treaty interpretation under Article 31 of the Vienna Convention[21] supports reading "device" to include malware that is intended to damage or endanger a ship.[22] That avenue gives States a basis for arrest, extradition and prosecution of perpetrators, but it does not itself displace the flag-State rule over the ship.

Deconstructing the Tripartite Governance Gap

The failure of UNCLOS to anticipate intangible threats, combined with the cyber risk management-focused IMO response,[23] has created three legal governance gaps.

The first gap relates to the core duty of the flag State. UNCLOS Article 94 requires a flag State to "effectively exercise its jurisdiction and control" over its ships, including measures concerning their "construction, equipment and seaworthiness." The legal concept of seaworthiness is evolutionary; a ship must be "fit to meet and undergo the perils of the sea" by the standards of the time, as assessed by a prudent owner at the commencement of the voyage.[24] This article argues, in line with emerging doctrine, that this principle should now be extended to "cyber-worthiness." A ship operating with known, unpatched vulnerabilities in its critical OT systems—whose navigation can be spoofed or engine disabled—is as unseaworthy as one with a structural defect or an incompetent crew. This aligns with carriage conventions like the Hague-Visby Rules[25] and Rotterdam Rules,[26] where cyber-compromised systems could breach warranties.

The problem is not the existence of the duty, but the enforcement deficit. The flag State's "effective control" under Article 94 is undermined by the very mechanism chosen to enforce it: the ISM Code audit, which is almost universally delegated to ROs (Classification Societies). These ROs, experts in hull integrity, are not historically cyber-auditors. Their audit can verify that a cyber-risk plan exists on paper. It is generally ill-equipped to perform technical validation, such as penetration testing of OT networks or code review of the ECDIS. This creates a high risk of paper compliance (formal certification without substantive technical assurance). Consequently, the flag-State duty of "effective control" risks being reduced to a largely nominal, procedural exercise unless administrations build or procure genuinely technical verification capacity; IMO guidance stresses the need for effective flag-State control, but capacity and practice vary widely. The International Convention on Standards of Training, Certification and Watchkeeping for Seafarers (STCW) requires crew competency, which should extend to cyber training, but lacks mandatory provisions for the same.[27]

The second gap is the unresolved jurisdictional right of the coastal State, which the IMO's ISM framework leaves untouched. Within the Territorial Sea, the coastal State is caught in a legal vice. UNCLOS Article 25 grants the right to "take the necessary steps" to prevent non-innocent passage, and a cyber-vulnerable ship is an undeniable threat to the coastal State's "peace, good order or security" (Article 19). However, the coastal State's primary legislative tool, Article 21, is neutralised by the CDEM limitation in Article 21(2). Because the IMO's procedural requirement is not a concrete GAIRS, the coastal State law mandating specific cybersecurity software would be a law relating to "equipment." The coastal State thus has the responsibility to protect its ports, but lacks the clear authority to pre-emptively act against the digital threat.

In the EEZ, the ambiguity persists. The coastal State's right to protect its marine environment[28] is pitted against the ship's freedom of navigation.[29] The right of a coastal State to prescribe minimum cybersecurity standards for ships in its EEZ to avert a catastrophic, cyber-induced pollution event remains a profound and unresolved legal question, challenging the foundational jurisdictional balances of UNCLOS. Linkages to the SUA Convention could apply if spoofing is "active," but attribution remains challenging.[30]

The final gap is structural: the misallocation of responsibility. The ISM Code makes the shipowner the primary duty-holder for cyber risk. This is legally problematic, as the shipowner is often the party with the least control over the core technological vulnerability. This creates a significant upstream liability gap. First, the OT manufacturers who design the ECDIS, GNSS, or integrated bridge systems are not held accountable under the international maritime framework. If a system is sold with known vulnerabilities, default passwords, or "insecure-by-design" architecture, the manufacturer has created the primary risk, yet the shipowner bears it. The absence of a product liability regime removes a powerful market-based incentive for manufacturers to build secure systems from inception, as highlighted in supply chain attacks. Second, the Recognised Organisations (ROs) are shielded. If an RO, lacking requisite cyber-expertise, approves a deficient SMS and a catastrophic incident occurs, their liability is deeply uncertain. By focusing liability almost exclusively on the end-user (the shipowner), the current legal landscape fails to distribute responsibility to the "upstream" actors most capable of mitigating the risk. This gap is exacerbated in cyber-physical systems, where upstream flaws cascade to kinetic harms, unaddressed in carriage regimes like the Hamburg Rules or Rotterdam Rules.

Proposing a Reconceptualised Legal Architecture

Addressing these gaps requires moving beyond procedural checklists toward a reconceptualised legal architecture. This necessitates a multi-tiered approach.

First, the international community must pursue interpretive clarification of UNCLOS. Given the impracticality of amending the Convention, the most effective path is for a group of States parties to request an Advisory Opinion from the International Tribunal for the Law of the Sea (ITLOS).[31] This request should seek clarification on the central ambiguities:

1. What are the conditions under which a ship's cyber-vulnerability or operations render its passage "prejudicial" under Article 19(2)?
2. What is the full extent of a coastal State's prescriptive jurisdiction under Articles 21 and 56 to protect its security and marine environment from cyber-physical threats?[32]

Second, the legal concept of seaworthiness must be given a contemporary, binding technical meaning. The IMO's ISM-based approach is insufficient. What is required is a mandatory, baseline cybersecurity standard for critical OT systems, incorporated via a new "Maritime Cyber Resilience Code," modelled on the structure of the Polar Code. This would provide a clear, technical benchmark for flag States to fulfil their Article 94 duties, integrating quantitative metrics. Critically, to make "effective control" meaningful, this regime must include mandatory cybersecurity competency standards for ISM auditors and RO surveyors, perhaps via amendments to the STCW Convention, to ensure substantive technical assessments, not paper-based reviews. "Cyber due diligence" clauses in BIMCO contracts could enforce this, verifiable via encrypted logs and AI anomaly detection.

Third, a new international civil liability regime for maritime technology manufacturers is necessary to close the "upstream liability gap" and incentivise security-by-design. Dialogue within the competent international legal forum could establish a framework for limited but proportionate responsibility for vulnerabilities introduced at the manufacturing stage. This framework should also clarify the liability of ROs in their capacity as cyber-auditors, ensuring negligence in certification carries appropriate legal consequences. A Zero Trust Architecture (ZTA) could serve as a technical defence against negligence claims and be integrated into supply contracts to formalise shared accountability.

The Role of Regional Mechanisms: India's IORA Chairmanship as a Catalyst for Reform

Under India's 2025-2027 Chairmanship of the Indian Ocean Rim Association (IORA), there is a strategic opportunity to address these gaps, aligning with IORA's priority on Maritime Safety and Security. India can leverage its SAGAR (Security and Growth for All in the Region) vision to transform vulnerabilities into cooperative resilience.

Priorities include harmonising standards and capacity-building. India should draw on SAGAR's capacity pillar to initiate training programmes for OT audits and penetration testing, targeting vulnerable members like Comoros or Seychelles. This could foster regional cyber-worthiness benchmarks, supplementing IMO guidelines with practical tools.

Clarifying jurisdictional boundaries is essential. India should advocate for an ITLOS advisory opinion on cyber applications of UNCLOS Articles 19, 21, and 56, coordinated via IORA. This would provide legal clarity for coastal States, fostering protocols for information sharing on vulnerable ships and resolving EEZ/high seas ambiguities.

India should establish a working group to discuss upstream liability, modelled on existing conventions, to hold manufacturers accountable. This incentivises security-by-design, emphasising sustainable development through resilient supply chains.

Cyber-physical threats represent a paradigm shift in Indian Ocean Region (IOR) maritime security, exposing gaps in global frameworks. India should offer a coherent vision for leadership, transforming IORA into a platform for resilient governance. By advancing harmonised standards, jurisdictional clarity, liability reforms, and enforcement mechanisms, India can foster a stable maritime order, transforming IOR into a model for cooperative stability in an interconnected world.

Conclusion

The digital transformation of shipping through IT/OT convergence has created a severe class of risk that the international legal order is not equipped to manage. The foundational treaty, UNCLOS, is beset by critical jurisdictional ambiguities, a product of its pre-digital origins. The IMO's response, while necessary, is procedural and insufficient to fill the underlying public international law gaps.

This results in a fragile regime defined by a tripartite governance gap: a flag State enforcement deficit for "cyber-worthiness"; an unresolved jurisdictional dilemma for coastal States; and an upstream liability gap that shields the technology manufacturers and certifiers best placed to mitigate the risk.

Closing this gap requires a deliberate, multi-faceted effort. This involves clarifying UNCLOS through an ITLOS advisory opinion, giving binding technical meaning to "cyber-worthiness" through a mandatory IMO code, and establishing a new liability framework to distribute responsibility across the entire maritime ecosystem. Without urgent, multilateral action to build this holistic architecture, the international community risks sailing into increasingly dangerous digital waters with a legal compass that is no longer fit for purpose. Regional platforms like IORA, under proactive leadership such as India's, can catalyse these reforms, ensuring a secure and sustainable maritime future.[33]

NOTES

1 Wesley, David T.A. and Alexandra Roth., "Developing a Culture of Cybersecurity," International Journal of Technology, Knowledge and Society 21, no. 1, 29-48. 2024; Knowler, Greg. "All MSC Systems Back Online After Easter Malware-Caused Outage." Journal of Commerce. April 15, 2020. https://www.joc.com/article/all-msc-systems-back-online-after-easter-malware-caused-outage-5208384.

2 Kimberly, Tam, Hopcraft, Rory, Moara-Nkwe, Kemedi, and Jones, Kevin. "Case Study of a Cyber-Physical Attack Affecting Port and Ship Operational Safety." Journal of Transportation Technologies 12 (1): 1-27. 2022. https://doi.org/10.4236/jtts.2022.121001.

3 Kowalewsky, Erik M., and Ramkissoon, Brian. "Safeguarding the Marine Transportation System: New Cybersecurity Rules." Insurance Journal, April 23, 2025. https://www.insurancejournal.com/news/national/2025/04/23/820817.htm.

4 "Comprehensive Review of the 1978 STCW Convention and Code: Proposed Addition of Navigational Competence to Navigate Safely in a Global Navigation Satellite System

(GNSS) Compromised Environment." International Maritime Organization. November 29, 2023. https://www.intertanko.com/images/imo-submissions/2024/HTW%2010-6-6.pdf

5 Karahalios, Hristos. "Cybersecurity Threats of Remote Autonomous Ships While Approaching Ports." Journal of Transportation Security 18 (1): 2. 2025.

6 Kowalewsky and Ramkissoon, "Safeguarding the Marine Transportation System," Insurance Journal. April 23, 2025.

7 "United Nations Convention on the Law of the Sea". 1982.

8 The International Maritime Organization (IMO) is a UN specialised agency established in 1948, headquartered in London, setting standards for shipping safety and pollution prevention. In the UN Convention on the Law of the Sea (UNCLOS), the IMO is primarily referred to as the 'competent international organisation' responsible for establishing 'generally accepted international rules and standards' for maritime activities, safety, and environmental protection.

9 "Guidelines on Cyber Security Onboard Ships". Version 4. International Chamber of Shipping. 2021. https://www.ics-shipping.org/wp-content/uploads/2021/02/2021-Cyber-Security-Guidelines.pdf.

10 "Maritime Cyber Risk." International Maritime Organization. https://www.imo.org/en/ourwork/security/pages/cyber-security.aspx.

11 "24th Indian Ocean Rim Association (IORA) Meeting of the Council of Ministers (CoM)" Ministry of External Affairs, Government of India. May 21, 2025. https://www.mea.gov.in/press-releases.htm?dtl/39511/24th_Indian_Ocean_Rim_Association_IORA_Meeting_of_the_Council_of_Ministers_COM_May_21_2025.

12 Durai, Suchitra. "India's Maritime Vision: From SAGAR to Indo-Pacific to MAHASAGAR." Embassy of India, Dili. August 13, 2025. https://www.indembassydili.gov.in/section/articles-commissioned-by-xpd-division/india-s-maritime-vision-from-sagar-to-indo-pacific-to-mahasagar-by-amb-suchitra-durai/.

13 "United Nations Convention on the Law of the Sea". Article 92. 1982.

14 "International Maritime Organization." 2021.
Guide to Maritime Security and the ISPS Code. 2021 ed. London: IMO Publishing. Within the framework of the ISPS Code, the provisions most relevant to cybersecurity are found in Part A, Sections 8 and 9, which establish the mandatory requirements for the Ship Security Assessment (SSA) and Ship Security Plan (SSP). Section 8 requires each ship to assess vulnerabilities in its systems, a process that, under current IMO interpretation, extends to cyber vulnerabilities in radio, telecommunication, computer, and networked systems. Section 9 obliges the SSP to include measures to counter the threats identified in the SSA, which now encompasses cyber threats and the corresponding mitigation, detection, and response procedures..Although the Code's original text does not expressly mention cyber risks, IMO's guidance treats these provisions as an "all-risks" framework, allowing integration of cyber risk assessment and mitigation within the existing mandatory SSA/SSP structure, thereby aligning cyber security obligations with the Code's foundational security management requirements.

15 Into these void steps the IMO's response, Resolution MSC.428(98), which leverages the mandatory ISM Code to require that a ship's Safety Management System (SMS) address cyber risks. This was a pragmatically effective move, forcing cyber into the existing audit cycle. However, this ISM-based approach is a safety management solution, not a public

international law solution. It regulates the relationship between the shipowner, the flag State, and its Recognised Organisation (RO). It does not—and cannot—resolve the underlying UNCLOS jurisdictional gaps. It provides no new legal tools for a coastal State confronted by a cyber-vulnerable foreign-flagged ship in its waters. The Convention on the International Regulations for Preventing Collisions at Sea (COLREG, Rule 5: proper lookout) could extend to cyber anomalies, but lacks specificity for enforcement.

16 "United Nations Convention on the Law of the Sea." Article 25(1). 1982.
UNCLOS grants the coastal State the right to take necessary steps in the territorial sea to prevent passage that is not innocent, as defined in Article 19.

17 "United Nations Convention on the Law of the Sea." Article 21(1)(a). 1982.
The coastal State's legislative authority under Article 21(1)(a) UNCLOS to adopt laws concerning the "safety of navigation" is significantly limited by Article 21(2). Specifically, Article 21(2) strictly prohibits the coastal State from applying its laws and regulations to the design, construction, manning, or equipment (DCME) of foreign ships in the territorial sea, unless such standards implement generally accepted international rules and standards (GAIRS). Given that the current IMO cyber security framework consists of non-mandatory guidelines and a procedural ISM Code requirement, they do not constitute the hard-law GAIRS necessary to overcome the Article 21(2) limitation. Consequently, while a coastal State may have a clear security interest under Article 19 to mandate equipment like encrypted AIS signals or anomaly detection systems, its primary enforcement mechanism under Article 21 is nullified by the DCME constraint.

18 "United Nations Convention on the Law of the Sea." Article 21(2). 1982.
The strict limitation in Article 21(2) UNCLOS prevents a coastal State from unilaterally mandating specific cybersecurity "equipment" standards in the territorial sea, as the current IMO framework lacks a hard-law GAIRS to override this constraint.

19 "United Nations Convention on the Law of the Sea." Article 56. 1982
This conflict extends to the EEZ, where prescribing cybersecurity standards as a preventive measure under the coastal State's environmental jurisdiction under Article 56 remains a highly controversial challenge to the flag State's exclusive regulatory domain.

20 "Convention for the Suppression of Unlawful Acts against the Safety of Maritime Navigation." 1988. Opened for signature March 10, 1988. Article 3(1)(d). 1678 U.N.T.S. 221.

21 "Vienna Convention on the Law of Treaties." 1969. Opened for signature May 23, 1969. 1155 U.N.T.S. 331.

22 Petta, Michael. "Malware, a Device under the 1988 SUA Convention." International Law Studies 100: 110-47. 2023.

23 "Guidelines on Maritime Cyber Risk Management." International Maritime Organization. April 4, 2025.

24 *McFadden v. Blue Star Line*. 1 K.B. 697 (K.B.). 1905.

25 "International Convention for the Unification of Certain Rules of Law Relating to Bills of Lading (Hague-Visby Rules)." 1968.
Article III (1) carrier's duty to exercise "due diligence" to make the ship seaworthy and to "properly man, equip and supply" it is plausibly read to encompass cyber-resilience of IT/OT systems and crew cyber competence.

26 "United Nations Convention on Contracts for the International Carriage of Goods Wholly

or Partly by Sea (Rotterdam Rules, not in force)." 2008.
Article 14's continuing duty to make and keep the ship seaworthy during the sea leg plausibly includes maintaining cyber-resilience systems and crew competence, thus imposing ongoing cyber-risk diligence on carriers.

27 "International Convention on Standards of Training, Certification and Watchkeeping for Seafarers (STCW)." Opened for signature July 7, 1978. 1361 U.N.T.S. 2. 1978.

28 Op. cit. note no. 19.

29 Ibid. Article 58 (2).

30 "Convention for the Suppression of Unlawful Acts against the Safety of Maritime Navigation." Article 3. 1988.

31 ITLOS advisory opinions have repeatedly interpreted UNCLOS and specified States' duties under it. Notably, the Seabed Disputes Chamber (2011) imposed a high due-diligence standard on sponsoring States for activities in the Area; the full Tribunal (2015) applied a due-diligence framework to flag-State obligations in relation to IUU fishing; and in May 2024 ITLOS characterised anthropogenic greenhouse gases as "pollutants" under UNCLOS and affirmed States' obligations to prevent, reduce and control marine pollution (including differentiated responsibilities).

32 While UNCLOS lacks a provision for general advisory jurisdiction for the full Tribunal, ITLOS has affirmed such jurisdiction exists when conferred by an "international agreement related to the purposes of the Convention" (ITLOS Statute, Art. 21; Rules, Art. 138). This procedure was utilised in the 2015 SRFC and 2024 Climate Change opinions.

16

Deep Ocean Exploration and Science-Based Cooperation with Indian Ocean Rim Countries

Dr. Rasik Ravindra

The Indian Ocean Rim countries form a part of the larger Indo-Pacific Region that refers to a vast biogeographic region of Earth encompassing the tropical waters of the Indian Ocean, the western and central Pacific Ocean, and the seas connecting the two. The region is marked by a display of rich marine habitats extending from Madagascar to Japan and Oceania as different from the Atlantic Ocean. It is also rich in non-living resources in terms of energy and poly-metallic mineral resources. Geopolitically, the Indo-Pacific construct comprising Australia, India, the United States and other East Asian states, has emerged as key partnership of likeminded nations in forming a grouping to advance economic and strategic partnership in this region to counter growing naval and economic influence of China. It is worth mentioning that the Indo-Pacific region caters for 66 per cent of world's trade and movement of 35 per cent of world's cargo.

The Indo-Pacific is evolving fast as a strategic region of multi-lateral cooperation among both state and non-state stake holders who appreciate that the oceans are a shared responsibility of mankind and that the benefits from oceans can be best reaped only through international cooperation and sustainable means that lead to preserving the marine biodiversity and balance between environment and development. Impact of climate change on global energy security, supply chain resilience, large-scale submergence of littoral areas and resultant forced migration - are likely to aggravate the situation making it necessary to evolve a regional cooperative model.

Figure 1: The Indo-Pacific Region

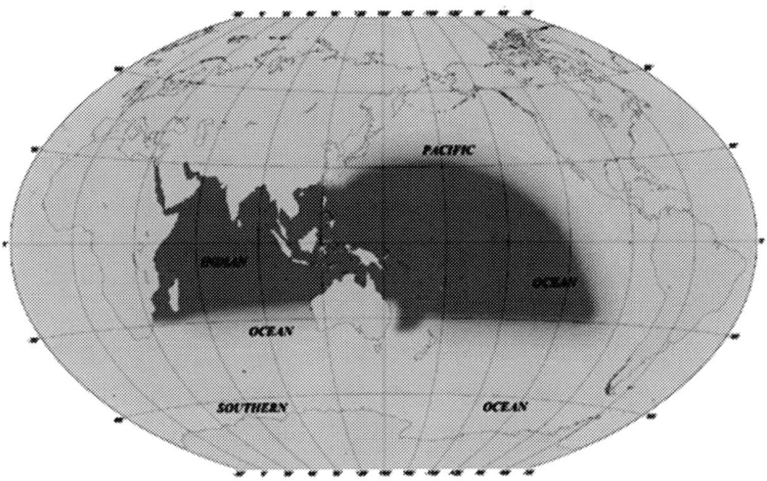

Source: Wikipedia

The essay focusses on the status and exploration of the living and non-living resources in deep oceans surrounding India and the contributions that science and technology can make in the Indo-Pacific region to enhance geoeconomic potential of States and improve livelihood for millions of people in this part of the world through sharing information (warnings) on weather, cyclones, tsunami and earthquakes etc.

In this regard, it is appropriate that the Indo-Pacific region remains open with freedom of navigation, inclusive and free from coercion, thereby strengthening the ASEAN led policy of "inclusive regional security architecture". The vision of fostering a favourable environment for trade and resource exploration and utilisation is propagated through two Indian doctrines of SAGAR (Security And Growth For All) and MAHASAGAR (Mutual And Holistic Advancement For Security And Growth Across Regions).

Several policy decisions taken in last few years by India, such as Deep Ocean Mission aim to focus on harnessing ocean wealth and strengthening the Blue Economy. The Deep Ocean Mission of India is one such step towards realisation of this goal that will enhance blue economy through development of deep-sea technology, exploration and sustainable exploitation of living and non-living resources, integrated ocean observing systems, modelling, forecasting and by issuing advisories to coastal communities for their financial health and disaster mitigation as also improve general connectivity and navigation throughout the Indo-Pacific.

Non-Living Resources

The oceans are store house of several mineral deposits such as oil and gas, ferrous ad non- ferrous metals, rare earth and critical metals etc. The deep-sea areas are especially rich in poly metallic nodules and hydrothermal deposits that contain manganese, iron, nickel, cobalt along with gold, silver, platinum and rare earth minerals. The offshore rare earth minerals are found enriched in deep sea mud, near-shore carbonaceous clay with high metal content and in cobalt-rich Fe–Mn crusts and nodules deposited on the volcanic seamounts/ridges and in the abyssal plains respectively.[1]

Figure 2: Non-Living Resources Of Oceans

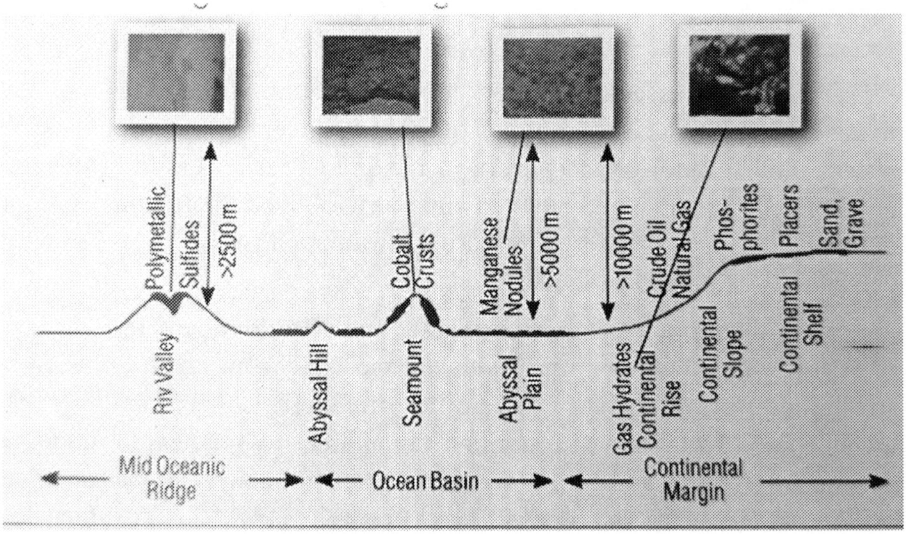

Source: Ramadass, G. A., S. Ramesh, G. Kuttikrishnan, N. Vedachalam, N. R. Ramesh and M. A. Atmanand. "Technologies for Deep Ocean Exploration." Geog. And You.Vol. 19. Issue 13. No 124. pp 39-43. 2019.

Cobalt-rich ferromanganese crusts (Cobalt Crust) and Polymetallic (ferromanganese) nodules are the chemical precipitates from seawater. Iron hydroxide and Manganese oxide form nodules on the surface of sediments, while the cobalt crusts are formed on the surface of basement rocks. Mineralogy and chemistry of these deposits are similar except their minor elements' contents. Both ores are enriched in Fe, Mn, P, Cu, Co, Ni, Pb, REE, Ti, and Pt (refer Table 1). The distribution of these deposits in different parts of oceans is shown in Figure 2, Rare Earth Minerals (REE) often associated as accessories, are proving critical in modern industries especially in clean energy devices, space technology, electrical automobiles, computer and allied products.

Poly Metallic Nodules (PMN): These are small nodules found on the deep-sea bed, which are rich in minerals such as nickel, cobalt, copper, manganese. The PMN also contain minerals like Molybdenum, Vanadium, Titanium, Platinum, Rhodium in small quantities. These deposits of PMN are known to occur in Pacific and central Indian ocean (Figure 3). India is one of the pioneer investors to have undertaken exploration of allotted site in Indian ocean by the International Sea bed Authority. Detailed geophysical surveys in the allotted area, 2,000 km away from the southern tip of India, have shown an estimated reserve of about 380 million metric tonnes.

Figure 3: Showing areas of PMN and Sulphide deposits in Indo-Pacic Region

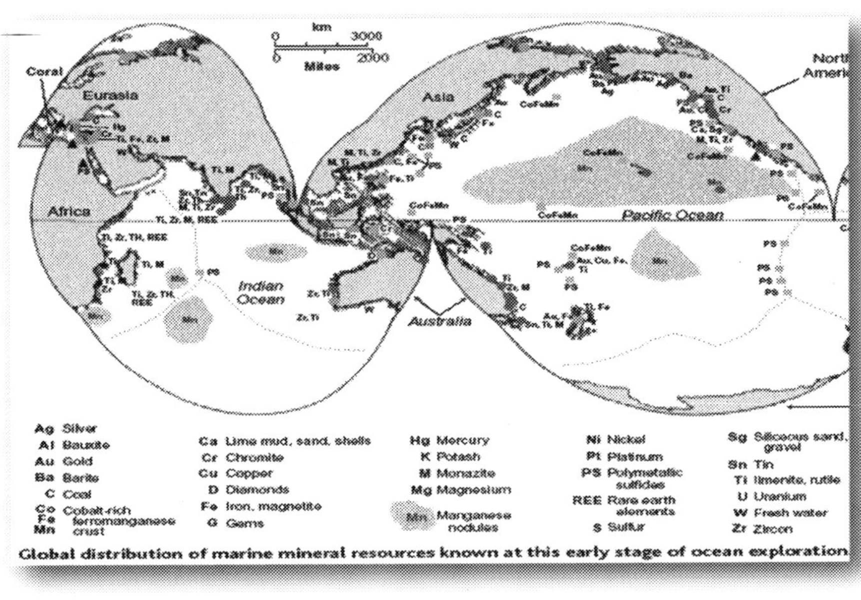

Source: Rona, P.A. "Resources of the Ocean Floor." Science. 299:673-4. 2003.

Hydrothermal Sulphides: Massive sulphide deposits occur at the deep oceanic realms along the mid -ocean ridges formed through the interaction of sea water with a heat source beneath the seabed. At water depth up to 3,700 m, hydrothermal fluids having seeped from the ocean into subterranean chambers, get heated by the molten rock beneath the crust. When these fluids are discharged through the chimneys or vents, these mix with the cold sea water leading to precipitation of minerals such as galena, sphalerite and chalcopyrite, on the sides of chimneys or nearby sea beds. These vents also mark the presence of dense biological communities (> 700 species), on the deep ocean beds.

The minerals contain base metals- copper, lead and zinc along with minor amounts of noble metals gold, silver, platinum (Pt) and palladium (Pd). The Pt and Pd are used in applications like automobile catalytic converters and pharma industry. India is exploring southwest and central Indian Ridge areas for these sulphide deposit. Significant hydrothermal plumes have been discovered over the Carlsberg Ridge and central Indian Ridge.

Figure 4: Distribution of Hydrothermal sites

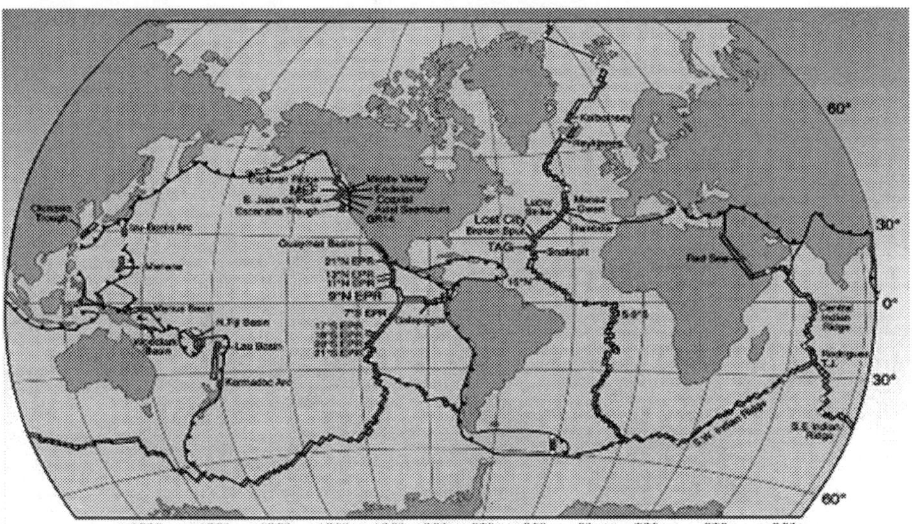

Source: Tivey, Margaret. "Generation of Seafloor Hydrothermal Vent Fluids and Associated Mineral Deposits." Oceanography. 2007. https://doi.org/10.5670/oceanog.2007.80.

There are about 400 known and inferred sites of hydrothermal deposits, 80 per cent of which are on mid-ocean ridges and the rest are in arc and back-arc settings (Figure 4).

Cobalt Crust: A cobalt rich crust is formed by hydrogenetic precipitation of manganese and iron from the ambient ocean water as colloidal particles. These particles form nucleus to adsorb trace and rare earth elements such as cobalt, platinum, cerium, tellurium etc. The minerals are formed on elevated rock surfaces called seamounts. Such deposits have been found to occur at Afanasiy-Nikitin Seamount about 1,000 km south of India. The potential area for these deposits could be around 10,000 sq. km.

Table 1: Fact Sheet on Ocean Mineral Resources

Name	Ferromanganese Nodule	Cobalt-Rich Ferro-manganese Crust	Seafloor Massive Sulfide
Shape	Sphere (1-10 cm μ)	Coating (1-10 cm)	Chimney, mound
Major components	MnO_2+Fe-hhydroxide	MnO_2+Fe-hydroxide	Sulfides + sulfates
Metals of interest	Cu, Ni, Co, Mn, REE	Co, Cu, Ni, REE, Pt	Cu, Zn, Au, Ag, Pb
Water depth	3500–6000 m	1000–3000 m	700–3500 m
Resources	5×10^{11} ton (?)	5×10^{10} ton (?)	10^{8} ton (?)
Geology	Sediment hiatus of deep-sea floor	Bare rock of sea-mount & plateau	On volcanic center of MOR and arc
Age	< 80 Ma	< 120 Ma	< 0.1 Ma
Ore genesis	Chemical precipitates from seawater	Chemical precipitate	Precipitates from high-temp fluid
Mining Technology	Developed and tested	Not yet tried	Seriously planned

Source: Compiled by Author

Energy Resources: The energy resources—oil, gas and gas hydrates are known to exist in wide areas within the Indo-Pacific region (Figure 5 and 6).

As a result of joint partnership between US, Japan and India, potential deposits of highly enriched accumulations of natural gas hydrate were located in in the Bay of Bengal. These Gas Hydrates are located in coarse-grained sand-rich deposits in the Krishna-Godavari and Mahanadi Basins. Reserve estimation and feasibility studies on the development of the prospects are currently being made by several research institutions of India such as National Geophysical Research Institute (NGRI), National Institute of Oceanography (NIO), National Centre for Polar and Ocean Research (NCPOR), Directorate General of Hydrocarbons (DGH) and National Institute of Technology (NIOT).

Figure 5: Distribution of Known and inferred deposits of Gas Hydrates, globally.

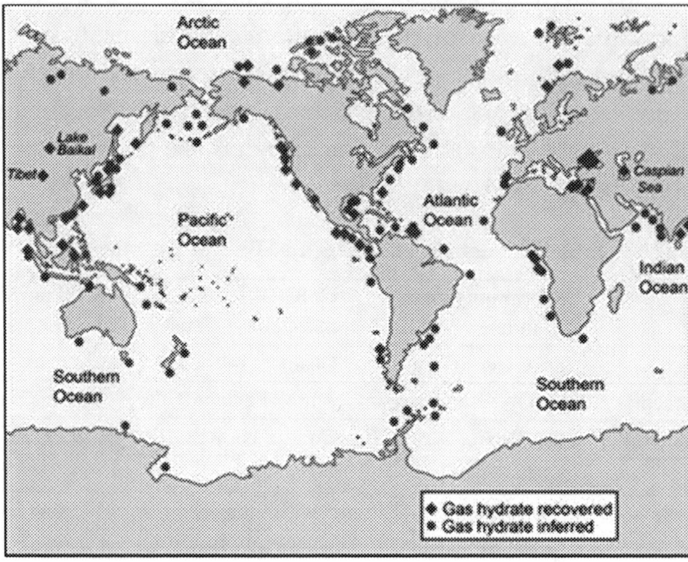

Source: Li, Yuanyuan, Jingyi Chang, and Hailong Lu. "Geochemical Characteristics of Gases Associated with Natural Gas Hydrate." Frontiers in Marine Science 9 (2022). https://doi.org/10.3389/fmars.2022.968647.

As regards oil and gas deposits, the Pacific coast of US, specifically federal waters off California, has some offshore production, though it is much smaller than in the Gulf of Mexico. The possible sites of such resources in the Extended Continental Shelf are shown in the Figure 6, below.

Living Resources*:* Fisheries play an important role in the global food chain system and livelihood of the coastal population. Indian Ocean Rim countries' catches have grown continuously over 300 per cent from 1.9×10^6 tonnes per year in 1950 to 6.5×10^6 tonnes per year by 2018.[2]

India is world's second largest fish producer, contributing 8 per cent to the global output, ranks second in aquaculture production and leads in shrimp production and export. It is one of the largest producers in capture fisheries, with nearly 30 million people involved in fish production across the value chain. The fish production has nearly doubled since 2014 to 17.5 million tons. The fisheries and aquaculture sector have great impact on the food security, nutrition, employment and economic stability in the global context and more so for IOR, considering the density of population and their poverty levels.

Figure 6: Locations of likely and possible Extended Continental Shelf of US in Pacific Ocean

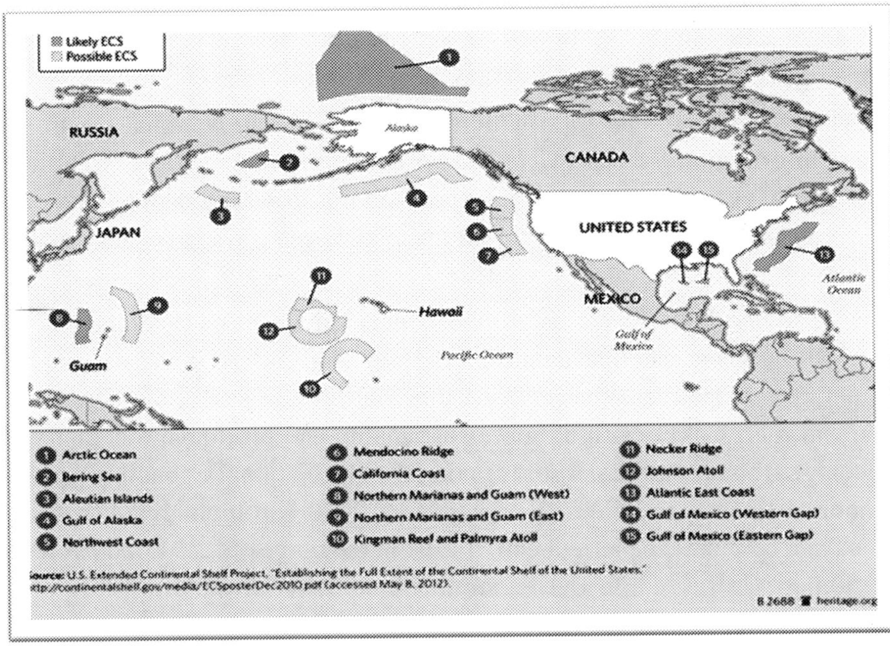

Source: Groves, Steven. "U.S. Accession to U.N. Convention on the Law of the Sea Unnecessary to Develop Oil and Gas Resources." The Heritage Foundation. 2012. https://www.heritage.org/report/us-accession-un-convention-the-law-the-sea-unnecessary-develop-oil-and-gas-resources.

India has endorsed the Regional Plan of Action on Illegal, Unreported and Unregulated Fishing (IUU) jointly in cooperation with Sri Lanka, Bangladesh and Maldives to prevent IUU fishing in the Bay of Bengal Region. It has also joined the International Maritime Organisation-Food and Agricultural Organisation (IMO-FAO) 'GloLitter Partnership Project' to combat marine plastic litter, and framing Standard Operating Procedures (SOP) for retrofitted LPG kits to promote energy-efficient-low carbon emissions and low-cost marine fishing in the region.

Dissemination of Information for Societal Benefit

The in-situ data collected through a network of Ocean Moored Buoys, drifting platforms (buoys), research vessels, ships of opportunity and remote sensing observing systems from northern Indian Ocean forms the foundation for understanding the state of the ocean and predicting the changes using different models. The dissemination of data and information under international data exchange policy helps the Indian Ocean rim countries in vessel movement, fishery operations, disaster mitigation, Search and Rescue etc.

The Ocean Data and Information System of Indian National Centre for Ocean Information Services (INCOIS)- an institute under Ministry of Earth Sciences (MoES) serves as the one stop shop for providing data on physical, chemical, biological and geological parameters of ocean on spatial and temporal domains.

The advisories issued to fishermen in local languages on Potential Fishing Zone (PFZ) using satellite data, chlorophyll concentration and sea surface temperature helps them to identify zones rich in fish stock, thereby saving time and fuel, making fishing more sustainable and profitable together with reducing carbon footprints. A study undertaken by National Council of Applied Economic Research (NCAER) way back in 2010 had highlighted that total annual net economic benefit due to PFZ lie in the range of Rs 34,000 Crores to Rs 50,000 Crores while the economic benefit from the use of weather information was estimated to be around Rs 2,11,000 crores if all the farmers receive such information.[3] To add to these gains, the improved severe weather warning and the early warning of cyclones, has saved lives of hundreds of vulnerable coastal populations.

The Tsunami Early Warning System operational at INCOIS, Hyderabad is another world class facility that serves not only India but greater regions of Indian Ocean Rim countries in issuing timely warning about large scale disturbances in the ocean floor that can produce high waves capable of causing massive inundation and destruction. The System uses a network of broadband seismic stations and data from more than 300 seismic stations spread over the world, a network of tsunami buoys deployed in Indian Ocean and several tide gauge stations to compute the travel time of waves to coastal regions.

In addition to this, a national network of 160 seismological stations spread over India that includes 20 stations in northeastern region, is monitored on 24×7 basis by National Centre for Seismology, to make real time data available on any seismic activity in Indian subcontinent.

The Way Forward

India can ink bilateral or trilateral Memorandums of Understanding (MoUs) with like-minded nations within the Indo-Pacific Region on sharing our expertise, exchange of data and information on subjects of mutual interest such as weather and early warnings of extreme events, ocean information, seismic activity, tsunami, etc. This can provide us an opportunity to spread the data collection from widely spread platforms which in turn will benefit the communities at large.[4]

NOTES

1 Wadhawan, Sudesh Kumar. "Marine Geology and Coastal Surveys for Seabed Mapping and Mineral Resource Evaluation in India – an Overview." Proceedings of the Indian National Science Academy. 2016. https://doi.org/10.16943/ptinsa/2016/48476.

2 Zeller, D., M. Ansell, V. Andreoli, and K. Heidrich. "Trends in Indian Ocean Marine Fisheries since 1950: Synthesis of Reconstructed Catch and Effort Data." Marine & Freshwater Research. 2023. https://doi.org/10.1071/mf22148.

3 Ravindra, Rasik. "Earth Sciences: How Far Is India?" Governance Today, 16–19. 2014.

17

Environmental Attributes of the Indian Ocean: Opportunities for Strengthening Regional Cooperation

Dr. K. Kathiresan and Dr. J. R. Bhatt

The Indian Ocean is the third-largest ocean, covering about 70 million square kilometres, bordered by 38 countries, stretching from Africa's east coast to Australia's west coast.[1] The Indian Ocean has a strategic location for global trade, through the transportation of 40 per cent of the world's oil supply, and 64 per cent of global oil trade.[2] This region is home to 30 per cent of the global human population, but the dense coastal population is vulnerable to disasters. The Indian Ocean is rich in natural resources, producing about 40 per cent of the world's offshore oil, and more than 15 per cent of the world's total fishing. Mineral resources in sediments are considerably high, with nodules containing nickel, copper, iron and huge sulphide deposits of manganese, copper, iron, zinc, silver and gold.[3]

The Indian Ocean Region (IOR) is home to the most productive marine ecosystems—including mangroves, coral reefs, seagrasses, estuaries, open and deep-sea habitats. These ecosystems are rich in biodiversity, supporting fisheries and coastal livelihoods for over 2.5 billion people living there, besides promoting tourism, coastal protection and global climate regulation. However, overexploitation, pollution and climate change affect the marine environment, and hence its conservation is of top priority in the Indian Ocean region.

Mangroves of Indian Ocean

Covering half of the world's mangrove areas, containing 85 per cent of the world's mangrove species, occurring in a variety of habitats, the mangrove ecosystem plays a vital role in coastal biodiversity of the countries bordering the Indian Ocean. This region is unique in having the Sundarbans—the world's largest mangrove forest, and it is the only mangrove-tiger kingdom of the world. Indonesia, a country bordering the Indian Ocean, has about one fifth of the global mangrove cover.[4] However, the mangroves of the Indian Ocean are facing heavy human pressures and natural stressors. This calls for urgent measures of conservation and restoration.

In the Indian Ocean, about 89 per cent of mangrove area is present in South and Southeast Asia and 10 per cent in Eastern and Southern Africa. However, only 0.3 per cent of the area occurs in each of the Middle East and East Asia [Table 1]. In a 20-year period from 2000-2020, there was a net annual gain of 2.2 per cent mangrove area. An annual loss of 0.17 per cent occurred in south and Southeast Asia, but an annual gain of 2.32 per cent was recorded in East Asia.[5] There was no change in other sub-regions [Table 2].

Table 1: Mangrove area by sub-region of the Indian Ocean [FAO, 2023]

Sub-region	Annual mangrove area change [million ha]	Per cent of total area in the Indian Ocean region	Per cent of total area in the world
Eastern & southern Africa	0.73	10.06	4.92
Middle east	0.02	0.28	0.10
South Asia & South East Asia	6.48	89.38	43.80
East Asia	0.02	0.28	0.14
Total	**7.25**	**100**	**48.96**

Source: Compiled by the Author[6]

Table 2: Rate of annual mangrove area change, by region between the years 2000-2020 [FAO, 2023]

No.	Sub-region of Indian Ocean	Annual mangrove area change [Per cent] During 20 years [2000-2020]	Inference
1	Eastern & southern Africa	0	No net change
2	East Asia	+2.32	Gain of forest cover
3	South & South East Asia	–0.17	Loss of forest
4	Western and Central Asia	0	No net change
Overall change in mangroves of the Indian Ocean region		**+2.15**	**Net gain**

Source: Compiled by the Author[7]

Mangrove ecosystems of the Indian Ocean support a rich species diversity. For example, the mangrove ecosystem of India has perhaps the highest record of biodiversity of any country, with a total of 5,746 floral and faunal species. Of these, 12 species groups dominate the numbers, and these include plants [mangroves and associates], marine algae [phytoplankton and seaweeds], fungi, protozoa, nematodes, polychaetes, arachnids, crustaceans, molluscs, insects, birds, and finfish.[8]

Commercial fisheries are highly dependent on mangroves. Approximately one third of all wild fish landings in Southeast Asia are mangrove-dependent species. In addition to aquatic fauna, terrestrial fauna, such as insects, amphibians, reptiles, and mammals, take refuge in the mangrove habitats. Insect diversity in mangroves has been shown to be particularly high even when mangrove plant diversity is low. For example, more than 3,000 insect species have been recorded in Singapore's mangroves alone.[9]

Mangrove waters are home to various species of critically endangered sawfish, and are important refuges for dugongs, manatees, and some coastal cetaceans. The Sundarbans supports globally threatened species, including tigers, fishing cats, Gangetic dolphins, estuarine crocodiles, horseshoe crabs, water-monitor lizards, and river terrapins. According to the IUCN Red List of Threatened Ecosystems, 11 mangrove species (16 per cent), 48 birds, 14 reptiles, one amphibian, and six mammals of mangrove ecosystems are at an elevated threat of extinction in the world, mostly in the sub-regions of Indian Ocean [Asia and Australia]. Little is known about the effects of mangrove loss on biodiversity at local or regional scales.[10]

Biodiversity in mangroves remains astonishing, but more data is required at the local and regional scales. The actual species richness of different mangrove regions in the Indian Ocean remains poorly documented due to the lack of systematic and extensive field surveys.

Management: Mangroves of the Indian Ocean region is conserved through regional cooperation with the Indian Ocean Rim Association (IORA) initiatives, and international frameworks [Ramsar Convention, UNEP's Regional Seas Programme, Blue Carbon Initiative]. At the national level, the mangroves are protected by regulatory measures, and restored by people's participatory approach.

Way-forward: It is necessary to strengthen regional cooperation under IORA. A special focus is required for integrated coastal zone management, community participation, and mangrove-positive business development, including blue carbon finance.

Coral Reefs of Indian Ocean

overing only <1 per cent of the ocean floor, but supporting 25 per cent of marine life, the coral reef ecosystem plays a vital role in the biodiversity of the countries bordering the Indian Ocean. The coral reefs strongly support tourism, fisheries, and coastal protection during storms and extreme climate events. But the coral reef ecosystem is facing heavy pressures from unsustainable fishing, marine pollution (including sedimentation) and climate change. One-third of reefs are rated at high or very high risk and more than 65 per cent of reefs in the Indian Ocean are at risk from local threats.[11] This calls for urgent measures of conservation and restoration.

The Indian Ocean region has 28,000 square kilometres of reefs providing economic benefits of US$2 billion annually. About 70 per cent of this value is derived from tourism, and the remaining from fisheries. Almost 3,000 businesses depend directly or indirectly on coral reef health. Annually, almost 1.4 million visitors enjoy the beauty of coral reefs and pay for it. At least 1.5 million people rely on reef fisheries for their livelihood. For some countries, coral benefits can represent up to 20 per cent of their GDP.[12]

Healthy reefs in the Indian Ocean region could support a maximum yield of 4 tons of fish per square kilometre per year. In contrast, the yield from degraded reefs is 5.7-fold lower [0.7 tons per square kilometre per year]. Hence, healthy reefs are to be protected. However, the coral reefs of the Indian Ocean suffer from bleaching events in several instances. Healthy coral populations may recover within 15 years from severe bleaching events.[13]

Coral reefs are conserved in the Indian Ocean region, through developing networks of about 330 marine protected areas [MPAs], covering 19 per cent of the coral reefs. The benefits of MPAs implementation outweigh the costs of protection up to 20:1. However, 75 per cent of MPAs are considered to be only partially effective for protection.[14] In addition, there are other local methods of conservation such as implementing sustainable fishing practices (especially protecting herbivores), and improving water quality.

Management: The coral reefs of the Indian Ocean are conserved through regional cooperation with the IORA initiatives, and the Indian Ocean Commission [IOC], and UNEP's Regional Seas Programme (Nairobi & South Asia Regional Seas). The coral reefs are also conserved with global support of the Coral Reef Conservation Programme (NOAA), Global Coral Reef Monitoring Network (GCRMN), and blue carbon initiatives. At the national level, the coral reef is protected in MPAs, monitoring, and restoration efforts.

Way-forward: It is necessary to strengthen regional cooperation under IORA and IOC for reef monitoring, restoration and blue economy initiatives. It is vital to implement adaptive reef management and climate resilience strategies. A special focus is required for promoting artificial reefs, coral gardening, and marine protected area networks.

Seagrasses of Indian Ocean

The Indian Ocean hosts extensive and diverse seagrass ecosystems, supporting fisheries, biodiversity, and coastal livelihoods. An estimated 7 per cent of seagrass habitat is being lost worldwide each year, and at least 22 of the world's 72 seagrass species are in decline.[15] The seagrasses are affected by coastal development, pollution, climate change, destructive trawling and drag-net fishing that uproots the seagrass beds. The Maldives is a rare seagrass 'bright spot' of the Indian Ocean as it has shown a threefold increase in seagrass areal extent over the last 20 years, which is against the backdrop of global seagrass decline.[16]

Management: The seagrasses of the Indian Ocean are conserved through regional cooperation with the IORA initiatives, and the UNEP Regional Seas Programme (Nairobi & South Asia Regional Seas). The seagrasses are also conserved with international partnerships with UNEP–GRID Arendal's Blue Forests Project, IOC–UNESCO, and Global Seagrass Watch. At the national level, the seagrasses are protected in MPAs, community-based restoration, blue carbon projects, seagrass mapping and dugong conservation programmes.

Way-forward: It is necessary to enhance regional cooperation under IORA and IOC for monitoring and data sharing. It is vital to integrate seagrasses into Nationally Determined Contributions (NDCs), and coastal zone policies.

Seaweeds of Indian Ocean

The Indian Ocean supports a rich diversity of marine macroalgae (seaweeds) due to its extensive tropical and subtropical coastlines, hardy substrates [coral reefs], and nutrient upwelling zones. These resources are vital for coastal livelihoods, aquaculture, fisheries, pharmaceuticals, climate regulation, and marine-based industries. One third of the Indian Ocean's seaweed resources is present in the Gulf of Mannar on the southeast coast of India.[17]

Seaweeds significantly contribute to the economic development of rural coastal areas. The seaweeds are consumed as food in some Asian countries, but their utilisation for production of phycocolloids [agar, algin, carrageenan] is widespread across the world as well in India. Recently the seaweeds have been used in India for the production of plant growth promoters for agricultural applications.

Major seaweed-producing countries in the Indian Ocean include India, Sri Lanka Indonesia, Tanzania, Madagascar, Kenya, Seychelles, and Western Australia. Seaweed farming is rapidly expanding in India, Indonesia, and East Africa for promoting coastal livelihood and climate resilience initiatives. Large-scale seaweed farming is encouraged in India's blue economy policy. Total seaweed production in India was 72,385 tonnes (wet weight) in 2023.[18]

Policy InitiativesL IORA Blue Economy Agenda promotes seaweed as a priority bio-resource. There are country-wise programmes: National Seaweed Mission in India; Seaweed Industry Development Program in Indonesia; and, Women-led community farming programs in Tanzania and Kenya.

Dugong of Indian Ocean

The Indian Ocean has a significant population of dugongs, especially in areas with extensive seagrass habitats. The dugong plays a vital ecological role by maintaining seagrass health through grazing, and nutrient recycling. They are present in abundance in the Arabian Gulf region (Abu Dhabi, Qatar; (~7,000 individuals), East Africa's Bazaruto Bay, and in the Southeast Asia [Thailand, Myanmar, and Indonesia]. The dugongs are locally extinct in the western Indian Ocean islands [Comoros, Mauritius]. Listed as Vulnerable (IUCN Red List), the dugongs face regional decline of populations due to seagrass habitat loss, fishing-related mortality, and climate change.[19]

Dugong is legally protected in 9 countries of the Indian Ocean, and these are India, Kenya, Tanzania, Mozambique, Indonesia, Thailand, UAE, Qatar, and Oman. The key frameworks used for protection of dugong are the Convention on Migratory species [CMS], the ASEAN Dugong Conservation Programme, and the East African Conservation Network & CMS initiatives

Conservation Initiatives: The IORA promotes community-based conservation of dugongs. This is implemented by participatory monitoring, seagrass restoration, and awareness in Indonesia, India, and East Africa. Twenty-seven countries signed a Memorandum of Understanding [MoU] for promoting internationally co-ordinated actions to ensure conservation of dugong and their seagrass habitats under the Convention on Migratory Species (CMS).

Way-forward: It is necessary to strengthen the regional co-operation through IORA, IOC and CMS networks for monitoring and data sharing for dugong conservation. Marine Protected Areas are to be expanded to include feeding and breeding sites of dugong. Community-led conservation is to be encouraged through awareness programmes on habitat protection and by-catch reduction. It is vital to integrate dugong and its seagrass habitats into the National Coastal Management plans, NDCs, and coastal zone policies.

Whale Shark of Indian Ocean

The whale shark is the largest fish in the sea, widely distributed across tropical and warm-temperate waters of the Indian Ocean. It is found in surface and near-surface waters with high plankton density and around upwelling zones, coral reefs, and island groups. The whale shark is of ecotourism and socio-economic importance especially in the Maldives, Seychelles, Mozambique, and Western Australia. It has seasonal aggregation behaviour: during March-May in India, October–April in Seychelles and Tanzania, May–December in Maldives, March-July in Australia. Key hotspots are Western Indian Ocean [Mozambique, Seychelles, Madagascar, Tanzania, Kenya], Central Indian Ocean [Maldives], and Eastern Indian Ocean [India, Sri Lanka, Indonesia, Thailand, Western Australia].[20] Its conservation status is Endangered in the IUCN Red List, due to over-fishing and vessel strikes.

Conservation Initiatives: India has successfully conserved the whale sharks along the Gujarat coast through awareness and rescue operations. The campaign conducted by Shri Morari Bapu, a spiritual leader, convinced the fishermen that the whale shark is like their daughter who comes home to give birth, and it is their duty to take care of the animal. This sentiment has turned fishermen, turning from hunters to protectors. Fishermen are paid a compensation amount of ₹ 25,000/- (twenty-five thousand rupees) in lieu of nets that are damaged or cut during rescue operations involving trapped whale sharks.[21]

Regional efforts include the by-catch mitigation programs under the Indian Ocean Tuna Commission [IOTC]; the marine mega-fauna conservation initiatives under the Indian Ocean Rim Association [IORA]; and, the population monitoring through photo-identification, tagging, and satellite tracking.

Way-Forward: Research is required on estimating the whale shark population across the Indian Ocean basin, and on understanding its migration corridors and breeding grounds. Community participation in conservation is to be encouraged through responsible tourism for the regulation of tourist numbers and boat conduct near feeding aggregations.

Whales of Indian Ocean

The Indian Ocean supports a diverse range of whales including baleen whales and toothed whales as well as resident populations (e.g., Arabian Sea humpback whale), and migratory species (e.g., blue and fin whales). In the Indian Ocean, the key whale hotspots are found in Arabian Sea, Bay of Bengal, Western Indian Ocean, Southern Indian Ocean, Maldives, and Chagos Archipelago. Whale watching is a major source of tourism revenue: blue and sperm whales in Sri Lanka; blue whales in Maldives; and, humpback whales in Madagascar and Seychelles.[22]

The India Ocean provides feeding, breeding, and migration routes for many populations of whales. Many species migrate between high-latitude feeding grounds (Antarctic) and tropical breeding grounds in the Indian Ocean. For example: Southern Hemisphere humpback whales breed off Madagascar and Mozambique, while they feed in the Southern Ocean. Arabian Sea humpback whales are unique—they remain year-round residents, due to upwelling productivity along Oman's coast.[23]

Several species are included in the IUCN Red list: Blue whale—Endangered; Fin whale—Vulnerable; Humpback whale—Least Concern; but Arabian Sea population is Endangered; and, Sperm whale—Vulnerable. The whales are affected by entanglement in fishing gear and nets, ship strikes near ports (e.g., Sri Lanka, India, and Oman), noise pollution from shipping and sonar, climate change altering prey distribution, and pollution [micro-plastics].

Conservation and Management: Whales are protected under wildlife laws in India, Australia, South Africa, and island nations. Monitoring is done by using acoustic techniques, satellite tagging, and photo-identification of blue whales in Sri Lanka and Chagos. Community-based ecotourism is implemented for whale watching in Maldives, Sri Lanka, and Madagascar.

Commercial whaling is banned in the entire Indian Ocean by the Indian Ocean Whale Sanctuary (IOWS), established by the International Whaling Commission (IWC) in 1979. Regional collaboration has been established under IORA and IWC Scientific Committee.

Dolphins of Indian Ocean

The Indian Ocean has a rich diversity of dolphin species due to its warm tropical and sub-tropical waters, productive coastal ecosystems, and extensive continental shelves. Dolphins are found from the coasts of East Africa and the Arabian Sea to Southeast Asia, Australia, and the islands of the Indian Ocean. The hotspots of dolphins are found in India, Mauritius, Seychelles, Tanzania, Western Australia, and Maldives.[24] However, several dolphin species are Vulnerable or Near Threatened under the IUCN Red List, due to by-catch in tuna and gillnet fisheries, habitat degradation from coastal development, noise pollution from shipping and sonar activities, plastic ingestion, and climate change. The dolphin plays an ecological role of controlling fish and squid populations. It is an important component of marine tourism in Maldives, Mauritius, and Sri Lanka.

Conservation Efforts: In the Indian Ocean, dolphins are protected under CMS and CITES. National initiatives include the Wildlife Protection Act in India, marine mammal sanctuaries, and community and NGO initiatives for conducting awareness campaigns, dolphin watching guidelines, and stranding monitoring.

Sea Turtles of Indian Ocean

The Indian Ocean supports nesting and foraging habitats of sea-turtles. It has six of the seven global species. India has the world's largest nesting site of the Olive Ridley Turtle in Odisha. Other hotspots are Seychelles and Aldabra Atoll for green turtle nesting grounds, Madagascar and Comoros for hawksbill nesting, Maldives and Sri Lanka for hawksbill and green turtle.[25]

Sea turtles are vital indicators of marine ecosystem health and have deep cultural and ecological importance across the Indian Ocean Region. Turtle watching is of cultural and tourism value (e.g., Maldives, Sri Lanka). The sea-turtle maintains the health of seagrass and coral reefs, and controls populations of jellyfish, which otherwise eat away the fish eggs and larvae.

Major threats include by-catch in trawl, gillnet, and long-line fisheries; poaching and illegal trade for meat, shells, eggs; coastal development that destroys nesting beaches; plastic pollution that leads to plastic ingestion and entanglement; and, climate change [Rising temperatures affect hatchling sex ratios].

Conservation and Management Initiatives

All the sea turtles of the Indian Ocean are legally protected under CITES and CMS. The Indian Ocean–South-East Asian Memorandum of Understanding (IOSEA MOU) is a regional venture for the protection of marine turtles. Community-based conservation is implemented by the turtle protection groups in Odisha (India), Seychelles, Zanzibar; and, ecotourism-based conservation is implemented in Maldives and Sri Lanka. Sea-turtle monitoring is done through satellite tracking in Seychelles, Sri Lanka, India, and Australia. Beach management is practiced in collecting eggs, developing hatcheries, turtle-safe lighting, nest relocation, and predator control programmes.

Estuaries Of Indian Ocean

Estuaries of the Indian Ocean are among the most productive ecosystems, serving as nurseries for fish, crustaceans, and molluscs; providing habitats for migratory and resident birds; supporting mangroves, seagrasses, and saltmarshes. The estuaries act as natural filters, trapping sediments, nutrients, and pollutants from the water before it reaches the sea. They also serve as socio-economic hubs of fishing, trade, and tourism.

Threats to estuaries include mangrove destruction for aquaculture and development, overfishing, climate change, urbanisation, and pollution due to industrial and sewage discharges.[26]

Conservation and Management: Estuaries are conserved through integrated coastal zone management as practiced in India, Sri Lanka, and East Africa to balance development with ecological integrity. Community participation and sustainable fisheries are vital for the conservation of estuarine systems.

Deep Sea of the Indian Ocean

The deep-sea zone with depth >200 meters, covers vast areas between Africa, Asia, Australia, and Antarctica in the Indian Ocean. The deepest part is found at up to 7,258 metres, near Java.[27]

The Indian Ocean's deep sea is rich in polymetallic nodules (manganese, cobalt, nickel, copper), which are found in the Central Indian Basin. It is also rich in cobalt-rich crusts and hydrothermal sulphides, which are potential sources of rare metals.

India has ventured into deep sea mining to explore the non-living resources by using a manned submersible vehicle (*Samudrayan*) at a depth of 6,000 meters. It has also achieved the status of a 'pioneer investor' by holding an area of 75,000 square kilometres in the Central Indian Ocean Basin for nodule exploration. India has also initiated exploring new drugs from deep sea organisms.

Fisheries of Indian Ocean

The Indian Ocean is home to rich pelagic, demersal, and coastal fisheries, contributing significantly to seafood supply, providing employment for over 12 million people in the fisheries sector, supplying over 25 per cent of global tuna catches, and supporting the blue economy through aquaculture and fisheries.[28] However, over-fishing has resulted in the decline of tuna, sharks, and demersal fish. The loss of coral reefs and mangroves has reduced fish nursery habitats. In addition, climate change and pollution affect fish health.

Fisheries Management and Cooperation: IORA enhance regional cooperation in sustainable fisheries, aquaculture, and the blue economy. Indian Ocean Tuna Commission [IOTC] manages tuna and related species in the Indian Ocean. South West Indian Ocean Fisheries Commission (SWIOFC) promotes sustainable fisheries management among the western Indian Ocean nations. FAO Regional Fishery Bodies support capacity building, data collection, and sustainable management. Regional Commission for Fisheries deals with fisheries in Arabian Gulf and adjacent waters.

Sustainable Fisheries: MPAs and Fishery Restricted Zones are helpful to protect spawning grounds. Local fishers are empowered in fisheries management in Kenya and Tanzania. Ecosystem-based management of fisheries is encouraged to balance harvest and ecosystem health. Blue Economy Initiatives are promoted by integrating fisheries with conservation, tourism, and renewable energy.

International agreements: The principles of sustainable management of marine capture fisheries and the protection of marine biodiversity were established by the United Nations Convention on the Law of the Sea. Building on it, Agenda 21 of the UN Earth Summit in 1992 in Rio De Janeiro and the Johannesburg Plan of Implementation from 2002 summit set targets relating to the marine environment. Further, the 17 Sustainable Development Goals, the Kunming Montréal Global Biodiversity Framework, and the Biodiversity Beyond National Jurisdiction (BBNJ) agreement are yet other global efforts to invoke multilateralism for sustainable management of the oceanic resources.

Way-forward: It is necessary to strengthen regional governance and data-sharing frameworks through IOTC and IORA. Small fishers are to be supported through access to markets, technology and finance. Climate-resilient fisheries and adaptive management are to be promoted.

Climate Change Impacts

There are 23 countries, brought together under the IORA. They are Australia, Bangladesh, the Comoros, France, India, Indonesia, Iran, Kenya, Madagascar, Malaysia, Maldives, Mauritius, Mozambique, Oman, Seychelles, Singapore, Somalia, South Africa, Sri Lanka, Tanzania, Thailand, the United Arab Emirates and Yemen. All are non-annex I countries except Australia and France, and these two are Annex I countries. The Climate Risk Index [CRI] and cumulative GHG emission during 1850-2024 of the IORA members are shown in Table 3.[29]

There are 12 dialogue partners of IORA. There are 8 Annex I countries—USA, EU, Russia, Germany, UK, Japan, Italy, Turkey. There are 4 non-annex I countries—China, Egypt, Saudi Arabia, South Korea. The cumulative GHG emissions during 1850-2024 of the dialogue partners are shown in Table 4.

Table 3: CRI ranking in 2024 and cumulative GHG emission between 1850 and 2024 in 23 IORA member states [Source: CRI, 2025]

No.	Name of IORA member state	CRI 2024	Cumulative GHG emission [1850-2024]	
			Gg CO_2 eq.	Per cent of world
1	Australia	55	33978990	1.26
2	Bangladesh	13	9495600	0.35
3	The Comoros	76	34913.1	0.001
4	France	97	60791200	2.25
5	India	15	128929000	4.78
6	Indonesia	27	33868200	1.25
7	Iran	69	33310560	1.23
8	Kenya	45	2343850	0.09
9	Madagascar	29	2586160	0.10
10	Malaysia	112	10086952	0.37
11	Maldives	144	39798.69	0.00
12	Mauritius	67	191167.6	0.01
13	Mozambique	53	2025220	0.08
14	Oman	74	2615132	0.10
15	Seychelles	115	20216.19	0.00
16	Singapore	89	2198603.7	0.08
17	Somalia	82	2490180	0.09
18	South Africa	162	30213920	1.12
19	Sri Lanka	52	1602890	0.06
20	Tanzania	23	3960900	0.15
21	Thailand	17	14627950	0.54
22	UAE	103	6955316.3	0.26
23	Yemen	-	1786080	0.07

Source: Compiled by the Author[30]

1. Most vulnerable IORA [Indian Ocean Rim Association] Member States

- The IORA member countries that are the most climate-vulnerable in the world are Bangladesh, India, and Thailand with the CRI ranks of 13,15 and 17 respectively [Climate Risk Index {CRI}, 2024).
- Despite the low per capita emissions, these countries are highly affected in climate-sensitive sectors (agriculture, fisheries, and tourism), and by sea level rise, and frequent natural disasters.

- This underscores the unjust climatic regime, where the countries that are least responsible for emissions face the greatest climate-induced disaster risks.

Table 4: Cumulative GHG emission during 1850-2024 in 12 dialogue partners of IORA

No.	Dialogue partner	Annex	Cumulative GHG emission [1850-2024]	
			Gg CO_2 eq.	Per cent of world
1	USA	Annex I	575607000	21.32
2	China	Non-Annex I	413539000	15.32
3	EU	Annex I	410767000	15.22
4	Russia	Annex I	177255600	6.57
5	Germany	Annex I	117033200	4.34
6	UK	Annex I	99440000	3.68
7	Japan	Annex I	80211400	2.97
8	Italy	Annex I	35236400	1.31
9	South Korea	Non-Annex I	26998610	0.99
10	Saudi Arabia	Non-Annex I	20524887	0.76
11	Turkey	Annex I	19975700	0.74
12	Egypt	Non-Annex I	12804690	0.47

Source: Compiled by the Author[31]

2. *Adaptation Challenges and Capacity Gaps*

- Climate adaptation is constrained by limited financial, technological, and institutional capacities in many IORA members.
- Poor adaptation financing and weak access to climate technology from Annex I partners deepen the dependency and vulnerability of non-annex countries of IORA.
- Rising sea-levels, coastal erosion, and extreme weather events threaten livelihoods and national development goals.

3. *Mitigation burden on member states*

- IORA members are increasingly undertaking mitigation commitments—renewable energy transitions, blue economy strategies—often without adequate external support.

- This reflects a reversal of responsibility, where non-annex I countries shoulder the burden of climate action, instead of high GHG emitting Annex I countries.
- The situation amplifies the North–South divide, revealing inequities in global climate governance.

4. Means of Implementation and the Role of Annex I Discussion Partners

- Annex I countries (13 IORA discussion partners, including the USA, UK, EU, and Australia) are obligated under the UNFCCC to provide finance, technology transfer, and capacity building to non-annex I states.
- Yet, means of implementation to the IORA region remain insufficient, fragmented, and slow, weakening trust and solidarity.
- Australia's unique position—as an Annex I state within the Indian Ocean—highlights the geo-political tension between developed countries' responsibility and regional belonging.
- Annex I countries need to support non-annex I countries with finance, technology transfer, and capacity building—consistent with the UNFCCC's principle of Common but Differentiated Responsibilities and respective capacities.

India's Importance in Indian Ocean

The name 'Indian Ocean' was aptly given by European explorers in the 16th century in recognition of India that had a strong influence over the region' economy. The Indian Ocean holds importance for India. This country is the most populated, geographically located at the Ocean's centre, and strategically situated for maritime benefits to support 95 per cent of India's trade by volume, and 68 per cent of trade by value in the Indian Ocean. India has a great potential for the **blue economy,** due to its extensive coastline of 11,099 kilometres, 1,382 islands, and a vast Exclusive Economic Zone (EEZ) of 2.3 million square kilometres**.** It is one of the few countries in the world to have detailed maps of coastal habitats, mangroves, coral reefs, coastal land use, and shore changes for the entire country's coastline. India's sea dependence for oil is about 93 per cent for its offshore oil production and petroleum exports. It is also the fourth-largest importer of liquefied natural gas (LNG), with about 45 per cent coming by sea.[32]

India is a founding member of the IORA, established in 1997. It hosted the IORA Leader Summit in Jakarta [2017] and adopted the IORA Action Plan, aligning with India's SAGAR vision. It has contributed to the IORA's agenda on maritime security, blue economy, and disaster management. It has supported IORA's priority areas, including trade and investment facilitation, fisheries management, tourism, academic and scientific cooperation, cultural exchanges, and gender empowerment. India is sharing the interests of IORA countries in preserving freedom of navigation for commercial shipping, assessing the natural resources, and supporting disaster relief and rescue operations.

India is recognised as a maritime power in promoting, peace, prosperity and security across the Indian Ocean Region through its naval strength, cooperative diplomacy, and developmental initiatives. It also strengthens partnerships with Indian Ocean Island nations especially Mauritius, Seychelles, Maldives. It is strongly diplomatic in maintaining balanced relations with U.S, China, ASEAN and Africa for maritime stability.

Conclusion

The Indian Ocean region is crucial to the global economy. The region is rich in natural resources—fisheries and mineral wealth—which are important for livelihoods, trade, and economic growth. It is a vital trading hub especially for energy, connecting the Middle East to Southeast and East Asia, as well as Europe and the Americas. Any disruption along its trading routes will impact the global energy security. Indian Ocean's challenges remain in piracy, illegal fishing, climate change impacts and marine pollution. There is a need for strong regional coordination and naval modernisation.

There are several global commitments for sustainable management of the ocean living resources. They are the United Nations Convention on the Law of Sea, the Agenda 21 of the UN Earth Summit in 1992, the Johannesburg Plan of Implementation from 2002 summit, the 17 Sustainable Development Goals (SDGs), the Kunming Montréal Global Biodiversity Framework and the Biodiversity Beyond National Jurisdiction (BBNJ) agreement. But these can succeed only if all nations endeavour to act, based on the principles of Equity, Justice and Inclusivity within the backdrop of their evolving national circumstances. Unfortunately, the implementation of many of the above-mentioned commitments has been difficult, ineffective or even practically non-existent, especially in the developed countries, despite of having the necessary wherewithal to do so.

While the Indian Ocean region is beset with issues and concerns of evolving geopolitics, maritime safety and security threats, it also presents owing to its rich environmental attributes, unique opportunities for regional cooperation through smart partnerships and collaborative efforts. Countries with their shores in the Indian Ocean will do well to ensure peace, security and prosperity as well as empathy for all life forms and not turn it into a theatre of war.

NOTES

1 Wikipedia. "Indian Ocean," November 17, 2025. https://en.wikipedia.org/w/index.php?title=Indian_Ocean&oldid=1322637471.

2 "World Oil Transit Chokepoints," U.S. Energy Information Administration. November, 2014. https://www.scribd.com/document/678134733/Indian-Ocean

3 Op. cit. note no. 1

4 Kathiresan K and N. Rajendran. "Mangrove ecosystems of the Indian Ocean region." Indian Journal of Marine Sciences, 34: 104-113. 2005.

5 "The World's Mangroves 2000–2020." FAO. July 26, 2023. https://doi.org/10.4060/cc7044en.

6 Ibid

7 Ibid

8 Kathiresan, K. "Mangroves of India." Current Sciences, 114, 1–6. 2018.

9 Leal, Maricé and Spalding, Mark D (eds). "The State of the World's Mangroves 2024." Global Mangrove Alliance. 2024. https://doi.org/10.5479/10088/119867

10 Polidoro, Beth A., Kent E. Carpenter, Lorna Collins, Norman C. Duke, Aaron M. Ellison, Joanna C. Ellison, Elizabeth J. Farnsworth, et al. "The Loss of Species: Mangrove Extinction Risk and Geographic Areas of Global Concern." PloS One 5, no. 4. 2010. https://doi.org/10.1371/journal.pone.0010095; Luther, David A., and Russell Greenberg. "Mangroves: A Global Perspective on the Evolution and Conservation of Their Terrestrial Vertebrates." Bioscience 59, no. 7, 602–12. 2009. https://doi.org/10.1525/bio.2009.59.7.11.

11 Ministry of the Environment and Energy, Government Offices of Sweden. "Indian Ocean Factsheet." ICRI, n.d. https://icriforum.org/wp-content/uploads/2019/12/ICRI%20Indian%20Ocean%20Factsheet_0.pdf.

12 Ibid

13 O. Lindén and N. Sporrong (ed.), "Coral Reef Degradation in the Indian Ocean: Status Report and Project Presentation." Cordio, IUCN. 2002.

14 Ibid

15 "Protection of seagrasses-key-building-resilience-climate-change." UNEP. 2000. https://www.unep.org

16 Floyd, Matthew, Holly K. East, Dimosthenis Traganos, Azim Musthag, James Guest, Aminath S. Hashim, Vivienne Evans, Stephanie Helber, Richard K. F. Unsworth, and Andrew J. Suggitt. "Rapid Seagrass Meadow Expansion in an Indian Ocean Bright Spot." Scientific Reports 14, no. 1. 2024. https://doi.org/10.1038/s41598-024-61088-1.

17 Saxena A. "Marine biodiversity in India: Status and issues." International Day for Biological Diversity, Uttar Pradesh State Biodiversity Board. p127-134. 2012

18 Ibid

19 Marsh, Helene (ed). "Dugong: Status Report and Action Plans for Countries and Territories." UNEP. January 1992.

20 Andrzejaczek, Samantha, Jessica Meeuwig, David Rowat, Simon Pierce, Tim Davies, Rebecca Fisher, and Mark Meekan. "The Ecological Connectivity of Whale Shark Aggregations in the Indian Ocean: A Photo-Identification Approach." Royal Society Open Science 3, no. 11. 2016. https://doi.org/10.1098/rsos.160455.

21 Singh, H. S. "Mangroves Conservation and Whale Shark Protection - An Unique Initiative." Gujarat Government. https://forests.gujarat.gov.in/writereaddata/images/pdf/23_Mangrove-and-Whale-shark-conservation.pdf.

22 "New Regulations Help Protect Whales from Entanglement in Fishing Gear in the Indian Ocean." March 26, 2024. World Wildlife Fund (WWF). https://www.worldwildlife.org/news/stories/new-regulations-help-protect-whales-from-entanglement-in-fishing-gear-in-the-indian-ocean/.

23 Roman, Joe, Andrew J. Abraham, Jeremy J. Kiszka, Daniel P. Costa, Christopher E. Doughty, Ari Friedlaender, Luis A. Hückstädt, Milton Marcondes, Emma Wetsel, and Andrew J. Pershing. "Migrating Baleen Whales Transport High-Latitude Nutrients to Tropical and Subtropical Ecosystems." Nature Communications 16 (1): 2125. 2025. https:/ /doi.org/10.1038/s41467-025-56123-2.

24 Webber, Thomas, Tim Lewis, Sheena Talma, Shaama Sandooyea, Laura Meller, Violaine Dulau-Drouot, and Kirsten F. Thompson. "Cetaceans of the Saya de Malha Bank Region, Indian Ocean: A Candidate Important Marine Mammal Area." Regional Studies in Marine Science 66 (103164): 103164. 2023. https://doi.org/10.1016/j.rsma.2023.103164.

25 Shanker, Kartik, and Nicolas James Pilcher. "Marine Turtle Conservation in South and Southeast Asia: Hopeless Cause or Cause for Hope?" Marine Turtle Newsletter. January 2023. https://www.researchgate.net/publication/291867080_Marine_turtle_conservation_in_South_and_Southeast_Asia_hopeless_cause_or_cause_for_hope.

26 "Estuary." Wikipedia. November 14, 2025. https://en.wikipedia.org/w/index.php?title=Estuary&oldid=1322177666.

27 Thomas, Elin A., Todd Bond, Jess L. Kolbusz, Yakufu Niyazi, Denise J. B. Swanborn, and Alan J. Jamieson. "Deep-Sea Ecosystems of the Indian Ocean >1000 m." The Science of the Total Environment 957, no. 176794. 2024. https://doi.org/10.1016/j.scitotenv.2024.176794.

28 De Young, Cassandra. "Review of the State of World Marine Capture Fisheries Management: Indian Ocean." FAO. October 2025. https://www.fao.org/4/a0477e/a0477e04.htm.

29 "Climate Risk Index 2026," German Watch. https://www.germanwatch.org/en/cri.

30 Ibid

31 Ibid

32 "India's Role in Indian Ocean." GS Score. 2025. https://iasscore.in/current-affairs/indias-role-in-indian-ocean.

Index